MODERN MARKETING STRATEGY

EDITED BY
EDWARD C. BURSK
Editor, *Harvard Business Review*

JOHN F. CHAPMAN
Executive Editor, *Harvard Business Review*

A MENTOR EXECUTIVE LIBRARY BOOK

Published by The New American Library, New York and Toronto
The New English Library Limited, London

Published as a MENTOR EXECUTIVE LIBRARY BOOK
by arrangement with Harvard University Press,
who have authorized this softcover edition.
A hardcover edition is available from
Harvard University Press.

FIRST PRINTING, MAY, 1965

MENTOR TRADEMARK REG. U.S. PAT. OFF. AND FOREIGN COUNTRIES
REGISTERED TRADEMARK—MARCA REGISTRADA
HECHO EN CHICAGO, U.S.A.

MENTOR EXECUTIVE LIBRARY BOOKS are published *in
the United States* by The New American Library of World Literature, Inc., 501 Madison Avenue, New York, New York 10022,
in Canada by The New American Library of Canada Limited,
156 Front Street West, Toronto 1, Ontario, *in the United King-
dom* by The New English Library Limited, Barnard's Inn,
Holborn, London, E.C. 1, England

PRINTED IN THE UNITED STATES OF AMERICA

"Since World War II, American factories in general have been able to produce far more goods than marketing departments have been able to move along to the consumer. What has been needed seems to be new ways of finding out in advance what the consumer wants and will buy and new ways of getting it to him more cheaply. Marketing, in the last dozen years, has become the concern of the entire executive hierarchy, and involves the planning, organization, integration, direction and control of the whole marketing effort."

In this invaluable book, outstanding specialists throughout the country describe the radical changes that have occurred in modern marketing patterns and what management must do to meet their challenge. They outline all the factors involved in successful marketing, from the psychological impact on the consumer to media costs and commission fees. They stress systematic analysis and planning of the marketing function rather than individual patterns of marketing research . . . scientific thinking rather than scientific technique. For the forward-looking manager, here are the trends that seem likely to shape effective marketing methods for the future.

Other MENTOR Books
for Executive Libraries

CONTENTS

INTRODUCTION   vii

GENERAL

1. CONDITIONS OF MARKETING LEADERSHIP
   (March–April 1956)   1
   Arthur P. Felton

2. MARKETING MYOPIA (July–August 1960)
   Theodore Levitt   24

3. SHOWDOWN IN THE MARKET PLACE
   (July–August 1956)   49
   Edward M. Barnet

4. THREE-IN-ONE MARKETING
   (November–December 1956)   69
   Reavis Cox

THE CONSUMER

5. IT'S TIME TO RESEARCH THE CONSUMER
   (July–August 1955)   84
   Pierre Martineau

6. COMPUTER SIMULATION OF CONSUMER BEHAVIOR
   (May–June 1963)   104
   William D. Wells

THE PRODUCT AND PRODUCT
STRATEGY

7. THE PRODUCT AND THE BRAND (March–April 1955)   115
   Burleigh B. Gardner and Sidney J. Levy

8. BRAND LOYALTY—WHAT, WHERE, HOW MUCH?
   (January–February 1956)   128
   Ross M. Cunningham

CONTENTS

9. FUNCTIONAL FEATURES IN PRODUCT STRATEGY
(March–April 1959)   155
John B. Stewart

10. THE STRATEGY OF PRODUCT POLICY
(July–August 1955)   179
Charles H. Kline

11. STRATEGY OF PRODUCT QUALITY
(November–December 1962)   199
Alfred A. Kuehn and Ralph L. Day

THE ROLE OF RESEARCH

12. PHASING RESEARCH INTO THE MARKETING PLAN
(May–June 1960)   219
Lee Adler

13. MARKET TESTING (September–October 1958)   238
Ernest J. Enright

THE ECONOMICS OF ADVERTISING

14. HOW TO EVALUATE ADVERTISING'S CONTRIBUTION
(July–August 1962)   256
Cyril Freeman

15. SQUEEZING THE WASTE OUT OF ADVERTISING
(September–October 1962)   271
Russell H. Colley

PRICING POLICY AND PROFIT GOALS

16. MULTISTAGE APPROACH TO PRICING
(July–August 1960)   300
Alfred R. Oxenfeldt

17. PRICING POLICIES FOR NEW PRODUCTS
(November–December 1950)   319
Joel Dean

18. HOW TO SET REALISTIC PROFIT GOALS
(September–October 1958)   336
Bruce Payne

INDEX   353

INTRODUCTION

Business management is undergoing a radical reorganization as it seeks to adapt itself to the new environment which has been precipitated by the rapid postwar development of technology.

Just as the high-speed electronic computer and the more intensive use of mathematics and the social sciences are developing all forms of decision making into a more scientific process,[1] so the almost miraculous step-up in the speed of communications along with the insistent demand of peoples everywhere for more of the amenities of life are turning the whole world into a potential market for every business, with all of the critical competitive implications this has for marketing executives.

Repercussions from these rapid environmental shifts are already apparent. In company after company the marketing functions are being upgraded as management strives to meet the challenge of rapidly increasing competition and as the top executive team strives to bring its thinking into closer focus with the widening range and diversity of consumer needs and wants. The recognition is spreading that marketing managers must now base their plans on far more extensive and objective data and evaluate their actions by more constant and precise criteria.

Working in the environment of the Harvard Business School where, from its founding in 1908, the problems of marketing have

---

[1] See Edward C. Bursk and John F. Chapman, eds., *New Decision-Making Tools for Managers* (Cambridge, Mass., 1963).

been one focus of major research and analysis, the editors of the *Harvard Business Review* have had the benefit of expert research, analysis, and interpretation of each new development—from the widespread inauguration of large-scale installment credit to the blossoming of suburban shopping centers and the application of computer simulation of consumer behavior. In line with the editorial policy of the publication, the editors have attempted to transmit the best of this thinking to the broader business public in a flow of articles on all aspects of marketing.

The emphasis over the years has been on scientific thinking rather than on scientific techniques, on more systematic analysis and planning of the marketing function rather than on the dozens of individual patterns of marketing research which turn up every year. These are the concepts, the editors believe, which will be most useful to the managers who, in the face of today's rapidly changing world, recognize the need for bold and thoughtfully planned action at the highest level in the company. They are the concepts, too, which the aggressive young marketing manager needs to master if he is to guide his company's marketing strategy in a world where science and public taste can make half of a product line obsolete in ten years, where foreign competition has suddenly become a significant and growing factor in the domestic market, and where the greatest opportunity for future growth may lie in the vigorous and systematic development of overseas markets.

At today's tempo of change, no successful marketing policy can remain fixed for long. But, especially since the early 1950's, marketing philosophy has made some drastic but fundamental shifts which no alert executive in any part of the organization can afford to overlook.

Just as marketing research became the magic term for business about fifty years ago, so, now, "marketing management" is the phrase which commands the widest attention. It is based primarily on the realization that, since World War II, American factories in general have been able to produce far more goods than marketing departments have been able to move along to the consumer. What has been needed seems to be new ways of finding out in advance what the consumer wants and will buy, and new ways of getting it to him more cheaply. Marketing, in the last dozen years, has become the concern of the entire executive hierarchy, and involves the planning, organization, integration, direction, and control of the whole marketing effort.

With its audience of top management leaders, the *Harvard Business Review* has attempted to chronicle, describe, analyze, and interpret these developments by drawing on the skills of outstanding specialists throughout the country. Out of fifty or more articles on the changing concept of the marketing function, the editors of this volume have selected and updated eighteen which trace the transformation in the thinking of top-level marketers and highlight the trends which seem destined to help shape the most effective marketing patterns for tomorrow.

Four articles set the stage for the detailed discussion of the new concept of marketing and the role to be played by a new level of marketing management.

"Conditions of Marketing Leadership," by Arthur P. Felton, establishes the point which is basic to the whole new approach to marketing: "Technological progress is still outstripping marketing progress, and the peculiar nature of technological progress today is making the job harder." Citing automation as an example of the changing importance of marketing decisions and quoting Professor James R. Bright of the Harvard Business School, the article reports: "The marketing man is going to have to be *very* right or else he may have nothing to eat but a stream of unsaleable products." How to be "*very* right," how to establish in any business the qualities indispensable to marketing leadership are then described.

Because of Mr. Felton's long experience as a management consultant, he writes with the authority of a man who has faced actual problems in dozens of companies and who has distilled from this experience the three most important features of a successful approach to marketing. He is now assistant manager of home office marketing for the Tidewater Oil Company.

Certainly one of the most significant articles published in the *Harvard Business Review* in recent years, and undoubtedly the most quoted, is Theodore Levitt's thought-provoking "Marketing

Myopia." Pungently written to point out to complacent managements that there is no such thing as a growth industry, Mr. Levitt declares: "Every major industry was once a growth industry. But some that are now riding a wave of growth enthusiasm are very much in the shadow of decline. Others which are thought of as seasoned growth industries have actually stopped growing. In every case the reason growth is threatened, slowed, or stopped is not because the market is saturated. It is because there has been a failure of management." And then he adds this important warning to the executives in charge of every business: "In short, the organization must learn to think of itself not as producing goods or services but as buying customers, as doing the things that will make people want to do business with it. And the chief executive himself has the inescapable responsibility for creating this environment, this viewpoint, this attitude, this aspiration. He himself must set the company's style, its direction, and its goals. This means he has to know precisely where he himself wants to go, and to make sure the whole organization is enthusiastically aware of where that is. This is a first requisite of leadership, for unless he knows where he is going, any road will take him there."

Mr. Levitt, a lecturer in the field of marketing at the Harvard Business School and a prolific writer whose articles have appeared in popular as well as professional journals, is in wide demand as a speaker on the myopia which seems to be so widespread among would-be marketers.

Carrying the same theme a step further, Edward M. Barnet says in his vigorous discussion of the new innovistic competition versus the Maginot Line concept of fair trade: "The mass market awaits those who adapt to it." In his paper, "Showdown in the Market Place," Mr. Barnet challenges the attitude of management which struggles to maintain the status quo, to uphold fair trade in the teeth of the burgeoning success of the discount house, and to buck the trend toward the supermarket shopping center. In its place the author, drawing on his broad experience in both industry and the academic world, advocates a new fashion in competition, one that calls on management to see distribution problems in their totality instead of by departmental or institutional fragment, one which demands instead that top management focus its attention on total return on investment. The imaginative re-shuffling of functions and their costs between manufacturer and retailer and between retailer and consumer, he declares, can lead to substantially greater profits for everyone involved.

Mr. Barnet has taught at Columbia, Northwestern, and Michigan State, and is currently vice president in charge of planning for Kitchens of Sara Lee. His concept of "the market place," however, reflects a wide range of consulting work in this country and abroad as well as earlier executive positions with Saco-Moc Shoe Corporation and Marshall Field and Company.

Professor Reavis Cox rounds out the discussion of marketing backgrounds by drawing on a study he made for the Twentieth Century Fund. Out of his research on the nature and purposes of marketing, he came to the conclusion that there are three rationales of marketing—each one different but equally essential. In "Three-in-One Marketing" Mr. Cox explains these three rationales and points out clearly how, if they are considered together, they should assist the serious marketing executive "to understand better what these problems are and so set us on the road to solutions," and maintains that, while the ideas presented will not solve the problems of management in marketing, "without something of this sort we are not likely even to get started."

Professor Cox, Food Fair Stores Foundation Professor of Marketing at the Wharton School of Finance and Commerce, University of Pennsylvania, has a background of consulting and teaching which goes back to 1931.

Following the introduction to the "marketing concept" and the new responsibilities which rest on top management to reorganize to meet the new challenges in the areas of distribution, fourteen articles are presented under five functional subdivisions: The Consumer; The Product and Product Strategy; The Role of Research; The Economics of Advertising; and Pricing Policy and Profit Goals.

THE CONSUMER

J. W. Jewell, vice president in charge of marketing at Westinghouse Electric Corporation, told a marketing audience recently: "It must be made known that managing the market is just as critical as managing the mill; that we must first know what the customer wants before we plan; that our products must be, not those we want to make, but those the customer wants to buy; that our distribution system must be based, not on the habits of our particular industry, but on our customers' habits; and that our production and distribution decisions must be shaped by a constant flow of information from the marketplace."[1]

The editors have chosen two articles to demonstrate how this warning can be best applied by the alert management which wants to increase the efficiency of its marketing program.

When Pierre Martineau, the vigorous and imaginative director of research and marketing for the *Chicago Tribune*, presented "It's Time to Research the Consumer" in the *Harvard Business Review* in 1955, he introduced his article with a question: "Is it not strange that business, which uses product research, market research, and research in employee problems so extensively, does a complete about-face when confronted with consumer research?" And why, he continued, shouldn't business "try to unravel the underlying significance and the linkages between such surface phenomena as the flair for color in cars and men's shirts and refrigerators, the rise of discount houses and outlying shopping centers, the yearning for self-expression which emerges in new hobbies, new home designs, new places to travel to?"

In his outline of how this kind of research can be managed, what quality of results can be achieved, and how they can be interpreted and applied, he presents a dramatic record of an outstanding and varied research program which he organized and carried out for the *Chicago Tribune's* advertising clients.

Don't be misled into believing that, because his allusions to then current fads are now outdated, his concepts fall into the same category. When asked if he wished to update them for publication in this volume, his answer was "No." And the reason he gave was that 90 per cent of American business still gives nothing more than lip service to really serious consumer research. "The basic points I made in 1955," he declares, "are just as valid in the mid-1960's. Business still refuses to tackle this business seriously."

William D. Wells, associate professor of psychology at Rutgers University, considers the consumer research job from a quite different point of view. Where Martineau is primarily concerned with an exploration of why consumers think as they do, Wells is concerned with the applications of the new computer simulation techniques to the development of a sounder marketing strategy.

In "Computer Simulation of Consumer Behavior," he points out that, until recently, "attempts to simulate complex social systems have not met with much success. Analogies from physics prove to be too loose. Mathematical structures fail to represent the market with the fidelity required. And models couched only in words are much too vague. Computer simulation differs from these previous attempts in two important ways. First, every unit in the simulated system is represented as a separate entity in the machine. Second, the units 'behave'—they imitate the activities of the things they represent. Together these properties give computer simulation its unique power as a research tool [which can] . . . provide a way to conduct test-market experiments at extraordinary speed and at a fraction of their present cost . . . Because they will reduce the costs and risks of experimenting, they will encourage the unusual, but brilliant, plan."

THE PRODUCT AND PRODUCT STRATEGY

The essence of the modern marketing concept is the substitution of research-based planning for intuition and guesswork and the effective integration and coordination of all business activities with marketing. For this reason, the modern marketing manager must be actively involved in long-range planning of new products and company expansion as well as in the programing of current marketing strategy. To aid the manager directly concerned with such problems, a group of five articles on the product and product strategy are included.

Closely related to the Martineau article on "researching the consumer" is "The Product and the Brand," by Burleigh B. Gardner and Sidney J. Levy. The difference—and the reason the two articles are included in different sections of this book—lies in the emphasis Gardner and Levy place on a single facet of consumer psychology: loyalty to a specific brand of product.

Mr. Gardner, who is president of Social Research, Inc., and Mr. Levy, who is professor of marketing at Northwestern University and associate director of Social Research, Inc., pointed out to the editors when they prepared their article that counting noses and listening to what consumers say are their reasons for buying can be very misleading, especially since competing brands often show only minute quality differences and claim almost the same points of superiority in their advertising. Qualitative research into consumer motives, however, can produce for both company management and the advertising agency fresh insight into their joint task of building brand loyalty. Besides presenting a working pattern for the heads of marketing departments and advertising agency personnel, the article also provides a capsulization, with working examples, of the basic philosophy of "motivation" research, a Madison Avenue fad during most of the 1950's.

This same issue of brand loyalty has been the focus of almost continuous research by the late Professor Ross M. Cunningham, of the School of Industrial Management of the Massachusetts Institute of Technology. His article, "Brand Loyalty—What, Where, How Much?" reports the findings of a particular research project covering 402 families in the Chicago area, and shows that, while people have varying degrees of brand loyalty to different products, a significant amount of brand loyalty does exist within individual product groups. The exact tabulation of results by product areas will be of considerable interest to those who are concerned with this particular problem.

There is nothing quite like an eye-opening new product to overcome consumer inertia. Sometimes a new functional feature on an old product can achieve much the same results if wisely presented to the public. These functional changes, however, vary in impact. When the amount of operational effort that is required to use the product in terms of skill, work, and frequency is small, functional changes are of little help in improving salability. Water heaters and wrist watches, for example, require little work to operate, so operational features are a minor item in the planning of promotion. Automobiles, on the other hand, not only require a great deal of skill and effort to operate, but the circumstances of operation vary widely. For this reason, automobile manufacturers find some of their best advertising features in the functional improvements they are able to offer in their new models.

In "Functional Features in Product Strategy," John B. Stewart, professor of business administration at the University of Richmond, presents his findings from a study of approximately 5,000 functional claims made by 206 companies over a period of 26 years. His study not only sheds light on the marketing use of functional features but also points up some of their advantages over such other kinds of product differentation as styling and brand image. While consumer attitudes are of the utmost importance in the planning of product lines, management should not overlook the fact that consumer wishes cannot be the sole measure of the feasibility of adding a new product to the line. Of equal significance is the way in which the new product can be fitted into the company's existing resources. If this is not considered carefully and in detail, profit potential is jeopardized.

In "The Strategy of Product Policy," Charles H. Kline reviews his own experience at Climax Molybdenum and General Electric and sets up a list of nine economic areas in which company resources need to be measured before a product policy is determined. What these areas are, and how each should be weighted in the final policy decision, is discussed in detail. Mr. Kline is now president of Charles H. Kline & Company, Inc.

The final article in this section on The Product and Product Strategy is, significantly, "Strategy of Product Quality." Alfred A. Kuehn and Ralph L. Day point out the truism that marketing executives, if they are really "consumer-oriented," know that their marketing efforts face an uphill climb when the physical attributes of their product do not fit the preferences of a substantial group of consumers better than competing brands do. What makes their article of value to the marketing specialist is the concrete program of consumer-preference distribution which they lay out and explain. The paper includes elements of thinking and planning similar to those outlined by Martineau and Gardner and Levy, but they are focused completely on the issue of product quality. Mr. Kuehn is associate professor of industrial administration at Carnegie Institute of Technology and Mr. Day is professor of marketing at Pennsylvania State University.

THE ROLE OF RESEARCH

As a result of the commanding role played by science and technology, no aspect of business today is unaffected by the new importance which is attached to research. In the field of marketing, the emphasis has been especially significant because it has stretched from consumer taste analysis to organization strategy and has employed disciplines ranging from psychology to advanced mathematics.

While research has been a factor in many of the preceding articles in this series, in two it is the primary issue. "Phasing Research into the Marketing Plan" is designed specifically to point out to management that since marketing itself is being planned and conceptualized in new and exciting ways, it is critical now to see that each business develops a unified concept of marketing research which will make it possible for researchers to grapple with marketing problems as seen by top management.

Lee Adler, the author of this thoughtful article, is client service director for Marplan, the research affiliate of Interpublic, Inc. He writes from experience with numerous clients, as well as his own advertising firm, and charts dramatically a sample six-year marketing research plan for a new consumer product so that readers will understand exactly how his proposed four phases for new product marketing should be developed.

As he warns in his article, "If research executives want to assume more responsible positions in the corporate structure, they will have to find ways of increasing the contribution of their groups to the successful implementation of the marketing concept" rather than to limiting their research to such small pieces of a major problem that the relationship to the total problem is seldom demonstrated.

A second area of research which, though old in concept, is frequently ignored or badly used is market testing. In some cases, this is due to the fact that management is unwilling to allow time for an adequate test. In others, it is caused by a reluctance to reveal a new product to a competitor for fear it will be copied before an adequate test is possible. And occasionally marketing departments' emotional involvement in the campaign is so great that an objective appraisal of results becomes impossible.

In "Market Testing," Ernest J. Enright, director of research for the International Marketing Institute, reports the conclusions he reached after a study of fourteen market-testing campaigns of packaged consumer goods and on discussions with numerous executives of companies selling packaged goods and appliances.

The kernel of his findings is the fact that the determinant of success or failure in most market tests is to be found in the management of the details of a campaign. What to look for and how to handle problems as they arise are fully described.

"Whenever the executive committee begins to consider the design of a test campaign that can be questioned on grounds that it allows too little time for testing, testing in an off-season, testing on too limited a scale, testing before production can meet the inventory requirements of market testing, inadequate research methods to measure the results of the test campaign, or the closing of the campaign before research can do its work, it is time to stop and think," Mr. Enright believes.

"Market Testing" is included in this volume for those executives who are ready, openly and coolly, to consider the whole risk proposition with an accurate awareness of the pressures they feel and then to draw up a thoughtful plan of action.

THE ECONOMICS OF ADVERTISING

Because advertising is such an important factor in the over-all marketing picture, two thought-provoking articles which deal with the economics of advertising are included in this volume. Some of the questions that are raised and discussed are: How much is advertising worth? Why not spend the money on salesmen? Does it pay to advertise at all? How can you have more effective, more efficient advertising?

Cyril Freeman, advertising and sales promotion manager of Worthington Corporation, sets out in "How to Evaluate Advertising's Contribution" to show that it is possible to apply numbers to some of the subjective estimates which management is constantly asked to make in appraising the actual return from an advertising campaign. This includes an appraisal of the portion of over all cost which should be applied to each of the six selling tasks in a sales process.

Freeman's advertising yardstick approach is a firm, aggressive position, not a defensive one. It can be applied to all classes of business, and to both product and corporate program evaluations. Beyond this, it is a way for advertising to talk to top management in the same language as sales.

The same realistic approach to dealing with the so-called intangibles of advertising is pursued by Russell H. Colley, a management consultant, in "Squeezing the Waste out of Advertising." In his opening paragraph he boldly claims: "A shockingly large share of the $12 billion spent annually for advertising is wasted for one fundamental reason: lack of well-defined objectives."

"In search of profit and growth," he claims, "corporate management has focused its attention on the technological aspects of business. In the past, here was where the big productivity gains could be made; and here was where top management felt most competent and comfortable . . . [Today, it is] in marketing, which represents over 50% of United States economic activity, or more than $250 billion annually, [that] the opportunities for productivity gains are so large and numerous that we practically stumble over them. And," he adds, "the *crème-de-la-crème* lies in advertising." How to effect economies and how to measure results are described in detail. One of the most intriguing parts of Mr. Colley's article is his table showing the ratio of advertising expenditures to earnings for the hundred largest advertisers.

PRICING POLICY AND PROFIT GOALS

No book devoted to modern marketing strategy would be complete without consideration of pricing policy and profit goals, and three articles on these critically important problems are included.

In "Multistage Approach to Pricing," Alfred R. Oxenfeldt, professor of marketing at Columbia University, outlines for executives who seek a sound, long-range, policy-oriented approach to better prices a series of six successive steps which, though lacking a mechanical formula, are designed to make executive judgment in this area sharper and surer.

The author's six elements essential to sound pricing policy, placed in the sequence in which they need to be considered, are: (1) selecting market targets; (2) choosing a brand "image"; (3) composing a marketing mix; (4) selecting a pricing policy; (5) determining a pricing strategy; and (6) arriving at a specific price.

One of the oldest articles included in the series (1950), but one so basic in its concept that it has been in steady reprint demand ever since it was published, is "Pricing Policies for New Products," by Joel Dean, president of the management consulting firm of Joel Dean Associates and professor of business economics at Columbia University.

In contrast to the Oxenfeldt article on pricing, Mr. Dean deals almost entirely with the special problems which are involved in the early stages of introducing a new product. "Pricing in the pioneering stage of the cycle involves difficult problems of projecting potential demand and of guessing the relation of price to sales. The first step in this process is to explore consumer preferences and to establish the feasibility of the product, in order to get a rough idea of whether demand will warrant further exploration. The second step is to mark out a range of prices that will make the product economically attractive to buyers. The third step is to estimate the probable sales that will result from alternative prices."

Mr. Dean's step-by-step analysis of pricing policy will provide a valuable guide to the marketing man who is struggling to break away from the usual fuzziness which surrounds price planning.

Since the early 1950's one of managements greatest and most persistent problems has been the squeeze on profits. Since the beginning of the otherwise "Fabulous Fifties," our gross national product has almost doubled, but the profit segment in terms of the percentage share of GNP has shrunk by one third. Because there is no indication that the trend is likely to change soon, management will continue to need constructive guidance on ways to improve the profit picture.

"How to Set Realistic Profit Goals," by Bruce Payne, President of Bruce Payne & Associates, Inc., is included in this volume on modern marketing strategy for two reasons: first, it stresses the urgent need for long-range company planning—an essential for sound management of all business today—and second, it helps to shape executive thinking on the way in which both short- and long-term sales goals must be set as a part of the over-all strategy of every successful business.

No single volume can provide a full background to the revolutionary changes which have taken place in the last dozen years as marketing has evolved from the narrow functional role it once played to one of being today the organizational core of every well-run business. In a period of change and development which has ranged from installment credit policy to the cash policies of the discount house and from nose-counting research to highly sensitive consumer-motivation studies utilizing the whole gamut of the social sciences, only the highlights of change which seem essential to future patterns of marketing can be included. Each article, also, has been chosen for its clarity of interpretation for the men and women who are presently training themselves to occupy key positions in the new marketing management.

It must be reiterated, however, that in this age of rapidly changing technology, enormous population growth, and the general explosion of knowledge far beyond the realm of science, no body of principles can remain static. In the field of marketing, the throbbing center of our economic lives, this is least possible. For the marketing specialist, the most that these articles can provide is a discussion of some of the basic problems and their solutions which the editors feel are most likely to provide a sound foundation in which the individual can continue to build and update his knowledge in the future.

E. C. B.
J. F. C.

MODERN MARKETING STRATEGY

1

CONDITIONS OF MARKETING LEADERSHIP

ARTHUR P. FELTON

A tremendous number of companies are experiencing marketing difficulties these days. Businessmen know this. Consultants are made keenly aware of it because so many of the problems management gives them are marketing problems. Many consumers do not need to be told that companies have troubles in this area, for they have been on the "receiving end" of them—service difficulties, for instance.

But as we look ahead, the prospect is that business will have even more marketing difficulties next year, more still five or ten years from now. For technological progress is still outstripping marketing progress, and the peculiar nature of technological progress today is making the marketing job harder.

Take automation, for example. As James R. Bright pointed out in discussing its impact on management: "The marketing man is going to have to be *very* right or else he may have nothing to eat but a stream of unsalable products."[1] Indeed, in the years ahead we will probably see marketing become a more challenging problem than it has ever been in our industrial history, even though over-all sales volume continues to increase. It will be easier to make things but not to sell them.

It is quite true, of course, that marketing is not standing still.

[1] "Thinking Ahead (Some Effects of Automation)," *Harvard Business Review*, November–December 1955, p. 27.

We have come out of the doldrums of the 1940's. Companies are experimenting with new methods and techniques—motivation research, better sales training, various kinds of market audits, and so forth. However, none of them offers anything in the way of a basic solution to the marketing problem. None of them would relieve the real difficulties which so many companies are getting themselves into today, although they might prove very useful once other steps are taken.

THREE ESSENTIALS

Judging by the experience of a wide range of companies with all sorts of marketing problems, there are three essential conditions of marketing leadership—and they are becoming increasingly important:

(1) Top management must recognize that the nature of the marketing problem is fundamentally different from the nature of the production problem. This fact has vital implications for (a) executive selection, (b) marketing strategy, and (c) sales organization. Failure to take the differences into account has got countless companies into serious trouble.

(2) Management must recognize the dynamic quality of the marketing problem—all the constant change that is continually occurring not only in the market but also in channels to the market. The change is so continuous and so widespread that it makes every sales plan in the country out of date to some extent. Failure to grasp this point, perhaps more than anything else, has kept companies from getting out of sales trouble when they might otherwise have succeeded.

(3) The crying need in marketing management today is for greater conceptual skill—the ability to see the enterprise as a whole and to understand how the various functions of the company and its sales organization depend on one another.[2] The specialists who devise techniques and conduct studies have been "going to town," but the general managers have not.

The tendency has been to think in terms of formulas such as "working back from the market" or in terms of a particular group such as the distributors, rather than to consider all parts of the

[2] See Robert L. Katz, "Skills of an Effective Administrator," *Harvard Business Review*, January–February 1955, p. 33.

marketing problem in relation to each other and to the rest of the company—for example, executive resources, productive capacity, and procurement.

The aim of this paper is to describe the nature of these conditions in more detail and show how they can be met.

MARKETING VERSUS PRODUCTION

How do companies get into marketing difficulties? In all the cases with which my associates and I are familiar, ranging from small companies in the paper industry to large companies in the steel industry, certain causes keep recurring with almost demoniacal frequency.

One such cause is the failure to recognize that marketing calls for a different executive temperament than does production. A factory-trained executive usually follows a logical line of reasoning that works best in factual situations. By contrast, sales executives must often think with only intangibles as a guide. In general, they are not accustomed to a clinical or analytical approach. Although successful sales executives are practical men, with push and drive to get things done, they typically count more on an intuitive feel for situations than do executives in other departments.

The rules that work in selling are just not the same, in letter or in spirit, as the rules that work in other business areas. It is in companies where this fact is not appreciated that we often find production and financial influence to be greater than marketing influence. Sooner or later that situation usually leads to poor or unprofitable sales, large pile-ups of obsolete inventories, and high administrative overhead.

In addition, the physical aspects of a marketing problem are different in many respects from the physical aspects of a production problem. The four walls of the plant may bound a problem in manufacturing but scarcely ever do they confine a problem in marketing. Machines, materials, and skilled men are the usual elements of a production problem; but the uncertain attitudes of distant consumers or industrial buyers may dominate the marketing problem. There are not as many facts and figures in marketing as in production.

Moreover, the data that do exist are not so easily controllable,

3

nor can they be checked so easily. Perhaps more important, it has not been customary for marketing men to make the best use of their data; the sales executive works in the midst of quite different currents of thinking than does the factory superintendent or industrial engineer who works in a tradition of scientific management and careful methodology.

When management fails to recognize the important differences between marketing and production, and particularly when the production influence becomes stronger than the marketing influence, telltale symptoms of "production-mindedness" soon become evident. Here are a few of them:

Designing in isolation—There may be a tendency to believe that a couple of smart people can design products and packages in a sheltered laboratory, run as a wing of the production facilities—without regard to the often-learned lesson that the artists and designers can and should be supplied with market facts. For all their ability, the creative geniuses cannot ensure acceptance by consumers or industrial buyers unless they take into account people's habits, motives, and feelings.

Avoidance of consumer research—Attitudes about consumer research are an especially sensitive indicator in industries which are several steps away from the consumer, and in which it might seem plausible for manufacturers to leave it up to retailers, wholesalers, and jobbers to learn what their customers want and to pass this information back. In fact, this attitude was once prevalent in virtually all industries producing primary goods, but some of them—notably steel, asphalt, and chemicals—have now come to the conclusion that distributors either will not or cannot do the job for them, and so they have gone into basic market research themselves. They reason that if their customers down the line do not sell end products, they will not buy raw materials.

However, not all such industries have come around to this point of view. The textile industry is a well-known example. There is some well-informed opinion to the effect that textiles would not have run into so much trouble in the postwar years if they had not taken a "let-George-do-it" policy about consumer research.[3]

[3] See the editorial in *America's Textile Reporter*, June 24, 1954.

Misdirected advertising—Too much production influence in the company's marketing effort usually shows up in advertising copy. Is it aimed at the industrial buyer or consumer, whichever the case may be, or does it glorify the company's research and engineering effort? Compare automobile advertising, generally a good example, with textile advertising, all too often a bad one. The automobile ads aim to make last year's model obsolete in the consumer's eye; by contrast, during the "battle of the fibers" of the 1950's the manufacturers of wool, cotton, and man-made fibers, instead of trying to make wardrobes seem obsolete, vied with claims of longevity and durability.

Inadequate market investment—Another symptom is insignificant expenditures for developing consumer markets in comparison with tremendous sums spent on research, cost reduction, and new plant and equipment. Thus, when the can makers first attempted to get the public to use beer in cans rather than bottles, they spent huge sums developing the can but left it up to the brewers to do the selling job—and no progress was made. It was only when a leading beer-can manufacturer stepped heavily into consumer promotion based on preference studies that buying habits were revolutionized.

Perhaps what all this adds up to is a plea for taking a fresh look at the complexities of marketing. One who goes from company to company and from industry to industry working on marketing problems is continually impressed—or, more accurately, appalled —by the tendency among executives everywhere to simplify, to reduce to rules, or (using one of their favorite terms) to try to "engineer" a sales program. This is nearly always fatal. Systematic thinking—yes. Efforts to analyze a problem—yes. But the attempt to apply to marketing what has worked in production (or, for that matter, in finance)—no.

Why should management underrate and belittle its job? Marketing is an area for awe and wonder. It is full of questions, unsolved problems, and baffling inconsistencies. It is dominated by the whims of consumers and the fancies of buyers. When management recognizes marketing for what it is and then proceeds to try to master it, the credit for a job well done is the greater because the job is more difficult.

CHANGE AND COUNTERCHANGE

There is probably no marketing plan in industry today that is not out of date. This may seem like a startling statement, but we actually have not been able to find any exception to it. The reason is that there are so many constantly changing factors in any company's marketing situation that it is practically impossible to keep revising a plan so rapidly and so accurately that there is no lag in it. The factors that keep a plan dated are not only those of the "changing American market" which *Fortune* and other publications have discussed—suburbia, the new middle class, the Negro market, and so on.[4] The dating factors have also to do with changing selling problems in consumer psychology that necessitate different kinds of advertising and packaging, trends in distribution that affect the company's relations with wholesalers and jobbers, changes in the "customer mix" that affect the efficiency of the sales organization, and the like.

The practical significance of the foregoing is that if management does not have a carefully thought-out marketing plan, or has a program based on insufficient facts, or—worse yet—has no real plan at all, the company's selling effort may fall dangerously out of phase with the times and may precipitate a company crisis. What are the most important steps management can take so that this will not happen?

The keystone of a strong marketing plan—the part of the program on which all the others depend—is a long-range objective. It is difficult to overemphasize the importance of this cardinal principle. Many companies find themselves in the position of not knowing where they are going and of having only vague ideas as to how to get anywhere. These companies rock along from month to month taking expedient action for each problem. The sales department consequently rides from one crisis to another—and nothing is done to determine the underlying reasons for the crises.

Why does all this happen in the absence of objectives? The reason is largely human nature, and especially "executive nature." Managers are opportunistic, and unless counteracted their oppor-

---

[4] The Editors of Fortune, *The Changing American Market* (Garden City, N. Y., Hanover House, 1955); see also Chapter 5, below.

tunism tends to dominate decision making. Sales managers and salesmen seek to capitalize on short-run deals and on tempting but (as it so often turns out) only transient markets. Before long the sales organization is confused and unwieldy; the company is committed to too many projects, many of them fast becoming abortive; and production costs are rising because production is spread too thin or becomes out of balance. In effect, there is wasted effort in sales, which causes wasted effort in other departments of the company. The sales managers call louder, "Let's get out and make calls, men," and the men spin their wheels doing it.

For example, a manufacturing company that had specialized for 45 years in the production of certain kinds of engine parts began losing business when its jobbers began turning to competitors offering wider lines. (Also, a competitor had found a way to make one of the parts automatically.) Without formulating a long-range sales plan, management began a vigorous search for business in other lines. Orders were approved for many items which the company had not made before; if the new business looked profitable, and if production could find some way to get it out, the customer's order was solicited. In effect, the company tried to be all things to all people. However, it turned out that the plant was not equipped to make many of the new lines well or cheaply enough. Both production and sales costs rose to dangerous levels. In reorganizing the strategy of this company, the emphasis was put on concentration. What sections of the market was the company best equipped to sell to? What specific objectives in certain areas could the sales force best be set up to reach? Only when a marketing plan with long-range objectives was developed in such a manner could the company move back into a strong profit position.

Here it is important to stress that objectives can be stated in more ways than in terms of sales volume. For example, management's number one objective may be to become the quality leader in its field—and advertising copy, public relations, and the selection of new business may be governed by that criterion. (A management pursuing this kind of an objective knows full well, of course, that sales will eventually follow a reputation for quality; at the same time, the marketing history of such a company will

7

develop quite differently from that of the company which sets as its objective becoming the leader in sales volume. Objectives can also be translated into specific tactics.

To take one case, a few years ago it was announced that Indian Head Mills would spend $300,000 to advertise a tablecloth-making project, urging people to go to their neighborhood stores and request two yards of Indian Head's fabric. While management expected to sell enough fabric to justify the cost of the campaign, and accordingly set quotas high enough to do so, the objective was not just to sell tablecloth fabric. Management's main purpose was to solidify Indian Head's leadership in textile merchandising, in this case by initiating the largest single promotional campaign in piece-goods history. In addition, management knew that the campaign would sharpen up the "pitch" of company salesmen; they could refer to the numbers of people going into stores to request Indian Head and capitalize on the story to sell industrial buyers. In short, part of the objective was to gain dealer cooperation by a tie-in promotional campaign rather than to promote the company name through an institutional approach. This is the kind of shrewd tactic that only a management with its longer-range objectives clearly in mind is likely to seize upon.

Whatever its objectives, a management will probably want to set dollar-volume goals—for purposes of control, if nothing else. Progressive companies today are setting goals at least five years in advance and then programing sales objectives for each year. These objectives not only should be stated in total dollar sales and total unit sales but also should be subdivided by specific products and product groups—and even by number and type of distributors needed to achieve the objectives.

Why all this detail? One of the most important reasons has to do with changing market trends. Specific objectives make it possible to check the sales performance of each product (and distributor). A product's failure to live up to expectations may be a danger signal—the first sign that there are new consumer trends affecting design or general suitability, or the first sign that there are new selling problems with implications, say, for the sales or service organization. Maybe product B increased only 10% instead of 20%, but product C increased 30% against an expected 20%. In both cases, it is important to know why; "management by exception" should work both ways.

All of us are familiar with the hackneyed phrase "Know your market." But we sometimes tend to think of the market only in the static terms of the dictionary sense of the word. "Market" should mean to us not only today's customers but tomorrow's and those we will have in 1968; not only today's price but also the likely price (and quality) four years from now; not only present methods of reaching customers but also the methods we will be using when current living and working trends become established habits.

It is because there are so many constantly changing factors in sales that market information is the problem that it is. Often management gets into trouble—or cannot get out of trouble—simply because of its data. The data are not accurate enough, timely enough, or well enough organized to allow executives to realize the full significance of changes which have occurred or are in the making.

In one case, the managers of a company making an automotive product received many reports each month on total sales of their own products and of automobiles. No direct action was ever taken on the basis of the reports, however, although they were read "with interest." Then management got the idea of making the reports specific and, more important, of showing the figures "in motion." New reports began going out revealing that within total car sales of all makes, sales of model X were holding their own, sales of model Y were decreasing, but sales of model Z were rising. When the managers saw these consumer preference trends, they really sat up; Z was what their company was best equipped to manufacture parts for! Moreover, when price trends were portrayed, it appeared that the company could realistically shoot for a larger share of the market if the selling price could be reduced about 10%. Management cut its price on the basis of increased volume expectations and a determined cost-reduction program—and this turned out to be a very successful move.

Judging from industrial records and actual company case histories, it is hard to escape the conclusion that most firms do not know their market very well. Granted the data may not be hanging out in bunches ready to be plucked, but good market data can always be obtained. Often a rich source is government and trade association reports, and it is unfortunate that more managements do not take advantage of them.

For instance, a manufacturer of woolen goods who wants to size up the market for his fabric lines can use information compiled by the Department of Commerce, National Association of Wool Manufacturers, National Outerwear Association, Dun & Bradstreet, National Credit Office's Market Planning Service, Fairchild Publications, and several confidential trade sources. All of this material, except for the last of course, is published.

Forecasts are another good example of market data relatively easy to get—in almost any industry. According to a Federal Reserve Board study made several years ago, there were 437 trade associations providing some sort of economic or statistical information for their members; over 250 of these associations were regularly assembling and disseminating information on the future prospects of the economy, the industry, or both.

More often the trouble is not so much lack of sources as lack of imagination and skill in the use of sources, including tests of the representativeness of samples and checkbacks of results against predictions.

In the case of a firm making a product for interior decoration, an important factor in the market naturally was the number of interior decorators. In a market study, management turned to the Census, which indicated that there were some 1,300 interior decorators. According to this figure there was not a great deal of room for increasing sales of the present line, so the management, being aggressive, decided tentatively to branch into new product lines. As subsequent events showed, this would have been a sad mistake. But, fortunately, the management did what few managements do: it had a more professional survey made. By just taking the further steps of checking the circulation data of an interior decorators' magazine, talking with an informed credit service, interviewing company salesmen, and making a spot mail survey, it was learned that there were actually 9,700 interior decorators and that they spent some $75 million a year for this product alone. The company's biggest and best market for expansion was the one it was already selling!

Nowhere is constant change a more important factor to watch than in a company's channels of distribution. These will be periodically reviewed by alert managements, and modern techniques of distribution cost analysis will be used to aid in making policy decisions. Sometimes new trends will operate in the company's favor, sometimes not; but always there are in the making trends which do affect sales and profits, and because it is impossible to keep any plan completely in pace with them, it is never correct to say that "our marketing effort is more than 90% efficient." To mention just a few of the possibilities for change:

(1) The company's market may be changing from a few relatively large customers in a concentrated area to several thousand smaller customers all over the country, with the result that the existing distributor setup is becoming less efficient. In the case of one company where this recently happened, the trend was so pronounced that it led to hundreds of thousands of dollars' worth of obsolete inventory, heavy markdowns, and a sharp increase in administrative overhead.

(2) Distributors' lack of merchandising ability may emerge as a decisive factor in the market. Television is a case in point. In 1955 over 7 million television sets were sold (7½ to 8 million according to one source); yet many manufacturers, notably medium-size firms, were forced out of business. The larger companies were able to spend a good deal on advertising and promotion, and some ten heavily advertised makes became well known to the public.

The key is the fact that the distributors were able to sell the well-known sets, but lacked the merchandising ability to push the lesser-known sets. With the "squeeze" on to sell, distributors concentrated on the big ten and left many other makers stranded. Significantly, some of the medium-size manufacturers did do well in certain localities where there happened to be a larger number of good distributors.

(3) Many progressive distributors, wholesalers, and retailers are tending to concentrate purchases with a few suppliers. For

11

manufacturers dealing with these outlets, the trend means that management must either offer a complete and well-promoted line or else risk having to turn to other—and probably less progressive—distributors.

Some sales executives have become so deeply involved with one method of distribution that they overlook the possibilities of other methods which, though once inappropriate, are now more closely attuned to the company's needs. Often the answer is not a single method but a combination of methods. Thus, one large manufacturing company that recently found it could no longer afford to service a large percentage of its retail accounts has turned away from tradition and carefully selected several distributors to handle a large volume of small repetitive orders at an attractive discount—and at lower cost to the manufacturer.

In fact many companies today are in a position to undertake what they might consider "radical" approaches to distribution. For some firms, such approaches might be house-to-house selling or direct selling by mail; for others, merchandising nonfood products through supermarkets, rack jobbing, or allowing supplementary sales organizations to sell the company's regular products under different brand names (a policy which, new studies show, may be more practical than many businessmen are inclined to think[5]).

Retailers, too, are looking for better selling techniques. One large chain of building-supply outlets has found that a self-service retail lumberyard offering a complete line of home-building and repair products direct to home owners can be quite successful under certain market conditions—another reflection of the do-it-yourself trend. It is too soon to pass judgment on many of the specific new approaches in marketing, but let us look at some of the possibilities which an imaginative executive group might consider.

(1) In most states of the South, school buying practices have forced publishers to centralize their warehousing operations in "book depositories." All public schools and other educational institutions order and receive from this one control point. The book depository performs all the functions of a wholesaler or a branch

[5] See Chapter 8, below.

operation except owning and actually selling the merchandise; it receives and stores merchandise, controls the inventory, receives and processes orders, packs, ships, invoices, and collects.

Some alert manufacturers have adapted the book-depository idea to their own needs, particularly where individual volume is not sufficient to warrant a branch warehousing operation. The obvious economies in paper work are supplemented greatly by economies in warehousing and handling. Much special-purpose equipment (lift trucks with special clamps, for instance) can be justified because of the greater volume. The manufacturer can reserve for himself any functions that he wishes (invoicing, for example, to keep prices confidential).

Small or medium-size manufacturers of appliances, automotive parts, and home furnishings might well look into this idea of specialized warehousing. Its main limitation is that it is not always easy to get together manufacturers of similar enough merchandise.

(2) There is, in many industries, an increasing trend toward the use of specialty jobbers. These jobbers, who are sometimes set up with the backing of a single manufacturer in the early stages, handle a narrow range of products—in some cases, the products of only one manufacturer. In one case, a midwestern manufacturer got, as a captive specialty jobber distributing its products exclusively, a man who had formerly distributed 4,500 items of 110 manufacturers.

More and more companies are becoming dissatisfied with the mediocre sales effort of distributors who are spread too thin. These companies are selecting the outstanding men with the important contacts and setting them up as specialists in their own territories. Granted, the specialty jobber will make a good living on perhaps just one account; but the manufacturer will benefit from the increased profits that will come from the intensified sales effort of a topnotch representative.

In some cases, management might find the answer it is looking for in specialized warehousing and specialized jobbing.

(3) Another interesting approach that has been tried is the automobile supermarket. A large dealer in the Midwest offers—for drive-away delivery—any model of any make of car, at bargain prices and with a full guarantee. With the increased prac-

tice of preselling merchandise through national advertising and sales promotion, at least one school of thought believes that there is very little need for specialized sales training of retail personnel. It is felt that a large percentage of prospective customers have been sufficiently presold so that much "shopping" comes down principally to a comparison of quality and prices.

The automobile supermarket offers the buyer a chance to compare, at one location, all his alternative choices without visiting a myriad of showrooms. This is, in essence, an open-air discount house. The supermarket owner claims that his high turnover and low overhead justify his low prices, and his volume is so great that no manufacturer can afford not to sell to him.

Merchants experienced in selling reasonably high-price merchandise with a high gross margin might well consider applying the automobile supermarket principle to those of their own products which are presold at the national level.

To a certain extent, every sales organization is created on the basis of the past experiences and prejudices of top officials. It has to be. But when these influences completely displace analytical judgments based on present-day market facts and anticipated future trends, the firm's marketing effort is almost certain to suffer. As selling conditions become more fluid in these years of a growing population, greater consumer spending power, and other "accelerators" of change, and as production tends to become more inflexible (at least on a short-term basis) because of automation, the importance of analytical judgments in organizing the sales effort will increase.

The unsound sales organization is commonly found in companies where it is headed by a sales manager who was hired from another industry in which he was successful. He tends to impose a similar plan of organization in his new surroundings, overlooking the fact that the former plan was for a different industry, different products, or different marketing conditions. Transplanting set ideas is not the answer to the problem of building a good sales organization.

Where the nature of the marketing problem is such that, say, quick decisions and specialized knowledge are needed, it would not be good to have a functional type of organization, however satisfactory for the company in times past or for other companies at present. On the other hand, it might be profitable, as a stimulus to constructive thinking, to look around at different ways of decentralizing sales responsibility. Let us look at an example of what can happen if sales management is not on its toes, and of what can be done when the danger is recognized before it is too late.

A New England manufacturer of a household product marketed through a variety of outlets—department, furniture, chain, and general stores, mail-order houses, club plans, and house-to-house agents. The product, slightly modified, was also sold to institutions, hotels, and motels. Over the years, the sales organization had grown here and there, this way and that, as expediency directed. There was one salesman who specialized in wholesalers, another who concentrated on all outlets in New York City, others who sold any and all accounts in stipulated territories. All salesmen reported directly to the sales manager, who also handled all "important" accounts personally.

One day, after 21 years on the job, the sales manager died. The department found itself in a crisis as it tried to carry on. However, its troubles were only symptomatic of a much deeper crisis which had been building up under the era of sloppy control of the deceased manager. For many years, unrecognized by the company, distribution methods and market conditions had been changing. Inevitably, creeping inefficiency had advanced to the point where there seemed to be nothing that the new sales manager could do within the existing framework to save the corporate neck. Sales were slipping, selling costs were mounting, and the sales manager himself had no time for policy thinking and forward planning.

When this situation became clear, the sales department was reorganized completely. The new setup provided for an office manager, a field sales manager, several staff directors, and a manager for advertising and merchandising, all with clear-cut responsibilities and authority; this relieved congestion at the top. As for the salesmen, their jobs were set on the basis of territory and type of outlet. For instance, where in the same territory one salesman had been selling to retailers and another to wholesalers (with the result that in effect they had been fighting each other), now the salesman for a given territory sold to both types of customers. But where the outlet was a unique one requiring specialized merchandising methods, as in the case of institutional sales, the business wherever located was put in the charge of one salesman.

The results showed up almost immediately, with a rise in sales and a reversal of the selling cost trend.

THE CONCEPTUAL APPROACH

Whenever top management begins to get worried about the marketing outlook, it is only natural that slogans like "Think retail" and "No sale, no profit" gain appeal—especially if the company suddenly realizes that production, finance, and research have been playing too dominant a role. This is all very well. But suppose management carries its sales consciousness a good deal further; suppose it buys the view which holds, as one expert stated in a national magazine, that "today you start with the market—not the factory—as the base for your organization and then work back."[6] Is this bolder, more extreme position desirable in a competitive industry with a dynamic market?

At first glance, the answer might seem to be yes. And probably it is yes in certain cases—for example, a detergent soap or a ball-point pen may be purely a merchandising proposition. But in the great majority of cases the extreme point of view just described is a troublemaker. Marketing cannot be effective if considered from a marketing point of view alone.

For the marketing officer, this means continual compromise and negotiation with other departments of the company. These compromises—or, better, adjustments—will be less hard to take as he develops a company viewpoint and understands why they must be made. For the president or executive vice president, the proposition just described means that "coaching" all department heads in conceptual skill—the ability, as Robert L. Katz described it, to see the enterprise as a working whole—is one of the most effective ways of helping any department to be effective. The less the managers of any department, marketing included, have to battle narrow, specialist viewpoints, and can count in-

[6] *Business Week*, December 11, 1954, p. 67.

stead on a meeting of the minds in top-level conferences (not necessarily agreement), the better off they will be.

Here are two examples of the conceptual approach applied at the interdepartmental level:

Marketing and production—From a market survey the sales manager of a large midwestern company in the electrical industry learned that there was a substantial market for a new line of consumer products. The survey showed that the line should be offered in eight sizes, with a wide range between the two extremes. The sales department drew up tight and definite specifications for the manufacturing department. The engineers went over these specifications and determined that the products could be made as detailed—but at an extremely high cost.

At this critical point a serious impasse might easily have developed, as often happens. An impasse of sorts was in fact beginning to develop in this situation. It was broken in the only possible way—by informal talks between the persons at odds. The sales manager hinted that more automatic machinery might be the solution; the plant manager at first reacted negatively because he feared loss of flexibility, then thought it over and came back with the proposition that maybe it would be feasible if specifications were relaxed a little; the sales manager indicated he was willing to contemplate this possibility; and together they went to the engineers and found that by changing the design of some of the internal components and applying some automatic controls, costs could be cut 20%.

As a result, the company launched an entirely new line of products on the market. The price was competitive, and a good profit was earned.

Marketing and top management—Toward the end of World War II, an old, established New England manufacturer of fabricated metal parts looked ahead to postwar conditions and decided to market a line of consumer products to retail outlets. As plans for the new venture were developed, it became apparent that a large amount of imaginative promotion would be necessary through a wholly new type of sales organization.

One fact loomed ominously when a realistic appraisal of executive resources was made: the president was vigorous and healthy, but any abilities which the other managers (either rela-

17

tives or stockholders) had in relation to their jobs were purely a matter of coincidence. Tests and interviews conducted by psychological experts showed that the managers had neither the experience nor the aptitude for manufacturing and selling high-volume, low-cost consumer products.

The upshot of all this was that the president reversed his earlier decision. The postwar marketing plans had to be tailored more to the management resources that were available.

Having looked at marketing's relationship to other parts of the company, let us now look at the relationships of different activities within the marketing effort itself. Here the contribution of conceptual thinking is as important as it is anywhere else.

Take motivation research, for example. It is one of the most interesting developments in the field. It has great possibilities. But its values must all be realized through the agencies that design, distribute, sell, and influence opinion. The buying decisions which a motivation study seeks to analyze are affected by the number and type of outlets; by the merchandising abilities of the dealers; by the freshness of the advertising copy, salesmanship, and public relations of the company (what consumers may read about it in the newspapers and see on television, and the like); and by other factors.

If marketing executives really want to capitalize on new findings about purchasing behavior, they will not merely revise product design or advertising or packaging in the light of what the researchers tell them—they will revise all of these activities to reinforce each other and have a total impact on sales greater than the sum of the individual contributions.

Here is an illustration of the way conceptual thinking works at the intradepartmental level. An appliance manufacturing company with a tough sales problem to lick made a survey of its dealers. The dealers were part of the problem because they were more interested in competitors' lines than in this manufacturer's. The survey showed that three product features would appeal to dealers: (a) superior quality, which would reduce service costs, typically borne by the dealer in this particular industry, (b) highly salable design, and (c) high price and high gross margin consistent with the quality features, giving dealers more flexibility on trade-ins.

In revamping its line of appliances, management naturally worked hard to please the consumer, but it also tried to please the dealer. Why design for consumers if dealers lacked an incentive to handle the line? This way of looking at the problem made quite a difference. For instance, the company had been manufacturing appliances in the low-price range; now it withdrew these models but extended its line in the medium-price and high-price ranges. In addition, one luxury model was added as a prestige item.

As a result of the new strategy, dealers began giving much more support to the company's products, and sales rose. Significantly, the most popular model in the line now sells for nearly twice as much as the lowest-price competitive model.

A Summary Case

Now let us look at a case which ties together many of the ideas discussed in the preceding pages. It points up the "chain reaction" of questions that occur when conceptual thinking is used, the kinds of conflicts between points of view that arise, and, in short, what happens that is different when executives go at a marketing problem this way rather than some other way.

The case involves an eastern manufacturer of a well-known staple product. (As far as the basic problems are concerned, the company might just as well have been a midwestern furniture manufacturer, a West Coast lumber producer, or a southern plastics firm.) For our purposes, the story began several years ago when the management realized that its market was changing. Several important trends were seen to be in the making:

(1) The industrial market was becoming more important than the consumer market. Whereas two thirds of the company's output had been going through wholesalers to retailers, and one third to industrial users, it now looked as if the situation would completely reverse itself within another ten years.

(2) On the retail scene, independents were playing a less important role in the distribution of the product, and chains a more important role.

(3) Geographically the market was changing too. The consumer market, which bade to become less important, was growing faster in the plant's home territory. But the more important industrial market was expanding faster in an area 1,500 miles west (with an average annual growth trend projected at 3%).

(4) Transportation costs—in particular, freight rates—had been increasing, and it looked as if they would continue to increase.

These trends posed a series of important questions for marketing executives. First of all, *what about the company salesmen?* They had been selected and trained to sell to wholesalers; it appeared now that, if they were going to go after a bigger share of the growing industrial market, they would need to be well instructed in materials and materials handling, the problems of commercial users. Obviously, selection and training procedures would need revision.

But *would not the sales organization need to be changed too?* The existing system emphasized clearcut sales territories and strict "territorial protection" for the individual salesmen who called on jobbers and commercial dealers. Perhaps it would be better to organize a task force of industrial salesmen who would freewheel across the country showing prospects how to use and handle the company's product; or to reorganize sales into commercial and domestic divisions, with managers of each reporting to a senior manager who would not be bothered by individual salesmen's problems.

Then the question of supporting the direct sales effort with other efforts was raised. For example, *what about packaging?* As for retail sales, the important fact was that in chain supermarkets there was less personal selling in the stores and more impulse buying. Therefore, the traditional black and white package should take on a little color and eye appeal; and maybe the routine labels could be supplemented with some attractively printed information for consumers about uses of the product. As for commercial sales, it seemed desirable to explore new, improved means of bulk shipping.

But just what package designs and colors would be best? And what kinds of advertising appeals would add to the impression? These questions pointed to another, more basic one: *Was more market research needed?* Little had been done in the way of pretesting, motivation research, or "bird-dogging" market statistics.

And if greater efforts were made along this line, as well as in the areas of packaging, sales training, and organization, could they be managed efficiently? *Were existing controls adequate?* In particular, there seemed to be a need for getting the control data in such form that it would lend itself to better distribution cost analysis.

So much for the "chain reaction" within the marketing department. Now let us look at some of the questions which were raised and disputed outside or beyond marketing.

Was plant expansion needed? The general manager, who had come up through engineering and manufacturing, presented a plan to the board of directors calling for a 50% increase in capacity at the eastern site—the maximum possible within the land and technological limitations. His plan was based on the fact that the company was currently operating at 105% of capacity, and that a 45% increase in the market was projected for the next ten years.

But another plan presented to the board took a more "marketing-minded" viewpoint. *Should a new factory of equal capacity be built in the area 1,500 miles west, where the booming industrial markets were centered?* The supporters of this plan pointed to the usual advantages of proximity to the market, and also to the savings in transportation of the finished product. They estimated that a $1,800,000 freight bill would have to be absorbed in five years if the proposed plant was not built (this figure would have been offset somewhat by the fact that new material freight costs would have been less at the eastern site).

When this plan was presented, some of the production men immediately pointed to problems. In the area of the proposed site, there was comparatively little skilled labor available, and it looked as if there would be "one hell of a training job." In addition, the area was heavily unionized. These were difficulties that had not been serious at the eastern plant. *Would new management skills in industrial engineering and industrial relations be needed—and just who was going to manage all this work?*

Still another viewpoint had to be considered. A good percentage of owners and board members were financial men. *Was the proposed second plant a sound enough investment?* Projected earnings showed that it would take nine or ten years for the new plant to equal the return on investment that could be achieved immediately if the eastern plant were expanded. Moreover, there was always the risk of a depression or of revolutionary new methods being developed in the industry.

So, *would it be better to expand on a more limited basis in the more mature, slow-growing eastern sector and capture larger short-range profits?* The younger executives in the firm took issue with this conservative view. They were more inclined to "grow with the economy." Their views were held in great importance by the board because both the first-line and second-line managers were older men nearing retirement age.

Further, the balance in capabilities of the present management was an issue if any kind of expansion was undertaken. The present managers were generally men who had been "pushers" in production (the firm was operating on a seven-day week, with three shifts a day) but with something of a laissez-faire attitude toward other areas of management—research and development, for example, and public relations. They had matured in an era when competition, while very much present, had never been dangerous. If the company bid for a greater share of the market, it seemed bound to run into much more vigorous competition than it had ever experienced before. *Did executives need to be brought in from outside who could complement the talents of the present management—and what about the need for executive training?*

These and many other questions were considered. What might have seemed to some at first as a fairly straightforward problem of marketing stategy became, with further thought, a problem with company-wide repercussions.

When all the different viewpoints were carefully considered, the board decided on the general manager's plan to expand the present plant. However, when it appeared that many of the younger executives might leave the company as a result, the board hit upon another solution: merger with a larger corporation in a related but noncompeting field. That firm was willing to supply the risk capital needed for the new second plant venture; it could also supply some of the management reinforcements needed in industrial relations and marketing. The price for these advantages, of course, was that management control would now have to be shared with another group, but that did not seem as serious as the risk of going ahead with either of the two plans proposed.

The moral of this case is not that merger is a good solution, but that conceptual thinking is a good approach. Applied within the marketing department, it produced a broad, well-balanced attack that, whatever tactical errors might be made, was strategically sound. Applied to the company as a whole, it produced a solution which combined the marketing virtues of the original two-plant plan with the features demanded by the financial and production interests in the company.

Of course the conceptual approach is difficult. In the long run, it tends to build understanding and agreement among managers, but in the short run it may tend to create friction simply because of the multitude of questions raised. More conferences are needed; and so are more legwork and more painstaking planning. Discouragement may be encountered as once simple problems magnify in scope and difficulty. But if marketing is to be recognized as the very complex management problem that it really is—so different from production, so beset with change—then conceptual thinking is a necessity. And there is always this to be said in its favor: it pays.

2

MARKETING MYOPIA

THEODORE LEVITT

Every major industry was once a growth industry. But some that are now riding a wave of growth enthusiasm are very much in the shadow of decline. Others which are thought of as seasoned growth industries have actually stopped growing. In every case the reason growth is threatened, slowed, or stopped is not because the market is saturated. It is because there has been a failure of management.

FATEFUL PURPOSES

The failure is at the top. The executives responsible for it, in the last analysis, are those who deal with broad aims and policies.

Thus, the railroads did not stop growing because the need for passenger and freight transportation declined. That grew. The railroads are in trouble today not because the need was filled by others (cars, trucks, airplanes, even telephones), but because it was not filled by the railroads themselves. They let others take customers away from them because they assumed themselves to be in the railroad business rather than in the transportation business. The reason they defined their industry wrong was because they were railroad-oriented instead of transportation-oriented; they were product-oriented instead of customer-oriented.

Hollywood barely escaped being totally ravished by television.

Actually, all the established film companies went through drastic reorganizations. Some simply disappeared. All of them got into trouble not because of television's inroads but because of their own myopia. As with the railroads, Hollywood defined its business incorrectly. It thought it was in the movie business when it was actually in the entertainment business. "Movies" implied a specific, limited product. This produced a fatuous contentment which from the beginning led producers to view television as a threat. Hollywood scorned and rejected television when it should have welcomed it as an opportunity—an opportunity to expand the entertainment business. Today television is a bigger business than the old narrowly defined movie business ever was. Had Hollywood been customer-oriented (providing entertainment), rather than product-oriented (making movies), would it have gone through the fiscal purgatory that it did? I doubt it. What ultimately saved Hollywood and accounted for its recent resurgence was the wave of new young writers, producers, and directors whose previous successes in television had decimated the old movie companies and toppled the big movie moguls.

There are other less obvious examples of industries that have been and are now endangering their futures by improperly defining their purposes. I shall discuss some in detail later and analyze the kind of policies that lead to trouble. Right now it may help to show what a thoroughly customer-oriented management can do to keep a growth industry growing, even after the obvious opportunities have been exhausted; and here there are two examples that have been around for a long time. They are nylon and glass—specifically, E. I. du Pont de Nemours & Company and Corning Glass Works. Both companies have great technical competence. Their product orientation is unquestioned. But this alone does not explain their success. After all, who was more pridefully product-oriented and product-conscious than the erstwhile New England textile companies that have been so thoroughly massacred? The Du Ponts and the Cornings have succeeded not primarily because of their product or research orientation but because they have been thoroughly customer-oriented also. It is constant watchfulness for opportunities to apply their technical know-how to the creation of customer-satis-fying uses which accounts for their prodigious output of successful new products. Without a very sophisticated eye on the customer, most of their new products might have been wrong, their sales methods useless.

Aluminum has also continued to be a growth industry, thanks to the efforts of two wartime-created companies which deliberately set about creating new customer-satisfying uses. Without Kaiser Aluminum & Chemical Corporation and Reynolds Metals Company, the total demand for aluminum today would be vastly less than it is.

Some may argue that it is foolish to set the railroads off against aluminum or the movies off against glass. Are not aluminum and glass naturally so versatile that the industries are bound to have more growth opportunities than the railroads and movies? This view commits precisely the error I have been talking about. It defines an industry, or a product, or a cluster of know-how so narrowly as to guarantee its premature senescence. When we mention "railroads," we should make sure we mean "transportation." As transporters, the railroads still have a good chance for very considerable growth. They are not limited to the railroad business as such (though in my opinion rail transportation is potentially a much stronger transportation medium than is generally believed).

What the railroads lack is not opportunity, but some of the same managerial imaginativeness and audacity that made them great. Even an amateur like Jacques Barzun can see what is lacking when he says: "I grieve to see the most advanced physical and social organization of the last century go down in shabby disgrace for lack of the same comprehensive imagination that built it up. [What is lacking is] the will of the companies to survive and to satisfy the public by inventiveness and skill."[1]

SHADOW OF OBSOLESCENCE

It is impossible to mention a single major industry that did not at one time qualify for the magic appellation of "growth industry." In each case its assumed strength lay in the apparently unchallenged superiority of its product. There appeared to be no effective substitute for it. It was itself a runaway substitute for the product it so triumphantly replaced. Yet one after another

[1] "Trains and the Mind of Man," *Holiday*, February 1960, p. 21.

of these celebrated industries has come under a shadow. Let us look briefly at a few more of them, this time taking examples that have so far received a little less attention.

Dry cleaning—This was once a growth industry with lavish prospects. In an age of wool garments, imagine being finally able to get them safely and easily clean. The boom was on.

Yet here we are 35 years after the boom started and the industry is in trouble. Where has the competition come from? From a better way of cleaning? No. It has come from synthetic fibers and chemical additives that have cut the need for dry cleaning. But this is only the beginning. Lurking in the wings and ready to make chemical dry cleaning totally obsolescent is that powerful magician, ultrasonics.

Electric utilities—This is another one of those supposedly "no-substitute" products that has been enthroned on a pedestal of invincible growth. When the incandescent lamp came along, kerosene lights were finished. Later the water wheel and the steam engine were cut to ribbons by the flexibility, reliability, simplicity, and just plain easy availability of electric motors. The prosperity of electric utilities continues to wax extravagant as the home is converted into a museum of electric gadgetry. How can anybody miss by investing in utilities, with no competition, nothing but growth ahead?

But a second look is not quite so comforting. A score of non-utility companies are well advanced toward developing a powerful chemical fuel cell which could sit in some hidden closet of every home silently ticking off electric power. The electric lines that vulgarize so many neighborhoods will be eliminated. So will the endless demolition of streets and service interruptions during storms. Also on the horizon is solar energy, again pioneered by nonutility companies.

Who says that the utilities have no competition? They may be natural monopolies now, but tomorrow they may be natural deaths. To avoid this prospect, they too will have to develop fuel cells, solar energy, and other power sources. To survive, they themselves will have to plot the obsolescence of what now produces their livelihood.

Grocery stores—Many people find it hard to realize that there ever was a thriving establishment known as the "corner grocery store." The supermarket has taken over with a powerful effectiveness. Yet the big food chains of the 1930's narrowly escaped being completely wiped out by the aggressive expansion of independent supermarkets. The first genuine supermarket was opened in 1930, in Jamaica, Long Island. By 1933 supermarkets were thriving in California, Ohio, Pennsylvania, and elsewhere. Yet the established chains pompously ignored them. When they chose to notice them, it was with such derisive descriptions as "cheapy," "horse-and-buggy," "cracker-barrel storekeeping," and "unethical opportunists."

The executive of one big chain announced at the time that he found it "hard to believe that people will drive for miles to shop for foods and sacrifice the personal service chains have perfected and to which Mrs. Consumer is accustomed."[2] As late as 1936, the National Wholesale Grocers Convention and the New Jersey Retail Grocers Association said there was nothing to fear. They said that the supers' narrow appeal to the price buyer limited the size of their market. They had to draw from miles around. When imitators came, there would be wholesale liquidations as volume fell. The current high sales of the supers was said to be partly due to their novelty. Basically people wanted convenient neighborhood grocers. If the neighborhood stores "cooperate with their suppliers, pay attention to their costs, and improve their service," they would be able to weather the competition until it blew over.[3]

It never blew over. The chains discovered that survival required going into the supermarket business. This meant the wholesale destruction of their huge investments in corner store sites and in established distribution and merchandising methods. The companies with "the courage of their convictions" resolutely stuck to the corner store philosophy. They kept their pride but lost their shirts.

But memories are short. For example, it is hard for people who today confidently hail the twin messiahs of electronics and chem-

[2] For more details see M. M. Zimmerman, *The Super Market: A Revolution in Distribution* (New York, McGraw-Hill Book Company, Inc., 1955), p. 48.

[3] Zimmerman, pp. 45–47.

icals to see how things could possibly go wrong with these galloping industries. They probably also cannot see how a reasonably sensible businessman could have been as myopic as the famous Boston millionaire who 55 years ago unintentionally sentenced his heirs to poverty by stipulating that his entire estate be forever invested exclusively in electric streetcar securities. His posthumous declaration, "There will always be a big demand for efficient urban transportation," is no consolation to his heirs who sustain life by pumping gasoline at automobile filling stations.

Yet, in a casual survey I recently took among a group of intelligent business executives, nearly half agreed that it would be hard to hurt their heirs by tying their estates forever to the electronics industry. When I then confronted them with the Boston streetcar example, they chorused unanimously, "That's different!" But is it? Is not the basic situation identical?

In truth, there is no such thing as a growth industry, I believe. There are only companies organized and operated to create and capitalize on growth opportunities. Industries that assume themselves to be riding some automatic growth escalator invariably descend into stagnation. The history of every dead and dying "growth" industry shows a self-deceiving cycle of bountiful expansion and undetected decay. There are four conditions which usually guarantee this cycle:

1. The belief that growth is assured by an expanding and more affluent population.
2. The belief that there is no competitive substitute for the industry's major product.
3. Too much faith in mass production and in the advantages of rapidly declining unit costs as output rises.
4. Preoccupation with a product that lends itself to carefully controlled scientific experimentation, improvement, and manufacturing cost reduction.

I should like now to begin examining each of these conditions in some detail. To build my case as boldly as possible, I shall illustrate the points with reference to three industries—petroleum, automobiles, and electronics—particularly petroleum, because it spans more years and more vicissitudes. Not only do these three have excellent reputations with the general public and also enjoy the confidence of sophisticated investors, but their managements have become known for progressive thinking in areas like financial control, product research, and management training. If obsolescence can cripple even these industries, it can happen anywhere.

POPULATION MYTH

The belief that profits are assured by an expanding and more affluent population is dear to the heart of every industry. It takes the edge off the apprehensions everybody understandably feels about the future. If consumers are multiplying and also buying more of your product or service, you can face the future with considerably more comfort than if the market is shrinking. An expanding market keeps the manufacturer from having to think very hard or imaginatively. If thinking is an intellectual response to a problem, then the absence of a problem leads to the absence of thinking. If your product has an automatically expanding market, then you will not give much thought to how to expand it.

One of the most interesting examples of this is provided by the petroleum industry. Probably our oldest growth industry, it has an enviable record. While there are some current apprehensions about its growth rate, the industry itself tends to be optimistic. But I believe it can be demonstrated that it is undergoing a fundamental yet typical change. It is not only ceasing to be a growth industry, but may actually be a declining one, relative to other business. Although there is widespread unawareness of it, I believe that within 20 years the oil industry may find itself in much the same position of retrospective glory that the railroads are now in. Despite its pioneering work in developing and applying the present-value method of investment evaluation, in employee relations, and in working with backward countries, the petroleum business is a distressing example of how complacency and wrongheadedness can stubbornly convert opportunity into near disaster.

One of the characteristics of this and other industries that have believed very strongly in the beneficial consequences of an expanding population, while at the same time being industries with a generic product for which there has appeared to be no competitive substitute, is that the individual companies have sought to outdo their competitors by improving on what they are already doing. This makes sense, of course, if one assumes that sales are tied to the country's population strings, because the customer can compare products only on a feature-by-feature basis. I believe it is significant, for example, that not since John D. Rockefeller sent free kerosene lamps to China has the oil industry done anything really outstanding to create a demand for its product. Not even in product improvement has it showered itself with eminence. The greatest single improvement, namely, the development of tetraethyl lead, came from outside the industry, specifically from General Motors and Du Pont. The big contributions made by the industry itself are confined to the technology of oil exploration, production, and refining.

In other words, the industry's efforts have focused on improving the efficiency of getting and making its product, not really on improving the generic product or its marketing. Moreover, its chief product has continuously been defined in the narrowest possible terms, namely, gasoline, not energy, fuel, or transportation. This attitude has helped assure that major improvements in gasoline quality tend not to originate in the oil industry. Also, the development of superior alternative fuels comes from outside the oil industry, as will be shown later. Similarly, major innovations in automobile fuel marketing are originated by small new oil companies that are not primarily preoccupied with production or refining. These are the companies that have been responsible for the rapidly expanding multipump gasoline stations, with their successful emphasis on large and clean layouts, rapid and efficient driveway service, and quality gasoline at low prices.

Thus, the oil industry is asking for trouble from outsiders. Sooner or later, in this land of hungry inventors and entrepreneurs, a threat is sure to come. The possibilities of this will become more apparent when we turn to the next dangerous belief of many managements. For the sake of continuity, because this second belief is tied closely to the first, I shall continue with the same example.

The petroleum industry is pretty much persuaded that there is no competitive substitute for its major product, gasoline—or if there is, that it will continue to be a derivative of crude oil, such as diesel fuel or kerosene jet fuel.

There is a lot of automatic wishful thinking in this assumption. The trouble is that most refining companies own huge amounts of crude oil reserves. These have value only if there is a market for products into which oil can be converted—hence the tenacious belief in the continuing competitive superiority of automobile fuels made from crude oil.

This idea persists despite all historic evidence against it. The evidence not only shows that oil has never been a superior product for any purpose for very long, but it also shows that the oil industry has never really been a growth industry. It has been a succession of different businesses that have gone through the usual historic cycles of growth, maturity, and decay. Its over-all survival is owed to a series of miraculous escapes from total obsolescence, of last-minute and unexpected reprieves from total disaster reminiscent of the Perils of Pauline. I shall sketch in only the main episodes.

First, crude oil was largely a patent medicine. But even before that fad ran out, demand was greatly expanded by the use of oil in kerosene lamps. The prospect of lighting the world's lamps gave rise to an extravagant promise of growth. The prospects were similar to those the industry now holds for gasoline in other parts of the world. It can hardly wait for the underdeveloped nations to get a car in every garage.

In the days of the kerosene lamp, the oil companies competed with each other and against gaslight by trying to improve the illuminating characteristics of kerosene. Then suddenly the impossible happened. Edison invented a light which was totally nondependent on crude oil. Had it not been for the growing use of kerosene in space heaters, the incandescent lamp would have completely finished oil as a growth industry at that time. Oil would have been good for little else than axle grease.

Then disaster and reprieve struck again. Two great innovations occurred, neither originating in the oil industry. The successful development of coal-burning domestic central-heating systems made the space heater obsolescent. While the industry reeled, along came its most magnificent boost yet—the internal combustion engine, also invented by outsiders. Then when the prodigious expansion for gasoline finally began to level off in the 1920's, along came the miraculous escape of a central oil heater. Once again, the escape was provided by an outsider's invention and development. And when that market weakened, wartime demand for aviation fuel came to the rescue. After the war the expansion of civilian aviation, the dieselization of railroads, and the explosive demand for cars and trucks kept the industry's growth in high gear.

Meanwhile centralized oil heating—whose boom potential had only recently been proclaimed—ran into severe competition from natural gas. While the oil companies themselves owned the gas that now competed with their oil, the industry did not originate the natural gas revolution, nor has it to this day greatly profited from its gas ownership. The gas revolution was made by newly formed transmission companies that marketed the product with an aggressive ardor. They started a magnificent new industry, first against the advice and then against the resistance of the oil companies.

By all the logic of the situation, the oil companies themselves should have made the gas revolution. They not only owned the gas; they also were the only people experienced in handling, scrubbing, and using it, the only people experienced in pipeline technology and transmission, and they understood heating problems. But, partly because they knew that natural gas would compete with their own sale of heating oil, the oil companies pooh-poohed the potentials of gas.

The revolution was finally started by oil pipeline executives who, unable to persuade their own companies to go into gas, quit and organized the spectacularly successful gas transmission companies. Even after their success became painfully evident to the oil companies, the latter did not go into gas transmission. The multibillion-dollar business which should have been theirs went to others. As in the past, the industry was blinded by its narrow preoccupation with a specific product and the value of its reserves. It paid little or no attention to its customers' basic needs and preferences.

The postwar years have not witnessed any change. Immediately after World War II the oil industry was greatly encouraged about its future by the rapid expansion of demand for its traditional line of products. In 1950 most companies projected annual rates of domestic expansion of around 6% through at least 1975. Though the ratio of crude oil reserves to demand in the Free World was about 20 to 1, with 10 to 1 being usually considered a reasonable working ratio in the United States, booming demand sent oil men searching for more without sufficient regard to what the future really promised. In 1952 they "hit" in the Middle East; the ratio skyrocketed to 42 to 1. If gross additions to reserves continue at the average rate of the past decade (37 billion barrels annually), then by 1970 the reserve ratio will be up to 45 to 1. This abundance of oil has weakened crude and product prices all over the world.

Management cannot find much consolation today in the rapidly expanding petrochemical industry, another oil-using idea that did not originate in the leading firms. The total United States production of petrochemicals is equivalent to about 2% (by volume) of the demand for all petroleum products. Although the petrochemical industry is now expected to grow by about 10% per year, this will not offset other drains on the growth of crude oil consumption. Furthermore, while petrochemical products are many and growing, it is well to remember that there are nonpetroleum sources of the basic raw material, such as coal. Besides, a lot of plastics can be produced with relatively little oil. A 50,000-barrel-per-day oil refinery is now considered the absolute minimum size for efficiency. But a 5,000-barrel-per-day chemical plant is a giant operation.

Oil has never been a continuously strong growth industry. It has grown by fits and starts, always miraculously saved by innovations and developments not of its own making. The reason it has not grown in a smooth progression is that each time it thought it had a superior product safe from the possibility of competitive substitutes, the product turned out to be inferior and notoriously subject to obsolescence. Until now, gasoline (for motor fuel, anyhow) has escaped this fate. But, as we shall see later, it too may be on its last legs.

The point of all this is that there is no guarantee against product obsolescence. If a company's own research does not make it obsolete, another's will. Unless an industry is especially lucky, as oil has been until now, it can easily go down in a sea of red figures—just as the railroads have, as the buggy whip manufacturers have, as the corner grocery chains have, as most of the big movie companies have, and indeed as many other industries have.

The best way for a firm to be lucky is to make its own luck. That requires knowing what makes a business successful. One of the greatest enemies of this knowledge is mass production.

PRODUCTION PRESSURES

Mass-production industries are impelled by a great drive to produce all they can. The prospect of steeply declining unit costs as output rises is more than most companies can usually resist. The profit possibilities look spectacular. All effort focuses on production. The result is that marketing gets neglected.

John Kenneth Galbraith contends that just the opposite occurs.[4] Output is so prodigious that all effort concentrates on trying to get rid of it. He says this accounts for singing commercials, desecration of the countryside with advertising signs, and other wasteful and vulgar practices. Galbraith has a finger on something real, but he misses the strategic point. Mass production does indeed generate great pressure to "move" the product. But what usually gets emphasized is selling, not marketing. Marketing, being a more sophisticated and complex process, gets ignored.

The difference between marketing and selling is more than semantic. Selling focuses on the needs of the seller, marketing on the needs of the buyer. Selling is preoccupied with the seller's need to convert his product into cash; marketing with the idea of satisfying the needs of the customer by means of the product and the whole cluster of things associated with creating, delivering, and finally consuming it.

In some industries the enticements of full mass production have been so powerful that for many years top management in effect has told the sales departments, "You get rid of it; we'll

[4] *The Affluent Society* (Boston, Houghton Mifflin Company, 1958), pp. 152–160.

worry about profits." By contrast, a truly marketing-minded firm tries to create value-satisfying goods and services that consumers will want to buy. What it offers for sale includes not only the generic product or service, but also how it is made available to the customer, in what form, when, under what conditions, and at what terms of trade. Most important, what it offers for sale is determined not by the seller but by the buyer. The seller takes his cues from the buyer in such a way that the product becomes a consequence of the marketing effort, not vice versa.

This may sound like an elementary rule of business, but that does not keep it from being violated wholesale. It is certainly more violated than honored. Take the automobile industry, where mass production is most famous, most honored, and has the greatest impact on the entire society. The industry has hitched its fortune to the relentless requirements of the annual model change, a policy that makes customer orientation an especially urgent necessity. Consequently the auto companies annually spend millions of dollars on consumer research. But the fact that the new compact cars sold so well in their first year indicates that Detroit's vast researches for a long time failed to reveal what the customer really wanted. Detroit was not persuaded that he wanted anything different from what he had been getting until it lost millions of customers to other small car manufacturers.

How could this unbelievable lag behind consumer wants have been perpetuated so long? Why did not research reveal consumer preferences before consumers' buying decisions themselves revealed the facts? Is that not what consumer research is for—to find out before the fact what is going to happen? The answer is that Detroit never really researched the customer's wants. It only researched his preferences between the kinds of things which it had already decided to offer him. For Detroit is mainly product-oriented, not customer-oriented. To the extent that the customer is recognized as having needs that the manufacturer should try to satisfy, Detroit usually acts as if the job can be done entirely by product changes. Occasionally attention gets paid to financing, too, but that is done more in order to sell than to enable the customer to buy.

As for taking care of other customer needs, there is not enough being done to write about. The areas of the greatest unsatisfied needs are ignored, or at best get stepchild attention. These are at the point of sale and on the matter of automotive repair and maintenance. Detroit views these problem areas as being of secondary importance. That is underscored by the fact that the retailing and servicing ends of this industry are neither owned and operated nor controlled by the manufacturers. Once the car is produced, things are pretty much in the dealer's inadequate hands. Illustrative of Detroit's arm's-length attitude is the fact that, while servicing holds enormous sales-stimulating, profit-building opportunities, only 57 of Chevrolet's 7,000 dealers provide night maintenance service.

Motorists repeatedly express their dissatisfaction with servicing and their apprehensions about buying cars under the present selling setup. The anxieties and problems they encounter during the auto buying and maintenance processes are probably more intense and widespread today than 35 years ago. Yet the automobile companies do not seem to listen to or take their cues from the anguished consumer. If they do listen, it must be through the filter of their own preoccupation with production. The marketing effort is still viewed as a necessary consequence of the product, not vice versa, as it should be. That is the legacy of mass production, with its parochial view that profit resides essentially in low-cost full production.

The profit lure of mass production obviously has a place in the plans and strategy of business management, but it must always follow hard thinking about the customer. This is one of the most important lessons that we can learn from the contradictory behavior of Henry Ford. In a sense Ford was both the most brilliant and the most senseless marketer in American history. He was senseless because he refused to give the customer anything but a black car. He was brilliant because he fashioned a production system designed to fit market needs. We habitually celebrate him for the wrong reason, his production genius. His real genius was marketing. We think he was able to cut his selling price and therefore sell millions of $500 cars because his invention of the assembly line had reduced the costs. Actually he invented the assembly line because he had concluded that at $500 he could sell millions of cars. Mass production was the result, not the cause, of his low prices.

Ford repeatedly emphasized this point, but a nation of production-oriented business managers refuses to hear the great lesson he taught. Here is his operating philosophy as he expressed it succinctly:

Our policy is to reduce the price, extend the operations, and improve the article. You will notice that the reduction of price comes first. We have never considered costs as fixed. Therefore we first reduce the price to the point where we believe more sales will result. Then we go ahead and try to make the prices. We do not bother about the costs. The new price forces the costs down. The more usual way is to take the costs and then determine the price, and although that method may be scientific in the narrow sense, it is not scientific in the broad sense, because what earthly use is it to know the cost if it tells you that you cannot manufacture at a price at which the article can be sold? But more to the point is the fact that, although one may calculate what a cost is, and of course all of our costs are carefully calculated, no one knows what a cost ought to be. One of the ways of discovering . . . is to name a price so low as to force everybody in the place to the highest point of efficiency. The low price makes everybody dig for profits. We make more discoveries concerning manufacturing and selling under this forced method than by any method of leisurely investigation.[5]

The tantalizing profit possibilities of low unit production costs may be the most seriously self-deceiving attitude that can afflict a company, particularly a "growth" company where an apparently assured expansion of demand already tends to undermine a proper concern for the importance of marketing and the customer.

The usual result of this narrow preoccupation with so-called concrete matters is that instead of growing, the industry declines. It usually means that the product fails to adapt to the constantly changing patterns of consumer needs and tastes, to new and modified marketing institutions and practices, or to product developments in competing or complementary industries. The industry has its eyes so firmly on its own specific product that it does not see how it is being made obsolete.

The classical example of this is the buggy whip industry. No amount of product improvement could stave off its death sen-

---

[5] *My Life and Work* (New York, Doubleday, Page & Company, 1923), pp. 146–147.

tence. But had the industry defined itself as being in the transportation business rather than the buggy whip business, it might have survived. It would have done what survival always entails, that is, changing. Even if it had only defined its business as providing a stimulant or catalyst to an energy source, it might have survived by becoming a manufacturer of, say, fanbelts or air cleaners.

What may some day be a still more classical example is, again, the oil industry. Having let others steal marvelous opportunities from it (such as natural gas, as already mentioned, missile fuels, and jet engine lubricants), one would expect it to have taken steps never to let that happen again. But this is not the case. We are now getting extraordinary new developments in fuel systems specifically designed to power automobiles. Not only are these developments concentrated in firms outside the petroleum industry, but petroleum is almost systematically ignoring them, securely content in its wedded bliss to oil. It is the story of the kerosene lamp versus the incandescent lamp all over again. Oil is trying to improve hydrocarbon fuels rather than to develop *any* fuels best suited to the needs of their users, whether or not made in different ways and with different raw materials from oil.

Here are some of the things which nonpetroleum companies are working on.

Over a dozen such firms have advanced working models of energy systems which, when perfected, will replace the internal combustion engine and eliminate the demand for gasoline. The superior merit of each of these systems is their elimination of frequent, time-consuming, and irritating refueling stops. Most of these systems are fuel cells designed to create electrical energy directly from chemicals without combustion. Most of them use chemicals that are not derived from oil, generally hydrogen and oxygen.

Several other companies have advanced models of electric storage batteries designed to power automobiles. One of these is an aircraft producer that is working jointly with several electric utility companies. The latter hope to use off-peak generating capacity to supply overnight plug-in battery regeneration. Another company, also using the battery approach, is a medium-size electronics firm with extensive small-battery experience that it developed in connection with its work on hearing aids. It is collaborating with an automobile manufacturer. Recent improvements arising from the need for high-powered miniature power storage plants in rockets have put us within reach of a relatively small battery capable of withstanding great overloads or surges of power. Germanium diode applications and batteries using sintered-plate and nickel-cadmium techniques promise to make a revolution in our energy sources.

Solar energy conversion systems are also getting increasing attention. One usually cautious Detroit auto executive recently ventured that solar-powered cars might be common by 1980.

As for the oil companies, they are more or less "watching developments," as one research director put it to me. A few are doing a bit of research on fuel cells, but almost always confined to developing cells powered by hydrocarbon chemicals. None of them are enthusiastically researching fuel cells, batteries, or solar power plants. None of them are spending a fraction as much on research in these profoundly important areas as they are on the usual run-of-the-mill things like reducing combustion chamber deposit in gasoline engines. One major integrated petroleum company recently took a tentative look at the fuel cell and concluded that although "the companies actively working on it indicate a belief in ultimate success . . . the timing and magnitude of its impact are too remote to warrant recognition in our forecasts."

One might, of course, ask: Why should the oil companies do anything different? Would not chemical fuel cells, batteries, or solar energy kill the present product lines? The answer is that they would indeed, and that is precisely the reason for the oil firms having to develop these power units before their competitors, so they will not be companies without an industry.

Management might be more likely to do what is needed for its own preservation if it thought of itself as being in the energy business. But even that would not be enough if it persists in imprisoning itself in the narrow grip of its tight product orientation. It has to think of itself as taking care of customer needs, not finding, refining, or even selling oil. Once it genuinely thinks of its business as taking care of people's transportation needs, nothing can stop it from creating its own extravagantly profitable growth.

Since words are cheap and deeds are dear, it may be appropriate to indicate what this kind of thinking involves and leads to. Let us start at the beginning—the customer. It can be shown that motorists strongly dislike the bother, delay, and experience of buying gasoline. People actually do not buy gasoline. They cannot see it, taste it, feel it, appreciate it, or really test it. What they buy is the right to continue driving their cars. The gas station is like a tax collector to whom people are compelled to pay a periodic toll as the price of using their cars. This makes the gas station a basically unpopular institution. It can never be made popular or pleasant, only less unpopular, less unpleasant.

To reduce its unpopularity completely means eliminating it. Nobody likes a tax collector, not even a pleasantly cheerful one. Nobody likes to interrupt a trip to buy a phantom product, not even from a handsome Adonis or a seductive Venus. Hence, companies that are working on exotic fuel substitutes which will eliminate the need for frequent refueling are heading directly into the outstretched arms of the irritated motorist. They are riding a wave of inevitability, not because they are creating something which is technologically superior or more sophisticated, but because they are satisfying a powerful customer need. They are also eliminating noxious odors and air pollution.

Once the petroleum companies recognize the customer-satisfying logic of what another power system can do, they will see that they have no more choice about working on an efficient, long-lasting fuel (or some way of delivering present fuels without bothering the motorist) than the big food chains had a choice about going into the supermarket business, or the vacuum tube companies had a choice about making semiconductors. For their own good the oil firms will have to destroy their own highly profitable assets. No amount of wishful thinking can save them from the necessity of engaging in this form of "creative destruction."

I phrase the need as strongly as this because I think management must make quite an effort to break itself loose from conventional ways. It is all too easy in this day and age for a company or industry to let its sense of purpose become dominated by the economies of full production and to develop a dangerously lopsided product orientation. In short, if management lets itself drift, it invariably drifts in the direction of thinking of itself as producing goods and services, not customer satisfactions. While it probably will not descend to the depths of telling its salesmen, "You get rid' of it; we'll worry about profits," it can, without knowing it, be practicing precisely that formula for withering decay. The historic fate of one growth industry after another has been its suicidal product provincialism.

DANGERS OF RESEARCH AND DEVELOPMENT

Another big danger to a firm's continued growth arises when top management is wholly transfixed by the profit possibilities of technical research and development. To illustrate I shall turn first to a new industry—electronics—and then return once more to the oil companies. By comparing a fresh example with a familiar one, I hope to emphasize the prevalence and insidiousness of a hazardous way of thinking.

In the case of electronics, the greatest danger which faces the glamorous new companies in this field is not that they do not pay enough attention to research and development, but that they pay too much attention to it. And the fact that the fastest growing electronics firms owe their eminence to their heavy emphasis on technical research is completely beside the point. They have vaulted to affluence on a sudden crest of unusually strong general receptiveness to new technical ideas. Also, their success has been shaped in the virtually guaranteed market of military subsidies and by military orders that in many cases actually preceded the existence of facilities to make the products. Their expansion has, in other words, been almost totally devoid of marketing effort.

Thus, they are growing up under conditions that come dangerously close to creating the illusion that a superior product will sell itself. Having created a successful company by making a superior product, it is not surprising that management continues to be oriented toward the product rather than the people who consume it. It develops the philosophy that continued growth is a matter of continued product innovation and improvement.

A number of other factors tend to strengthen and sustain this belief:

(1) Because electronic products are highly complex and sophisticated, managements become top-heavy with engineers and scientists. This creates a selective bias in favor of research and production at the expense of marketing. The organization tends to view itself as making things rather than satisfying customer needs. Marketing gets treated as a residual activity, "something else" that must be done once the vital job of product creation and production is completed.

(2) To this bias in favor of product research, development, and production is added the bias in favor of dealing with controllable variables. Engineers and scientists are at home in the world of concrete things like machines, test tubes, production lines, and even balance sheets. The abstractions to which they feel kindly are those which are testable or manipulatable in the laboratory, or, if not testable, then functional, such as Euclid's axioms. In short, the managements of the new glamourgrowth companies tend to favor those business activities which lend themselves to careful study, experimentation, and control—the hard, practical, realities of the lab, the shop, the books.

What gets shortchanged are the realities of the market. Consumers are unpredictable, varied, fickle, stupid, shortsighted, stubborn, and generally bothersome. This is not what the engineer-managers say, but deep down in their consciousness it is what they believe. And this accounts for their concentrating on what they know and what they can control, namely, product research, engineering, and production. The emphasis on production becomes particularly attractive when the product can be made at declining unit costs. There is no more inviting way of making money than by running the plant full blast.

Today the top-heavy science-engineering-production orientation of so many electronics companies works reasonably well because they are pushing into new frontiers in which the armed services have pioneered virtually assured markets. The companies are in the felicitous position of having to fill, not find, markets; of not having to discover what the customer needs and wants, but of having the customer voluntarily come forward with specific new product demands. If a team of consultants had been assigned specifically to design a business situation calculated to prevent the emergence and development of a customer-oriented marketing viewpoint, it could not have produced anything better than the conditions just described.

The oil industry is a stunning example of how science, technology, and mass production can divert an entire group of companies from their main task. To the extent the consumer is studied at all (which is not much), the focus is forever on getting information which is designed to help the oil companies improve what they are now doing. They try to discover more convincing advertising themes, more effective sales-promotion drives, what the market shares of the various companies are, what people like or dislike about service station dealers and oil companies, and so forth. Nobody seems as interested in probing deeply into the basic human needs that the industry might be trying to satisfy as in probing into the basic properties of the raw material that the companies work with in trying to deliver customer satisfactions.

Basic questions about customers and markets seldom get asked. The latter occupy a stepchild status. They are recognized as existing, as having to be taken care of, but not worth very much real thought or dedicated attention. Nobody gets as excited about the customers in his own backyard as about the oil in the Sahara Desert. Nothing illustrates better the neglect of marketing than its treatment in the industry press.

The centennial issue of the *American Petroleum Institute Quarterly,* published in 1959 to celebrate the discovery of oil in Titusville, Pennsylvania, contained 21 feature articles proclaiming the industry's greatness. Only one of these talked about its achievements in marketing, and that was only a pictorial record of how service station architecture has changed. The issue also contained a special section on "New Horizons," which was devoted to showing the magnificent role oil would play in America's future. Every reference was ebulliently optimistic, never implying once that oil might have some hard competition. Even the reference to atomic energy was a cheerful catalogue of how oil would help make atomic energy a success. There was not a single apprehension that the oil industry's affluence might be threatened or a suggestion that one "new horizon" might include new and better ways of serving oil's present customers.

But the most revealing example of the stepchild treatment that marketing gets was still another special series of short articles on "The Revolutionary Potential of Electronics." Under that heading this list of articles appeared in the table of contents: "In the Search for Oil," "In Production Operations," "In Refinery Processes," and "In Pipeline Operations." Significantly, every one of the industry's major functional areas is listed, except marketing. Why? Either it is believed that electronics holds no revolutionary potential for petroleum marketing (which is palpably wrong), or the editors forgot to discuss marketing (which is more likely, and illustrates its stepchild status).

The order in which the four functional areas are listed also betrays the alienation of the oil industry from the consumer. The industry is implicitly defined as beginning with the search for oil and ending with its distribution from the refinery. But the truth is, it seems to me, that the industry begins with the needs of the customer for its products. From that primal position its definition moves steadily backstream to areas of progressively lesser importance, until it finally comes to rest at the "search for oil."

The view that an industry is a customer-satisfying process, not a goods-producing process, is vital for all businessmen to understand. An industry begins with the customer and his needs, not with a patent, a raw material, or a selling skill. Given the customer's needs, the industry develops backwards, first concerning itself with the physical delivery of customer satisfactions. Then it moves back further to creating the things by which these satisfactions are in part achieved. How these materials are created is a matter of indifference to the customer, hence the particular form of manufacturing, processing, or what have you cannot be considered as a vital aspect of the industry. Finally, the industry moves back still further to finding the raw materials necessary for making its products.

The irony of some industries oriented toward technical research and development is that the scientists who occupy the high executive positions are totally unscientific when it comes to defining their companies' over-all needs and purposes. They violate the first two rules of the scientific method—being aware of and defining their companies' problems, and then developing testable hypotheses about solving them. They are scientific only about the convenient things, such as laboratory and product experiments. The reason that the customer (and the satisfaction of his deepest needs) is not considered as being "the problem" is not because there is any certain belief that no such problem exists, but because an organizational lifetime has conditioned management to look in the opposite direction. Marketing is a stepchild.

I do not mean that selling is ignored. Far from it. But selling, again, is not marketing. As already pointed out, selling concerns itself with the tricks and techniques of getting people to exchange their cash for your product. It is not concerned with the values that the exchange is all about. And it does not, as marketing invariably does, view the entire business process as consisting of a tightly integrated effort to discover, create, arouse, and satisfy customer needs. The customer is somebody "out there" who, with proper cunning, can be separated from his loose change.

Actually, not even selling gets much attention in some technologically minded firms. Because there is a virtually guaranteed market for the abundant flow of their new products, they do not actually know what a real market is. It is as if they lived in a planned economy, moving their products routinely from factory to retail outlet. Their successful concentration on products tends to convince them of the soundness of what they have been doing, and they fail to see the gathering clouds over the market.

CONCLUSION

Less than 80 years ago American railroads enjoyed a fierce loyalty among astute Wall Streeters. European monarchs invested in them heavily. Eternal wealth was thought to be the benediction for anybody who could scrape a few thousand dollars together to put into rail stocks. No other form of transportation could compete with the railroads in speed, flexibility, durability, economy, and growth potentials. As Jacques Barzun put it, "By the turn of the century it was an institution, an image of man, a tradition, a code of honor, a source of poetry, a nursery of boyhood desires, a sublimest of toys, and the most solemn machine—next to the funeral hearse—that marks the epochs in man's life."[6]

Even after the advent of automobiles, trucks, and airplanes, the railroad tycoons remained imperturbably self-confident. If you had told them 65 years ago that in 30 years they would be flat on their backs, broke, and pleading for government subsidies, they would have thought you totally demented. Such a future was simply not considered possible. It was not even a discussable subject, or an askable question, or a matter which any sane person would consider worth speculating about. The very thought was insane. Yet a lot of insane notions now have matter-of-fact acceptance—for example, the idea of 100-ton tubes of metal moving smoothly through the air 20,000 feet above the earth, loaded with 100 sane and solid citizens casually drinking martinis—and they have dealt cruel blows to the railroads.

What specifically must other companies do to avoid this fate? What does customer orientation involve? These questions have in part been answered by the preceding examples and analysis. It would take another paper to show in detail what is required for specific industries. In any case, it should be obvious that building an effective customer-oriented company involves far more than good intentions or promotional tricks; it involves profound matters of human organization and leadership. For the present, let me merely suggest what appear to be some general requirements.

Obviously the company has to do what survival demands. It has to adapt to the requirements of the market, and it has to do it sooner rather than later. But mere survival is a so-so aspiration. Anybody can survive in some way or other, even the skid row bum. The trick is to survive gallantly, to feel the surging impulse of commercial mastery; not just to experience the sweet smell of success, but to have the visceral feel of entrepreneurial greatness.

No organization can achieve greatness without a vigorous leader who is driven onward by his own pulsating will to succeed. He has to have a vision of grandeur, a vision that can produce eager followers in vast numbers. In business, the followers are the customers. To produce these customers, the entire corporation must be viewed as a customer-creating and customer-

[6] "Trains and the Mind of Man," p. 20.

satisfying organism. Management must think of itself not as producing products but as providing customer-creating value satisfactions. It must push this idea (and everything it means and requires) into every nook and cranny of the organization. It has to do this continuously and with the kind of flair that excites and stimulates the people in it. Otherwise, the company will be merely a series of pigeonholed parts, with no consolidating sense of purpose or direction.

In short, the organization must learn to think of itself not as producing goods or services but as buying customers, as doing the things that will make people want to do business with it. And the chief executive himself has the inescapable responsibility for creating this environment, this viewpoint, this attitude, this aspiration. He himself must set the company's style, its direction, and its goals. This means he has to know precisely where he himself wants to go, and to make sure the whole organization is enthusiastically aware of where that is. This is a first requisite of leadership, for unless he knows where he is going, any road will take him there.

If any road is okay, the chief executive might as well pack his attache case and go fishing. If an organization does not know or care where it is going, it does not need to advertise that fact with a ceremonial figurehead. Everybody will notice it soon enough.

3

SHOWDOWN IN THE MARKET PLACE

EDWARD M. BARNET

The fashions in kinds of competition have been revolutionized three times since Adam Smith argued, in the spirit of '76, that if you let the people alone and removed the heavy hand of the king from the channels of trade, then each man striving for his own interests would inevitably produce the best goods in the most economical way.

This perfect competition, probably so designated because it never existed, was considered the ideal for a time, but it gave way to recognition of imperfect or monopolistic competition—that is, nonprice competition between two brands of the same article.

Then, with the long depression of the 1930's, the fashion became handicap competition, whereby "fair trade" laws (establishing manufacturer-set retail prices) protected small operators from large and efficient competitors who made their money on volume and turnover.

Now there has been another revolution in production and selling, although as yet the government, the courts, and too many manufacturers and retailers alike have refused to recognize the accomplished fact. Innovistic competition, a new force engendering radically different goods and services, is destroying markets for old products and methods, and a showdown in the market place must eventually result.

The fact of innovistic competition is not new, but the concept may be. What the new fashion means to management is the need for a new conceptual approach—a way of seeing distribution problems in their totality instead of by departmental or institutional fragments. This should help to make sense out of what looks like a hodgepodge of contradictory developments—and thus may provide manufacturers selling through retailers and retailers dealing with manufacturers some new and different guides for their marketing policy.

Specifically, competitors will have to stop thinking of market effectiveness in terms of the traditional markup percentage on sales. They will have to realign their strategies more closely with that of the discount house—the outstanding form of innovistic competition—and look instead at their total return on investment. They must realize that the best profit can be made under circumstances of the new, consumer-oriented competition, where continuous and omnipresent adaptation is taking place in response to consumer needs, and where constant research for new products, new applications, and new methods is giving the consumer more of what he wants at prices he can afford to pay.

Handicap Competition

In the most recent legal round on "fair trade," a respected tribunal has again upheld the concept of "handicap" competition. According to *Retailing Daily* of March 9, 1956:

Boston. March 8.—The full bench of the Massachusetts Supreme Judicial Court ruled that the State fair trade law is valid . . . The court . . . states General Electric is entitled to an injunction restraining the defendant from selling plaintiff's small appliances at lower prices than those now, or hereafter, permitted in its fair trade agreement with other retailers . . . that "trademarks, trade names and the accompanying good will are valuable property rights which the owner is entitled to have protected from those who would wrongfully impair their value."

Handicap competition, like a cross-country race set with "handicaps" on the swiftest, is designed to assure equality of opportunity to contestants of varying strengths vying for consumer acceptance in the market place.

By putting legal restraints on the efficient and powerful retailer, handicap competition provides protection for the slow or tradition-bound merchant. Retailers are compelled to maintain higher prices than they require to cover expenses and make a profit. They must complacently condone driving potential volume out of their stores in order to preserve the happy fiction that a guaranteed percentage gross margin will produce dollar income —regardless of turnover!

Like the famed Maginot Line, so-called fair trade (the producer's right to set retail prices on his nationally advertised branded merchandise) lulls those who hide behind it into the illusion of security.

This style of competition has been called "fair" because it seems to provide "equity" for the traditional versus the strategic retailer. But despite legal guardianship, it is a style that is almost outmoded. Thus, Westinghouse has abandoned the practice of price setting, and General Electric has likewise drastically revised its policies in this regard. And department stores, notably those in St. Louis, have attested to the importance of such moves by openly taking retaliatory measures.

The handicaps imposed do not hold back the innovator when it comes to performance in the market place. Comparing the situation of the traditional retailer vis-à-vis the innovator, take the case of a small appliance dealer with operating expenses of 28% of sales who is assured a 33⅓% markup on the retail list price of a $9 fair-traded electric fan. He is happy in the assurance that his 33⅓% is guaranteed. What is not guaranteed is his total dollar return. If he sells 12 dozen fans in one year, his gross margin is $432 (144 × $3). But if a nearby discount house sells 240 dozen fans at $7.50 each (20% markup on retail), it has $4,320 in gross margin (assuming the same $6 unit cost)—a dollar intake ten times greater! Even more dramatic is the difference in gross return on investment. Of course, the small dealer or even the large traditional retailer is not thinking of that! Conditioned to his concept of expenses at 28% of sales, he has his eye fixed on the margin as a per cent of sales. Turnover is also noted, but turnover and margin are not tied together.

Let us look closer at these two outlets. The traditional retailer carries an average inventory of three dozen of these electric fans, and he turns this investment of $324 (at retail) four times a year. With a margin of 33⅓% times turnover of 4, his gross return on investment is 133⅓%. Our discounter turns over an average stock of 12 dozen fans ($1,080 sales worth) 20 times a year. With a margin of 20% times turnover of 20, his gross return on investment is 400%—not counting possible savings arising from quantity discounts on purchases.

But the discounter is operating illegally if he sells these $9 fair-traded electric fans for $7.50. Why? Because this is a Midas electric fan (Midas is used here as a symbol for any and all brand names and does not intentionally denote that of any real company), and Midas has an expensively won reputation that should not be jeopardized by volume if this means a reduction of retail price.

This is handicap competition. Regardless of the number of times the inventory investment may turn, handicap competition seemingly preserves "equality of opportunity" between outlets with entirely different strategies for creating consumer magnetism. But do laws which fix manufacturers' suggested retail prices on branded items give equal opportunity to operators who make their money on volume and turnover? All they do is protect (or give the appearance of protecting) those dealers who want an assured gross margin percentage—when and if they ever realize it.

The handicap approach seeks to preserve competitors rather than competition.

Born of the depression 1930's, so-called fair trade coerced large manufacturers of nationally branded goods into assuring their retail satellites that, regardless of whether or not they sold any merchandise, their margins of gross profit percentage would be defended. And they are defended—by the illusion of security in a situation presumed to be static. If a fixed and restricted volume were all that could be expected by each firm in the market place, this would afford protection—especially if that volume, however limited, could be guaranteed also.

But innovistic competition, in the form of private-label price cutting, new highways luring trade to big city price cutters, and the nonprice competition manifested by such shifts as offering patent medicines and cosmetics in the new supermarkets, leaves the "fair trade"-minded retailer standing on his door with his guaranteed gross margin resting securely in his stockroom and on his display fixtures. The discounter who cannot sell Midas electric fans for $7.50 will stock other brands which are not fair-traded. The consumer is going to weigh price and quality, and like as not he will accept and buy a cheaper unit which he considers just as good for its purpose as the Midas fan. Even "green stamps" may not save the traditional retailer by their quasi-monopolistic hold on his clientele. The conversion of percentage gross margin into dollar gross margin requires sales. That is the handicap for the handicappers.

Monopolistic Competition

Handicap competition is an outgrowth of monopolistic competition, and the two exist side by side.

Monopolistic competition, of course, is not new. Long before Adam Smith advanced the notion of perfect competition in revolt against government-regulated trade, branding or marking was inaugurated by a British king to prevent cheats and swindlers from putting out shoddy merchandise and hiding behind their anonymity. By making craftsmen put an identifying mark on their products, the king could catch the one with adulterated goods, and hang him if need be.[1] By fate's ironic twist, the mark became the means for identifying the good craftsman, and consumers began to demand the sword with such-and-such a mark. Brand identification was the way in which a consumer could distinguish one artisan's product from another's claiming to be just as good.

The styles of competition continually grew more sophisticated. Monopolistic or imperfect competition reached its zenith in the 1930's with a recognition of the power of advertising and the manufacturer's vested interest in his propaganda-promoted brand.[2] This power is real, and it is valuable. It shifts competition from the drab monotony of one mere soap vying against another mere soap for consumer acceptance. Now people clamor for

[1] G. B. Hotchkiss, *Milestones of Marketing* (New York, The Macmillan Company, 1938), p. 45.
[2] See E. H. Chamberlin, *The Theory of Monopolistic Competition* (Cambridge, Harvard University Press, 1933); also R. S. Meriam, "Bigness and the Economic Analysis of Competition," *Harvard Business Review*, March 1950, p. 109.

Midas soap. Loyalty no longer attaches to a commodity but to a name which connotes "the skin you love to touch" and a host of other social values.

That old-fashioned kind of competition of soap versus soap, coffee versus coffee, shoe versus shoe on the mundane basis of price differentials may have been "free" or "pure," as it was labeled by the economists, but it certainly was not as vigorous as what we have today. With brand names and Pavlov-type conditioning of the mass market to "seeing" values breathed into these names, we enjoy the unique situation of recognizing for ourselves that "there is no Ford but Ford," "there is no Lucky but Lucky," and "there is no Midas but Midas."

To be sure, if a very large number of people have been persuaded to want the Midas brand, there is a bit of monopoly for Midas, and all other manufacturers are up against Midas unless they too create and sustain some advertising hypnosis about their products.

But there is nothing anticompetitive about this situation. In fact, it is almost mandatory in a market characterized by products competitively screaming for consumer recognition. It does hold competition within flag lines and lends some dignity to the mayhem in the market place.

At the same time, there is a lot of zest added to life—at least marketing life—by the creation of these transient monopolies over the minds of a fickle public. Does anyone remember Larkin Soap? With television, new names can come in and dump the old ones even faster than what happened to poor old Larkin. All that the new name needs is a million dollars or so for advertising, and it can establish its little monopoly until another name comes along with twice as many million dollars.

In theory, these monopolies lead to higher prices, for they "destroy the free market." Actually, what this building of partisanship and loyalties does is to shift competition away from a mere price basis to nonprice factors such as the name established on the product and the "values" built into that name by the art of the advertiser and the product and package designer. Without recourse to handicap competition (that is, without policing prices in retail stores), monopolistic competition is positively creative.

Monopolistic competition becomes handicap competition only when the name Midas gives the Midas Corporation the right and power to set and enforce the retail resale price. Manufacturers do, of course, have the right to defend their brands in the retail store. But some, not satisfied to engage in combat with the weapons of advertising, have successfully insisted that legal umpires should re-enforce the manufacturer's franchise in public recognition with the added sanction of retail resale price control even against retailers who are willing to sell for less. Handicap competition is thus a distortion of truly competitive monopolistic competition (if I may be realistic and combine the terms).

Innovistic Competition

By the very necessity for infusing meaning into its brand names, monopolistic competition has given birth to another and lustier offspring—competition by innovation. The very battle of protected price versus nonprice features spurs on this innovistic competition. And innovistic competition is so outgrowing and outdistancing handicap competition that the mightiest brand is now threatened by this showdown in the market place.

In general, the new competition takes the form of nonprice innovations to meet the changing patterns of consumer wants. Today's market is a buyer's market—this fact is evident in the ever-increasing number of improvements in terms of time, convenience, and comfort for the customer. And because people are buying instead of being sold, nonprice innovistic competition is a matter of adjusting demand to supply, in contrast to the traditional price merchanism which was supposed to keep supply in line with market demand.

Forced to compete without price as a weapon for maneuver, aggressive and determined dealers switch tactics, desert producers' brands which are fair-traded, and bring out their own private brands—often at lower prices. They go still further, carrying the notion of differentiation even to the architecture and location of stores. Types of services are altered, some being omitted altogether while new ones are added. Supermarkets, self-service, shopping centers, factory prepacks, and other variations of means and method emerge to confront the market with innovations galore. Innovistic competition rears its menacing head to challenge even the most deeply entrenched buggy maker with not a better buggy but a horseless carriage!

Where monopolistic competition refers to slight and trivial differences between like products ennobled with brand names, innovistic competition signifies revolutionary differences which actually destroy the markets for old products and old methods. Nylon makes silk obsolete. The corner grocer is forced to go "super" or "superette." Products must be redesigned for new ways of doing things in the home or combined with new services such as time payments or parking.

Innovistic competition, like handicap competition, places mere price competition as such in a subordinate role; in fact, it treats the total costs to the consumer in the same rational light which is common in dealing in industrial goods. In effect, the costs to the consumer for shopping time, travel time, and use time are reduced when goods are sold nearer home, or made accessible for purchase at night, or charged for in more convenient proportions to earnings in a given period, or packaged in the form in which they will be consumed.

All this results from the fact that innovistic competition is consumer-oriented, in contrast to handicap competition's fixation that products and prices must take care of the dealer first. Note in the following examples how continuing and, ramifying have been some of the responses to consumer needs.

The Big Bear markets, which originated as price cutters in obscure and dilapidated warehouses, paved the way for today's glossy but efficient supermarkets, whose chief appeal is the display of a wide range of brands and products.

Successful mail-order houses understood the significance of population movements from rural to urban locations and the evolution of the automobile from the buggy, and so they opened up chains of retail stores with neighboring parking lots.

Because automobiles are expensive investments for the average consumer, car dealers created instruments for time payment, and now this type of installment buying has been extended to the combined sales of deep-freezers and food.

Recognizing that modern families have shrunk in size and that today's smaller homes have only limited storage space, enterprising manufacturers are packaging food in smaller quantities.

In every case, the injection of newly discovered elements into an existing situation transforms the situation, and a new pattern results. Thus, the function of self-service in a store, in combination with an adjacent parking lot, results in a new institutional form which we know as the supermarket in a shopping center. Simple enough. Yet what this presents is a completely new complex of old and new marketing components which in their totality require new adjustments, internal and external. The new form generates opposition, compels emulation, and fosters further innovating. Department stores open suburban branches, competing grocery stores try to hold business by offering trading stamps, and rack jobbers come into being to serve the supermarket with household wares and dry goods.

In short, innovistic competition not only brings about the reallocation of known resources, but encourages and even compels continuous research for new products, new applications, and new methods. It is a dynamic which threatens the status quo, puts all known goods and methods potentially out of date, and makes hazardous all investments in specific production equipment and distribution alignments. It is the antithesis of handicap competition, which aims deliberately to preserve existing channels of distribution and to give security to competitors rather than to maintain competition.

New Profit Concept

While innovistic competition is not a recent phenomenon, both retail and manufacturing managements have failed to see how the new fashion must affect the entire philosophy of retailing. As Arthur Felton puts it in his discussion of the conceptual approach: "Marketing cannot be effective if considered from a marketing point of view alone."[3]

The trouble is that handicap competition may not really protect the dealer. The extraordinary rise of the discount house and other forms of innovistic competition such as the regional shopping center, the supermarket, and enterprises such as Sears, Roebuck and Co. prove this. The growth of voluntary chains and other forms of retailer cooperation is another indication of the

[3] Page 16, above.

need for thinking in terms of increasing consumer satisfaction. So the question is: How can the retail dealer be truly protected against his illusions?

While most traditional retailers are preoccupied with statistical controls based on per cent of sales, they should be watching how key operating factors affect return on investment—particularly via turnover. Exhibit I, illustrating the thinking of the Du Pont Company regarding its return on investment, may bring out the infinitely larger significance of this concept and its incentives to innovistic competition.

In terms of this chart, total investment, not merely inventories, is the basis for turnover. It is only earnings as a per cent of sales times this turnover of total investment which gives a true measure of marketing effectiveness—of the way in which capital is being put to use.

EXHIBIT I. RELATIONSHIP OF FACTORS MAKING UP TOTAL RETURN ON INVESTMENT

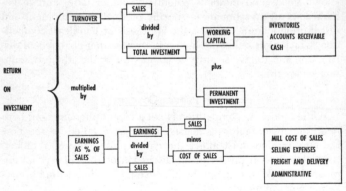

Source: William H. Newman, Administrative Action (New York, Prentice-Hall, 1953), p. 417.

In this light, a discount house with a total investment of $500,000 in plant, building, equipment, inventories, and accounts receivable, and sales of $10,000,000 enjoys a turnover of 20 times. Even with earnings at only 1.5% of sales, it has a 30% return on investment. (Sol Polk, famed Chicago "supermarket appliance dealer," is reported to achieve a return of 36% on his invested capital at 2% of sales and 18-times turnover.[4]) On the other hand, a department store with 3.5% earnings on its $20,000,000 sales and a total investment of $12,500,000 has a turnover of 1.6 times. Return on investment is only 5.6%. While there is, of course, almost five times more dollar profit in the department store till than in that of the discount house, it took a capital investment 25 times larger to achieve it!

It is in these terms that a dealer can reconcile percentage margins with turnover. He need not hide behind the camouflaged protection of percentages alone. Handicap competition will not shield him from the blasts of greater efficiencies on the part of his innovistic competitors. Only by appraising his plans in the light of return on all his resources can he build for realistic success.

Underlying the new conceptual approach to retailing, with its emphasis on return on investment, is the vital recognition of the manufacturer-retailer relationship as a whole. There is a great need for assembling the multiple efforts which make up the marketing process into a coherent scheme of thought so that the component parts may be understood in terms of their relationships to the over-all purpose.

Today there are too many specialists who know what they are doing but who do not know why what they do is important or relevant to the larger objectives. It is hardly conceivable that a producer of carburetors would not understand the purpose of a carburetor in a finished automobile. Yet there are many manufacturers who fail to see what their product's role may be as a component of a retailer's assortment of goods. There are many salespeople who do not know what is happening in their own store's delivery, accounting, or adjustment departments—or why.

In our highly refined division of labor we have succeeded in making firms and people more interdependent, and we have thus created a need for better understanding of the intertwining means for achieving the purposes of such joint effort. The purposeful coordination of component elements is what makes for a going concern instead of a random collection of specialized functions.

[4] Daniel Seligman, "Chicago's Red Hot Merchandiser," *Fortune,* September 1955, p. 130.

In the face of innovistic competition there is need for a new hypothesis regarding relationships in the market place. Efficiency can be truly measured only by the relationship of output to cost. By looking objectively at the various costs incurred in the manufacturing and selling process, by getting the total picture, and by sorting out and reclassifying the parts of what is too often a badly confused scheme of distribution, dollar gains for all concerned may be achieved.

At one time textbooks could announce the delightfully simple axiom that marketing began where production left off. This is, of course, no longer true. Innovistic competition, continually bringing out new products and services to displace those now on the dealer's shelves, has necessitated reorganization of the ways in which consumer needs and demands will be satisfied.

In order to discover how costs and activities can be most profitably allocated among the several components in the marketing process, it will be helpful to look at the traditional expenses of both retailers and manufacturers.

There are four categories of retailers' costs:

Acquisition costs, including price of goods acquired from the manufacturer; costs for buyers' time and travel; and costs of shipping to place of retail resale.

Counter costs, which involve the receiving, opening, and marking of goods; warehousing and stockroom service; and the getting of sample goods to the sales counters.

Explanation costs, including window and counter displays; advertising in newspapers, on radio and television, and by direct mail; and personal selling within the store.

Consummation costs, which involve packing and delivery; costs of a credit system for charge accounts and installment payments; costs of returns and adjustments; and the expenses incurred in markdowns and obsolescence.

The categories of costs generally allotted to the manufacturer include:

Designing costs, including research for determining what to make; designing of product and tools for making it; costs of machinery; arrangement of factory layout.

Production costs, which take into consideration procurement and warehousing of raw material; recruitment and training of labor; supervision and control of the work force; depreciation on machinery and plant.

Inventory unloading costs, such as storage of finished goods; selling, including advertising; packing, shipping, and invoicing; and customer service and repairs.

Innovistic competition requires understanding these categories of distribution costs. Return on investment points not only to sales income but also to expenses incurred in obtaining it. This can lead to a searching reappraisal of market relationships as well as of the internal divisions of labor within individual firms, both manufacturing and retail.

It is in terms of reshuffling these costs or activities among producers, distributors, and consumers that the greatest innovations affecting institutional forms of retailing have taken place. The supermarket, for instance, has pushed many counter costs and explanation costs back to the producers, while consumers have willingly shouldered a large share of the consummation costs in the form of cash-and-carry. Basic inventory costs have been materially reduced through large-scale purchasing and specification buying. Acquisition costs have been lowered through centralized buying.

The preceding classifications of costs should demonstrate how a reshuffling can be accomplished in the interest of both efficiency and economy. Specifically:

(1) These categories show up the need for thinking in terms of where such costs can be incurred most economically—in factory or store.

(2) They point to a more scientific assessment of operations actually performed, so that prices will include only those charges for which a manufacturing or retailing service is truly added.

(3) They help classify costs which may be considered as alternatives; for example, a markdown at retail represents an alternative to advertisement by the retailer—in this case a consummation cost can be substituted for an explanation cost.

(4) They demonstrate that there are a number of duplicate costs between production and sale which may be reduced and allow ultimately a lower price to the consumer. Between design by the producer and ultimate sale by the retailer there are many shifts in the burden of initiating and carrying costs which may result in greater effectiveness and economy. For example, pricing

61

need not include the wages of sales personnel if any item is to be sold exclusively by mail. A markup need not cover store warehouse costs if merchandise is sold from sample and delivered to the consumer from a manufacturer's own local plant.

Some manufacturers, alert to the new fashions in competition, now consider distribution through wholesalers and retailers as part of their total problem. Some outstanding retailers regard manufacturers' costs as within the purview of their acquisition costing. They consider merchandising as embracing both production and distribution, as being one problem. This kind of thinking is the bedrock of innovistic competition, transcending the ideas of those who still think in terms of preserving fair trade through legal handicaps. How have the innovistic competitors gone about reducing their costs?

First of all, it is the large retailers—who represent only about 1% of the total number of stores but who nevertheless make between one fifth and one fourth of all sales—who have been able to cooperate with manufacturers in cutting costs. This minority of retailers are, for producers, low-cost customers, while the majority of retail distributors are more expensive to reach. For example, one manufacturer found that 68% of his accounts, bringing in only 10% of his volume, were unprofitable. Most of these were dropped. Sales increased 76% as a result of more effective use of selling effort. Marketing expenses were cut in half, from 22.8% to 11.5% of sales, and a net loss of 2.9% was turned into a net profit of 15% of sales.[5]

The failure of small enterprises to buy in large quantities greatly raises the cost of selling. While orders from a large number of small buyers and a single order from a large purchaser might involve equal production costs, the costs of calling on the small buyers, lunching with them, invoicing, wrapping, shipping, and collection from them are what mount up.

Once a manufacturer and a retailer have agreed on the desirability of cooperation and coordination, they can take advantage of the great possibilities for innovation in the distribution process.

[5] See Ralph S. Alexander's chapter, "The Distributive Machine and Its Cost," in *Marketing by Manufacturers*, edited by Charles F. Phillips (Homewood, Illinois, Richard D. Irwin, Inc., 1951).

For instance, national advertising by the manufacturer reduces a retailer's explanation costs. Prepackaging in units adapted to retail sales and storage reduces counter costs and—to the extent that the packaging is adapted to delivery and other handling for shipping—consummation costs. The combination of many manufacturing firms into one company to provide a united front serving one kind of market is exemplified by circular chains such as General Foods: sales representatives calling on the grocery trade carry a diversified line from many factories, each of which formerly had its own sales representative. This not only reduces the manufacturer's selling cost, but also decreases the time spent by the retailer in buying these items, and so cuts acquisition costs.

Consider this example on the part of one leader in the competitive field. Ekco Products Company of Chicago retained Raymond Loewy at $75,000 a year to redesign its housewares, packaging, and catalogues.[6] The plan has paid off. Millions of kitchens now contain a paring knife or egg beater or one of the 1,600-odd Ekco implements. Whereas the company's sales in 1926 were $2,000,000 and profit was $348,000, sales in 1948 were $30,000,000 and profit was $4,422,000. Since a third of Ekco's output goes to such exacting customers as Sears, Roebuck and Co., Montgomery Ward, W. T. Grant, and J. C. Penney, the company cannot impair quality but it can improve design. By innovating in this way Ekco also manages, in effect, to reduce the price of even its fair-traded goods. It has, for instance, made a "terminal sterilizer" that sterilizes a baby's food and bottles while he is in the formula stage and then converts into a fair-sized pressure cooker. This not only gives the consumer a double use for the item; it also gives the retailer a story to tell. Here Ekco has managed to engage in innovistic competition even while under the fair-trade handicap. By re-examining processes, by eliminating superfluous operations, and by inventing machinery to meet specific needs, Ekco has cut production costs. A new woodworking machine that shapes, bores, cuts off, and ejects rosewood knife handles in one operation instead of four is but one example of how the pressure to meet consumer requirements of quality at a low price invites invention and innovation.

In short, the mass market awaits those who adapt to it. It is

[6] "Don't Fall in Love with Your Product," *Fortune,* October 1949, p. 80.

nonexistent for those who would simply try to hold the consumer to what they want to sell him—especially on the basis of fixed prices.

SEARS, ROEBUCK'S APPROACH

One excellent example of the revised and up-to-date philosophy of retailing, with its new concept of manufacturer-retailer relationships, is the experience of Sears, Roebuck and Co.

While most retailers and some manufacturers regard themselves as separate in their functions, Sears looks at the total picture. It cements close alliances with manufacturers—there is what might be called a "wedding" of the two—although Sears does not necessarily buy and own the producing firm.

In relieving the manufacturer of his distribution costs, Sears also assumes some of his other functions and risks. By predetermining the rate of production, by helping to finance tools, dies, and even plant, by engineering help, by large orders, by profit assurance, and by keeping the manufacturer informed of his rate of market acceptance as a guide to production scheduling and preproduction planning, Sears helps to reduce the manufacturer's unit costs.

Most retail buyers operate by pounding the pavements to find the best available product. Few of them will ask "Why is it best?", yet alone question "What would make it better?" Sears, which determines its own very strict merchandise specifications, which often produces its own goods in order to meet customer needs in the best possible way, and which is in no way hampered by preoccupation with the traditional retail markup percentages, does ask these important questions.

Suppose Sears is interested in stocking and selling kitchen dinette sets. The company has to figure out just what the product can be and what it cannot be—or, using Sears's terminology, "What is 'par' for the course?" First, the buyers determine their product specifications:

1. They buy a sample of every dinette set available.
2. They give these sets a full merchandise review, analyzing them as to function, appeal, special features, and weaknesses. The sets are taken to the laboratory for structural examination,

where they are taken apart and their component parts are carefully noted. The various styles are compared and weighed as to desirability—for instance, how does laminated plastic on steel compare with wood? Or, how effective would chairs with arms be?

3. They define the goals and minimal requirements for a Sears dinette set.

4. They settle on the number of varieties of dinette sets they wish to sell. If they concentrate on only three patterns, this simplicity of assortment greatly reduces costs. (As an example of Sears's technique, where Winchester has 400 guns in its line, Sears's primary supplier furnishes them with only four guns.)

Once the merchandise qualifications have been set, Sears goes about determining the costs of production. This includes:

1. Studying the basic costs of the ingredients. Supposing the buyers had decided on the steel and plastic dinette set, then their investigation would include steel in the raw state and its conversion into tubing, laminated plywood tops, and vinyl sheeting.

2. Making an analysis of labor needs.

3. Determining the amount which can be spent on overhead, including how much factory space will be needed and how much machinery will be required.

4. Setting costs for indirect labor and for supervision.

The third step for Sears's buying department is to determine the size and location of its factory or factories. Here the goal is to locate the plants to allow for the lowest freight costs, both in delivery of raw materials to the factory and in shipping finished products to Sears's warehouses and f.o.b. stores. Each plant is to be as small as possible while achieving the maximum of efficiency and assuring nothing more than full 12-month production at an even rate providing for expansion requirements and making up full needs by buying elsewhere.

Finally, Sears executives determine their desired profit. Taking their determined investment and carefully predicted sales, they set up a projected balance sheet and profit-and-loss statement. They compute their interest after taxes, set aside a sum for expansion, and estimate their percentage return on investment.

This might be a 15%, 20%, or 30% return on invested capital per annum, depending on margin and turnover. The profit will vary.

The preceding estimates give Sears its "par" costs and "par" facilities. On the basis of the figures, Sears decides that the dinette sets can be most economically produced in a single plant. They can be shipped knocked down, thus recapturing in distribution some of the advantages of decentralization.

The next problem is to find a plant to manufacture the sets according to Sears's specifications. Unable to find one to meet its predetermined criteria of location and size, it converts an old farm equipment plant, already owned by Sears, into a furniture division. A group is placed in charge of production, and the buying department negotiates with these people, submitting its estimates for volume and requiring the producer's estimated costs in return.

Once committed to an agreement, a contract is drawn, under the terms of which a standard cost statement and a monthly operating statement are required. Perhaps the first month's costs do not come down to the par the buyers had established; scrap is high and material variances appear as development progresses. Therefore a "mutual par" program is set up—the buyers revising their standards slightly to fit actual manufacturing conditions. No major revisions are made in the costing scheme, however.

Sears's elaborate merchandise analyses and production estimates allow for the greatest economies in manufacturing and distributing. In the case of the dinette sets, the buying department first ensured that the sets would fit the needs of Sears's customers and that they could be sold; risks were reduced by giving the manufacturer a guaranteed sale and a noncancelable order; and functions were either eliminated if unnecessary or shifted around so that they could be performed most economically.

This type of searching investigation is, of course, also vital in Sears's determination of whether or not it is worth going to the trouble of coexistence with a manufacturer. The par costs are a means of testing costs in the open market to decide whether there is sufficient differential to justify going ahead with the "wedding" between Sears and its manufacturer. The analysis provides not merely the aggregate cost of producing the dinette set, but also the costs of components on an item-by-item basis; this permits the exception principle to take effect, since it reveals areas needing special attention.

With such factual standards to go on, it is simple for Sears to choose between (1) attempting to influence and assist a proposed "affiliate" to make such changes in his plant as would be necessary to meet the buying department's par plant specifications, or (2) starting a brand new plant.

Sometimes there is a third alternative; perhaps a manufacturer with established customers other than Sears wishes to maintain his present plant without change, but would be willing to make an investment in a new plant. In this case Sears might go half way in financing the new factory and thus, without having or desiring a controlling interest in the company, gain a seat on the board of directors and share in the dividends of the enterprise. Sears is materially interested in the prosperity of the new plant, and indeed, even though it cannot prescribe production policy as closely as it could if it owned the factory, it has assured the supplier a return on his investment.

It is the type of thinking demonstrated by Sears's approach to buying dinette sets that has made this firm an outstanding example of innovistic competition. Here is no narrow preoccupation with traditional percentages. An annual $3 billion sales volume, without any "handicapped" merchandise, attests to the effectiveness of Sears's methods.

CONCLUSION

The issues arising from "fair trade" point up the changing fashions in kinds of competition. Four major styles have won sufficient public acclaim for each to be considered the fashion of its time: (a) perfect (or free) competition à la Adam Smith; (b) imperfect (or monopolistic) competition à la E. H. Chamberlin; (c) handicap (or fair trade) competition à la Miller-Tydings or Maguire (the legislators who sponsored the enabling laws); and (d) innovistic competition à la Ford, Du Pont, or Sears.

The judiciary have already awarded decisions for the acceptance of perfect, imperfect, and handicap competition. The decision for innovistic competition will be won, not in the courts, but by a showdown in the market place. Handicap competition can never withstand the successful innovation. The illusory protection of traditional percentage markups—even on the well-known nationally advertised Midas electric fan—produces a Maginot Line mentality.

Instead, the imaginative reshuffling of functions and their costs between manufacturer and retailer and consumer can lead to substantially greater profits for everyone involved. Low unit costs incurred in mass production can be realized in lower prices paid by consumers if retailers charge only for services truly rendered. Retailers can obtain profitable results if their thinking includes recognition of the relationship of both turnover and markup—not separately but in terms of total return on investment.

The need for and inevitability of innovistic competition are made explicit in the Du Pont chart. Spelling out the related factors involved in determining return on investment, it becomes obvious that a given amount of sales must be assured before investment in specialized equipment is rendered obsolete by another innovation. There is a great market pressure on manufacturers and dealers to get out from under before they are kicked out by competitors. There is need for constant vigilance, the use of all available advertising weapons, and channel strategy to move products that are already familiar. There is a compulsion to initiate innovation in order to avoid displacement by it.

The true measure of market effectiveness can never be in terms of mere sales volume, nor in terms of percentages of profit on that sales volume. The best measure is the return on all the assets employed in bringing about that return, and this demands what Arthur Felton has called "conceptual thinking" in marketing.

Handicap competition looks backward to preserving policies and procedures adequate for the past. It cannot stand up against the creative unknowns of the future. Innovistic competition, in contrast, keeps the eyes of management ever open to the possibilities for greater returns. It is not by setting handicaps in the paths of the efficient that one style of competition can win the final contest in the market place. Regardless of court leanings to fair trade, innovistic competition will eventually triumph, bringing success to those who seek — with total return on investment as their guideline—ever new and better combinations of means and methods for satisfying their customers.

4

THREE-IN-ONE MARKETING

REAVIS COX

Management of the marketing process is one of the toughest assignments in business today. Although marketing can easily be recognized for the major function of business that it is, the actual planning and controlling of one's own marketing operation is more difficult. Marketing becomes elusive when one tries to pin it down. This paper will present a rationale—or rather a combination of three different rationales—which may help businessmen to approach their marketing problems more intelligently and constructively.

THE DILEMMA

The difficulty arises not just because of incomplete understanding of the general concept of marketing, but also, and particularly, because of confusion about what specific items of expenditures a business should count as marketing cost.[1]

Even if businessmen do arrive at some satisfactory definition of what they want to control, they promptly run into another problem: how to control it. They can do little more than guess at the amounts that they ought to spend for the more conspicuous and expensive aspects of marketing—notably selling and advertising in their various forms. Of course, they have devised a num-

---

[1] See James W. Culliton, *The Management of Marketing Costs* (Boston, Division of Research, Harvard Business School, 1948); and "The Management Challenge of Marketing Costs," *Harvard Business Review,* January 1948, p. 74.

ber of formulas and procedures, especially for advertising. But it exaggerates very little to say that in the end they fall back on rough rules of thumb derived more or less arbitrarily from a combination of analysis, statistics, judgment, hunch, and hope.

At this point management runs into still more difficulties. Having made actual expenditures for marketing in accordance with the rules it has worked out, management needs meaningful measures of results. It soon finds that the measures available are likely to be uncertain and often superficial—limited to estimates of the immediate consequences of specific bits of technique. These help very little with the basic problem of determining what expenditures for marketing have contributed to profit or to the accomplishment of any other major objective of the enterprise.

The fact that really effective planning and control over marketing are very rare in such a setting, if indeed they exist at all, can hardly surprise us. Similarly, there is no reason to be particularly surprised that so many executives are dissatisfied with what they have achieved in this area. The astonishing thing is that they have done as well as they have.

Yet all of this is really quite extraordinary. We are talking about business management in the United States. American business has demonstrated over and over again that it can organize and control huge aggregations of capital, men, and facilities. That marketing persistently eludes its firm grasp must be a source of continuing chagrin to it.

The blame does not rest on indifference or indolence. On the contrary, the matter has been discussed endlessly, and has had much effort spent on it. So one may be tempted to conclude that we have here something fundamentally uncontrollable, destined forever to elude us. Although they do not say it outright, a good many people seem to have come precisely to this conclusion. Marketing, they tell us again and again, can never become scientific or be reduced to tight formulas. Its task is to work with the essence of human nature. So it must always be an art.

A Clue to Solution

There is much to be said for such an attitude. Before accepting it as definitive, however, we should ponder a little further whether management has really explored all of the possible avenues leading to solution of this dilemma. Particularly, we should consider a clue offered by Robert L. Katz's very perceptive article.[2]

Mr. Katz suggests that there are three different kinds of managerial skills: (1) *technical* skill—proficiency in the use of specific methods, processes, procedures, or techniques; (2) *human* skill—proficiency in operating as a member of a group, especially as the leader who induces peers and subordinates to work effectively as a team; and (3) *conceptual* skill—proficiency in visualizing what the enterprise really is and what it is supposed to do. This third skill, which runs more to thought than to action, leads to a deepening and broadening of the executive's ideas concerning the nature of his responsibilities.

It is evident that executives have used their human skill energetically in working with problems of marketing. Until fairly recent years, in fact, one could say that those who directed the marketing activities of companies possessed human skill above all else. Traditionally sales managers have been people blessed with a high degree of competence in organizing and directing salesmen, in dominating prospects, and in persuading them to "sign on the dotted line." The type has been caricatured in literature and art; but it did and does exist. Its way of getting things done has carried over into advertising, with a consequently heavy emphasis on persuasion and motivation.

One of the most striking developments in the management of marketing over the last four or five decades has been its effort to reduce the emphasis on technical skill. No one, to my knowledge, has made a systematic study of why the emphasis has changed, but it is a good guess that it can be traced to such forces as the extraordinary success of "scientific" management when applied to extracting, processing, and materials handling; the appearance in marketing itself of such techniques as sales analysis, distribution cost analysis, and marketing research; and the pervasive influence of collegiate schools of business.

Wherever the responsibility lies, the fact remains: applications of technical skill to the working out of bits and pieces of tech-

[2] "Skills of an Effective Administrator," *Harvard Business Review*, January–February 1955, p. 33.

nology, methodology, and procedures in marketing management are everywhere apparent.

Evidence that the third type of skill, conceptual skill, has been applied with energy and vigor to the management of marketing is by no means so easy to find. Quite the reverse; any observer who comes to marketing must be impressed by the extent to which businessmen have failed in their conceptual task. The most distressing facts is not that they fail to agree on the concepts they are to use when they talk about marketing or undertake to control it. Rather it is the extent to which they fail to have clear and workable concepts for their own use in the management of their own individual problems.

Before it surrenders to the dogma that marketing, because it is by nature not predictable, must be handled forever in terms of artistry rather than skill, perhaps business should take another look at its concepts. Perhaps, in the words of Arthur P. Felton, "conceptual thinking is a good approach" in this area.[3]

NEW PERSPECTIVE

A fresh look at marketing with the thought in mind that we need to do some new conceptualizing discloses some rather interesting things.

For example, we see immediately one reason why managements find it so difficult to determine what aspects of their operations to include and what to exclude when they talk about marketing; that is, when all of the usages of the term are put together, marketing includes an extraordinarily wide range of activities.

We also find a reason why the problem of conceptualizing marketing is particularly difficult for manufacturers as compared with wholesalers and retailers. Distributors can avoid running into serious difficulties by assuming that everything they do is marketing. Even if they engage in some manufacturing, they can distinguish it from the rest of the business easily enough for purposes of management.

However, the problem can be simplified by recognizing that what manufacturers in the aggregate consider distribution typically falls into one or the other of two broad categories: (1) a

[3] See page 23, above.

set of operations to be performed, largely physical in nature, such as sorting, storing, grading, transporting, and displaying; and (2) a set of forces that makes things happen, largely intangible in nature, such as promoting, merchandising, negotiating, and shopping.

Sometimes we can eliminate the physical operations from our consideration, just as many managers do when they try to spell out what it is they really mean by marketing. If we do this, we can put our full focus on the intangible forces. Here are activities that either sellers or buyers may engage in, but no one disagrees that, insofar as the seller performs them at all, they are part of his marketing responsibility.

The seller finds in these forces instruments he can use to mold the responses of buyers to serve his interests. To the buyer, and more particularly to the industrial buyer or the self-conscious and organized consumer buyer, they are forces to be resisted and redirected. Conflicts between seller and buyer arise from the fact that what benefits the seller most does not necessarily serve the buyer best.

This divergence of interest between seller and buyer is one source for the belief sometimes expressed that marketing (and more specifically selling) is a form of combat. Here is a highly important concept in marketing. The extent to which management accepts or rejects it plays a very important part in determining the responsibilities assigned to the manager of marketing, the instrument that he will use, and the standards against which his success or failure will be measured.

If management wants to establish effective controls over marketing, it must start by deciding what particular combination of operations and forces it is trying to control. Evidence that business is beginning to give thought to this conceptual problem may be found in a current tendency for large corporations to intro duce marketing directors into their organization charts—sometimes called managers of marketing or vice presidents in charge of distribution. Evidence that the problem is difficult may be found in the debates and confusion to which these efforts often lead.

In principle, what these companies are doing is to decide that all aspects of marketing, whether operations or forces, are intimately interrelated. They therefore must be subjected to some kind of common or over-all management. In practice, what managements do varies a great deal from company to company. Nearly everybody puts advertising and selling together under the new marketing director. Marketing research also will ordinarily be included. But there is much disagreement as to what should be done about such things as customer service, product development, packaging, pricing, and the physical operations of warehousing and delivery.

Conceptual problems cause much of the difficulty top management encounters when it introduces over-all management in marketing. This is not the only source of trouble, naturally, but it is an important one. Significant surely is the fact that at a recent conference of the American Management Association concerned with the manager of marketing, one theme came up repeatedly: in setting up this officer, a corporation should make every effort to obtain—at all levels of management—a clear understanding of what is being done, what its consequences are likely to be, and what exactly it is supposed to accomplish.

Whether an over-all manager of marketing is the best answer to a particular company's problems in marketing will always be debated vigorously. At least it has one very important advantage. It makes the conceptual task I have been talking about somebody's explicit responsibility. In setting up the arrangement, management must have someone look at the whole picture of marketing, break it into parts, assign each part to someone, see that it is done properly with relation to the rest of the work, and evaluate the results.

This over-all task of deciding what marketing is to include in any particular setting, how it is to be organized, and how performance is to be evaluated, difficult as it is, is complicated by a common tendency to mix up at least three different views concerning the nature and purpose of marketing. For convenience of discussion I shall call these the views of (1) the purchasing agent, (2) the investor, and (3) the horsetrader.

My point is not that any one is necessarily right and the others wrong, but rather that all three are right in their own way (as we shall see) and the only mistake is not to recognize them for what they are—different views with completely different implications.

The fact that there can be three such views obviously means that none of them can be really complete; just the same, they throw light on the over-all problem of marketing management—perhaps more light precisely because it comes from three different angles.

THE PURCHASING AGENT

When one adopts the view of the purchasing agent, marketing is something to be bought as effectively as possible. How this attitude affects management in marketing is easiest to see if we look first at a buyer rather than a seller of goods.

In a fundamental sense (and here we come to a very important departure from the concepts ordinarily used in talking about marketing) no one buys "goods" from the retailer, wholesaler, or manufacturer who provides them. The owner of a mine, forest, or farm from which raw materials are extracted does really sell "goods," but anyone else who adds value to these materials as they move down through the long channel of extraction, processing, and distribution sells services alone. For example, nine-tenths of the value of materials that went into building a typical house in 1950—perhaps 190 tons at a delivered cost of over $5,000—were contributed by some 300 "service" enterprises that converted the raw materials at their point of origin into form for use on the building site. Only 60 or so owners of trees, clay, iron ore, and so on, can properly be called "sellers" of the materials finally used in building and they provide only one-tenth of the accumulated value at the site.[4]

Looked at in this way marketing is simply one set of services out of many that provide the buyer with the particular combination of values he seeks. His essential problem as a buyer is to decide what combination of services he wants and what sources will provide those services most cheaply.

Taking the attitude of the purchasing agent makes it much easier to understand some of the bitter struggles and controversies that go on in business. From this point of view, a consumer who undertakes to buy through a consumer cooperative or a discount house is merely trying to get the particular assortment of services he wants at the lowest possible price. Whether he gets

[4] See Reavis Cox and Charles S. Goodman, "Marketing House-Building Materials," *Journal of Marketing*, July 1956, p. 36.

what he goes after is a question of fact in each particular case; but there is nothing inherently wrong or inherently unintelligent with what he is trying to do, and there is nothing evil or unintelligent about trying to sell him what he wants, no more and no less.

Similarly a businessman who undertakes to "buy direct" in some sense or to "circumvent the distributor," is merely operating as any good purchasing agent should. That he usually tends to think in terms of price allowances or advantages on the "goods" does not change the facts of the case. This way of thinking is unfortunate only because, like all imprecise concepts, it tends to divert management from the true substance of what is at stake.

Paradoxically, a seller of goods, and more particularly a manufacturer trying to sell his wares, is often well advised to take the attitude of the purchasing agent when he considers his problems of marketing. Here it is necessary to make still further conceptual adjustments of very great importance.

There is a strong tendency for businessmen and those who write about businessmen to think that marketing is effective if an enterprise succeeds in selling its products to its immediate customers in satisfactory quantities and at satisfactory prices. For many purposes, however, a much better concept substitutes the full channel for the immediate market as the entity to be controlled. In this view, effective marketing exists for a product only when the tasks of marketing are performed well all the way from extraction to final consumption.

The full-channel concept is particularly important for manufacturers because they hold a strategic position in determining how channels shall be organized and operated. Traditionally, students of marketing and businessmen themselves have assumed that effectiveness throughout the channel will follow if the manufacturer relies on the play of self-interest and free competition to get all the necessary jobs done and done well. In practice this assumption has become increasingly questionable. A manufacturer who undertakes to establish a strong consumer franchise for his products usually finds that he must take explicit steps to make sure that the goods move smoothly all the way into consumption.

It is in this situation that the marketing director finds himself acting very much like a purchasing agent. To do his job well he must work out clear ideas of the support his consumer franchise needs from the channel between him and the consumer. Having thought the problem out, he then finds himself under pressure to avoid having the ultimate consumer pay more than is absolutely necessary for the intervening services. Only in this way is he able to achieve full effectiveness in price competition at the crucial point where his products move out into consumption.

Looked at against this background, some explosive controversies in marketing become much easier to understand and more amenable to control. For example, consider the related problems of setting distributors' margins and deciding whether to fairtrade one's products or not. Many of the difficulties that have arisen in this area apparently spring from two sources: (1) changes in the services the manufacturer needs to buy from his distributors and (2) sharper competition among distributors on the prices they ask for the services.

Manufacturers may find it desirable for many reasons to establish margins somewhat higher than uncontrolled competition would set. On the other hand, any manufacturer is very foolish if he bases such decisions on assumptions that no longer apply to his market. If he no longer needs some of the services he once required from his distributors, there is no reason why he should pay for them. Similarly, if distributors have devised new methods of handling goods that reduce costs, or if newcomers are willing to work for lowered margins, why should the manufacturer insist on paying more simply because he used to do so?

He needs to remind himself that his task here is that of a purchasing agent. His responsibility is to determine what particular combination of services he needs, what combination of agencies can best provide them, what the costs should be under effective management, and who is willing to sell at the lowest price.

THE INVESTOR

The investor's attitude toward marketing in some ways resembles that of the purchasing agent. To the investor, marketing is an opportunity to buy earning assets. It is a set of expenditures made in the expectation that the money one sends out will come back with something added.

Here, as with the purchasing agent, one visualizes the marketing director as a rational, calculating, economic man. His central problem is to buy the best income available with the funds at his disposal—"best" being defined in terms of such characteristics as size, stability, and certainty. To do his job properly he seeks aggressively for opportunities to invest his resources, comparing alternatives not only within marketing but between marketing and other aspects of business.

His emphasis is likely to be on the long rather than the short run. Thus he must concern himself not with one-shot operations so much as with developing brands that live, preferably for years; establishing relations within his channels that persist indefinitely; and setting up sales organizations that operate effectively for long periods of time.

The conventional way of putting this aspect of marketing management is to say that it concerns itself with maximizing profit. But here again management needs to do a better job of conceptualizing. It needs to emphasize the presence of important weaknesses in the common assumption that the objective of an enterprise is simply to maximize profits.

Giving up this simple concept about the objective of business will not be easy. It is deeply entrenched in managerial thinking and comes up as an almost automatic response to the question, "What are you in business for?" Anyone who puts the question bluntly, whether to individuals or to groups, learns to expect a surprised: "Why that's obvious. We want to make as much money as possible."

It often takes a good deal of pushing to convince businessmen that they have here an important dogma of management that is badly in need of refinement. The first concession is likely to be a distinction between the short run and the long. Most, but not all, managers will agree that they aim for something more than a quick killing and prompt disappearance from the market. What they mean by making as much money as possible, they will say, is making as much money as possible during an extended period. They are not trying to squeeze every last dollar out of every transaction so much as some sort of maximum over a more or less explicitly defined future.

But the limitations of the concept of profit maximizing as a basic objective of business do not stop here. If one questions his executives still more vigorously, he will find them making many more modifications in their statement of their objectives. Few indeed, for example, are the businessmen who have no moral scruples concerning ways in which they might make an additional dollar. Their ethical standards, like those of other human beings, range over a wide spectrum; but almost every individual sets some sort of boundaries for himself.

Less generally recognized as a limitation on profit maximizing is what has been called in another connection "the luxury of not bothering." (This expression has been coined by students of marketing to explain why consumers do not always push their shopping to the point where they have drained the last penny of price advantage out of the market.) Profit objectives ordinarily appear not as absolute amounts but as increments to an income already being received. An individual who has already achieved a reasonably satisfactory level of living may find himself less than enthusiastic about exerting any considerable effort for a small addition to his compensation. In this connection, of course, the influence of steeply progressive income-tax rates is very important.

There also may be some difficulty in deciding whose income is to be maximized. By convention an enterprise or a firm is considered to have a single, unified set of objectives. In practice enterprises are combinations of more or less conflicting interests. History records more than one insider who has milked a business enterprise for his own benefit to the detriment of the enterprise as a whole and of other interests in it. Even if the management has no intention to defraud, it may find it extremely difficult to decide whether to maximize its own income, or the benefits received by the employees, or the profit accruing to stockholders, or to minimize the costs it imposes on customers. In such circumstances, it is hardly accurate to say that the company always tries to maximize its profits.

Still further, there may be a conflict within the management itself between the desire to maximize profits and other objectives. In times of crisis, simple survival may be a more important problem for a management than making any income. Irrational though it may be by some standards, preservation of a position of market leadership may dominate managerial decisions. Or managements may put their primary emphasis on restoring or maintaining peace within the enterprise, or providing amenities for the working force, or preserving and strengthening the managerial team as distinct from the enterprise.

Finally, management must maintain a working balance between amount of income and certainty or stability of income. Efforts to develop a mathematical theory of games applicable to business decisions have taught us that managerial choices do not ordinarily lie simply between smaller and larger amounts of profit. Each amount has a chance or probability associated with it. The manager must decide whether to play for large amounts at low odds or small amounts at high odds in his favor.[5]

Considerations such as these lie before the manager when he looks at expenditures for marketing as a form of investing. He may think of quick returns and fast turnovers of his capital, as when a merchant buys a particular lot of goods, advertises them aggressively, and tries to move them out of his store in a few days so as to make room for another promotion. Thus he moves his inventory quickly and at the same time always has something fresh to offer his customers. Alternatively, when a manufacturer undertakes to establish a consumer franchise for his brand or to build up a market that will support heavy investments in productive equipment, he must think in terms of long-term continuity.

THE HORSETRADER

The third attitude managers may take toward marketing—that of the horsetrader—contrasts sharply with the other two. Perhaps a suaver term that carries less connotation of sharp practice can be devised; but this one has the great merit of stressing the distinguishing characteristics of a particular way of looking at marketing.

The horsetrader attitude grows out of a very important but often neglected fact about marketing costs: what is a cost to one person is almost always income to someone else. To the one who counts it as income the problem is likely to be not how to reduce the expenditure but how to increase it to his own advantage. We

[5] See Edward G. Bennion, "Capital Budgeting and Game Theory," *Harvard Business Review*, November–December 1956, p. 115.

can again introduce questions as to the long run versus the short run, ethics, conflict of interest, and so on; but the basic problem of the individual in this view is to trade shrewdly in his own interest.

Here we come to vigorous rivalry and competition. Here the concept of marketing as a form of combat has its highest degree of validity. Aggressive bargaining, careful maneuvers for position, the attachment of great importance to slight advantages one way or the other, playing one's cards close to one's chest— these characterize the marketing man as a horsetrader. It need not surprise us to find here more than a trace of *caveat emptor*. Combatants in this arena deal with one another as equals. Each assumes that the others can look out for themselves.

Major emphasis in this view of marketing is likely to be put on the energetic use of forces to make things happen—considerably less on the tangible physical operations that bulk large in marketing as a whole. In this aspect of marketing lies the greatest danger that short-run views will come to dominate decisions and that ethical standards will be put aside in response to the urgencies of combat. As in all combat, there is a possibility that the original objectives may be overwhelmed, in the heat of battle, by a simple desire to win.

The horsetrader aspects of marketing are unquestionably the ones most difficult to bring under effective control. They are the areas of marketing that most stubbornly resist the efforts of engineers, technicians, accountants, and the like to reduce them to routine. Criticism from the outside is likely to find its most valid targets here.

Some of the greatest difficulties encountered in efforts to establish effective management of marketing arise from the difficulty of fitting the horsetrader into comfortable working relations with the purchasing agent and the investor. This is true because the controls appropriate to management in marketing must differ widely according to which parts of marketing are to be controlled and which point of view is to be taken toward them.

A satisfactory working relationship among the three attitudes is needed because most firms find that they must adopt each of the three at various times—if not simultaneously. Management may divide the job so that those parts calling for a particular attitude will fall to specialists with appropriate personal talents and traits. Over-all, however, all three attitudes must be provided for as they are needed.

Technicians are working out many devices to help managements plan and control marketing more effectively. These include long-established techniques, such as sales analysis, cost analysis, and marketing research. They also include novelties that have come in for very energetic discussion in recent years—motivation research, capital budgeting, and a whole set of mathematical devices summed up under such terms as operations research and mathematical programing. Some of these are very fashionable among academic and commercial research men, if not as yet among business managers.

These sorts of controls can be applied more easily to the physical operations than to the intangible forces of marketing. Similarly, they can be used more effectively to solve the problems of the purchasing agent and the investor than to cope with the problems of the horsetrader. Even with the horsetrader's problems, however, there seems to be some reason to hope for the development of more effective controls in such instruments as the theory of games.

CONCLUSION

What has been said here does not answer all the troublesome problems of effective planning in marketing. It does suggest, however, how we may hope to solve them. We must begin by improving our concepts of marketing and its problems. Only after this has been done can we expect to reduce the area to questions of technique and procedure.

Research has an old but often-stated governing principle. It says that asking the right question is the most difficult part of finding the right answer. Once the right question has been asked, the rest is likely to be more laborious than difficult. This is true because a correctly asked question carries with it a statement of what needs to be done to find the answer.

What little has been done along this line in marketing is only a start—but it is a promising start. The ideas here presented will not solve the problems of management in marketing; but they may help us to understand better what these problems are and so set us on the road to solutions.

At least one thing is certain. Without something of this sort we are not likely even to get started. And we can no longer delay.

5

IT'S TIME TO RESEARCH THE CONSUMER

PIERRE MARTINEAU

Is it not strange that business, which uses product research, market research, and research in employee problems so extensively, does a complete about-face when confronted with consumer research? Either it relies on lifeless, wooden statistics, or it clings stubbornly to a naive belief that human behavior cannot be studied on any scientific basis.

Wandering through the world of advertising and market research, one continually encounters the slogan "Markets are People." Advertising agencies stress the diversity, the underlying human quality of the American market, by showing crowd-shots in their reception rooms and their house advertising—but, amazingly enough, they seldom get around to exploring people as people.

Their implied conceptions are correct. Human beings are dynamic, complex creatures; irrational at least as often as rational; motivated in large degree by emotion, habit, and prejudice; differing widely in personality structure, in aspirations, ideals, and buying behavior even in our own society. Men differ from women not only biologically but in their fundamental interests and attitudes. Teen-agers approaching maturity and responsibility have a vastly different viewpoint from that of the middle-agers, who are gradually withdrawing from hectic competition. In countless respects there are broad gulfs among social classes, among racial and ethnic groups, among rural, small-town, and metropolitan dwellers, and among personality types in the same groups and classes.

Nor are human individuals static items like ingots. Rather, they constantly shift their values and their behavior. It is particularly necessary to understand this factor of change in view of the profound social and economic upheavals in our present-day society. Several Twentieth Century Fund studies have pointed out that we have experienced one of the greatest social revolutions in human history during the past two decades. Such books as *The Big Change*[1] and *The Changing American Market*[2] reveal that Americans not only have more money today; they also have very different values. When these are translated into buying behavior, they mean a demand for different cars, different homes in different areas, different paraphernalia for different recreations, different clothes, and different kinds of stores.

There is a definite relationship between consumers' purchase decisions and social and psychological changes. For instance, the tremendous sales success of Oldsmobile, Buick, and Ford is due to styling, not to any notable mechanical features. Car buyers are looking for designs that will express the new values which are characteristic of the changes indicated—modernity, color, individuality, self-expression, sophistication, youthfulness, gaiety, casual living. Cadillac's enviable sales picture stems from its realization that a different quality market exists today, a market much bigger than the *Social Register* set. Deliberately cutting loose from the narrow limits of social snobbery, Cadillac made itself the achievement symbol for the self-made executive.[3]

Why shouldn't business try to unravel the underlying significance and the linkages between such surface phenomena as the flair for color in cars and men's shirts and refrigerators, the rise of discount houses and outlying shopping centers, the yearning for self-expression which emerges in new hobbies, new home designs, new places to travel to?

In other words, why isn't it important to research basic reasons

[1] Frederick Lewis Allen, *The Big Change* (New York, Harper & Brothers, 1952).
[2] Editors of Fortune, *The Changing American Market* (Garden City, N.Y., Hanover House, 1955).
[3] See W. H. Whyte, "The Cadillac Phenomenon," *Fortune*, February 1955, p. 106.

85

for buying behavior? If our actions are determined not only by rational considerations but by underlying motivations, attitudes, feelings, and group norms, why aren't these valid fields for study?

THE FORGOTTEN HUMAN

How can we so ignore the consumer in our research?

Almost nobody is trying to understand him as a human being, as a creature who buys song hits like "Shake, Rattle and Roll" and "Let Me Go, Lover" by the million; who idolizes buffoons like Milton Berle and Jackie Gleason; who suddenly develops passions for lavender cars and sectional sofas; who spends his money for such illogical things as dog racing, filter cigarettes, and oversize cuff links.

Why are bigger families once more the style? Why has retail selling deteriorated almost to a wrap-up function? Why has there been such a tremendous shift to participation sports like hunting and skiing? Why aren't Packard and Lincoln accepted as success symbols in the same degree as Cadillac? Why are families who already owe money more likely to take on further debts through further purchases than those who are debt-free? Why have security and informality and leisure become such important values to so many people?

It is curious that even advertising, a major form of mass communication, overlooks research and theory in the many aspects of communication and makes most of its decisions about copy theme and art on an intuitive basis. I am perfectly aware that advertising is partly an art, and therefore must always be creative and, in large degree, intuitive. Freshness, imagination, novelty, drama, and daring are requisites and should never be shackled by stereotyped and rigid rules. Nevertheless, there are perfectly valid principles of successful communication which should serve as a framework for this creativity. And obviously it makes a tremendous difference to use relevant and effective motivational appeals.

Scholars in the field of communication point out that the success or failure of any message depends on so many other factors besides the rational content and the degree of attention the message receives.[4] Yet that is virtually all that advertising is concerned with. A tremendous part of meaning is conveyed below the verbal level; yet advertising seldom bothers to determine the impact of its nonrational symbols: art, color, tone, mood, and so forth.[5]

As adults we respond positively far more often to indirect than to direct suggestion. Except when we seek advice from an authoritative person like a doctor, direct suggestion affronts our ego. There are many things we can never say directly about ourselves without creating ridicule or resentment. Yet there is no systematized body of knowledge on how indirection in advertising can be achieved.

One of the principal objectives for any retail store is the establishment of a public personality. Buying specific merchandise always takes place within the climate of acceptance or rejection of this store personality. But retailing has never learned very much about how to work toward this objective of creating a positive personality with advertising. Retail advertising stays almost entirely on the item-and-price level.

The effectiveness of any one message in large part is determined by the amount of attention it receives and whether the message uses meaningful motivational appeals. Almost all of advertising's energy has been devoted to measuring this factor of attention. A few of the larger agencies have instituted motivation research, but putting it to use is more difficult. Far and away the greatest part of advertising content judgments are still made without determining if the motivational appeals are truly applicable.

There is really no research in advertising comparable to that which the propaganda experts would undertake. Does the message create any empathy? Are the symbols and the abstractions significant to the class we want to influence? What emotionality is created, if any?

---

[4] See Wilbur Schramm, "How Communication Works," in *The Process and Effects of Mass Communication* (Urbana, The University of Illinois Press, 1954), p. 3.

[5] See Pierre Martineau, "New Look at Old Symbols," *Printer's Ink*, June 4, 1954, p. 32.

SOME NEEDED RESEARCH

I should like to suggest, just at random, a number of broad areas for research which would prove to be most profitable for businessmen.

There is a rich literature on the American social class system which indicates how much each of us is conditioned by the norms of our own particular stratum. Sharp class differences in family stability, in moral codes, in educational and occupational aspirations, in political philosophy, even in physical and mental illness have been described in excellent studies.[6] Obviously since economic behavior is so important in human activity, there must also be significant differences in buying behavior by classes. Many products such as sausage and beer are typed as lower class, and have difficulty broadening their market upward. Conversely, instant coffee and frozen orange juice are viewed as quality products by the mass audience, and cannot expand downward. Savings banks, life insurance, and magazines are other instances of diverse institutions and products which have difficulty gaining acceptance in the whole lower half of the social hierarchy. On the other hand, some retail stores, institutions, and products have problems precisely because they have no social-class home, no strong loyalties in any one class.

Too often the executive plans his strategy on the assumption that all classes have the same outlook, the same attitudes, the same strivings as his own family. Usually they don't. He uses symbols to communicate with them which may be misunderstood or even completely meaningless. They have different word-comprehension levels and different degrees of ability to handle abstractions and to form imagery from symbols.[7] We assume we are a literate society. But possibly a third of the American market reads with difficulty.

The usefulness of any advertising varies with class. For example, middle-class families respond to advertising with com-

[6] See numerous monographs under the sections "Differential Class Behavior" and "Social Mobility in the United States" in *Class, Status and Power,* edited by Reinhard Bendix and S. M. Lipset (Glencoe, Illinois, The Free Press, 1953).

[7] See Leonard Schatzman and Anselm Strauss, "Social Class and Modes of Communication," *American Journal of Sociology,* January 1955, p. 329.

plete faith, while the lower-class man is suspicious and more apt to rely on the judgment of some friend.

Not only have huge segments of our population been boosted past the subsistence level, but their tastes and values have undergone tremendous change. The middle-class style of life has always been the goal of most Americans. With their economic gains, the new middle-income families are groping toward new standards, new symbols, new stores.[8]

Consider the disappearance of the class-mass cleavage in furniture. Gone is the hideous borax furniture which was standard in the mass-market home. Today the Sears, Roebuck catalogue emphasizes attractive modern furniture. Matching color schemes are available throughout the house. It is important that this market has moved up to modern furniture and interior decorating, modern dinnerware, and matching draperies. Obviously, its tastes are more discriminating, more sophisticated.

The enormous expansion of this mass purchasing ability presents a huge potential for businessmen who make some effort to comprehend the psychological characteristics and goals of these people. In my judgment, it is not only the aggressiveness of savings and loan associations that accounts for their incredible growth; the banks have helped by generally failing to understand the psychology of this new group of savers and so missing much of this market.

The feverish home-building in cow pastures and cotton fields, which has never stopped since 1947, should make studies of the new suburbanites imperative. Any observation at all will show that these people are not like the traditional prewar suburb-dwellers.[9] For instance, in some of the new suburbs around Chicago:

(1) There are many young married couples. There is a host of babies. There are very few adolescents and few old people.

(2) There is a very large proportion of mass-market families —bus drivers, printers, technicians. The suburbs represent a bet-

[8] See "The Rich New Middle Income Class," in *The Changing American Market*, p. 52.

[9] See W. H. Whyte, "The Consumer in The New Suburbia," in *Consumer Behavior* (New York, New York University Press, 1954), p. 1.

ter way of life which they feel they now can afford. Also, there is powerful pressure in the cities from a different type of migrant which causes them to move. As Mexicans, Puerto Ricans, poor whites from the South, and particularly Negroes move into their neighborhoods, they jump into something entirely new for them —suburban living.

(3) There are numbers of migratory families in these suburbs, the turnover in some of the newer ones running as high as 25% yearly. Many of these are families moving from city to city merely through transfer by the particular corporation for which they work. Naturally they develop few loyalties, few roots beyond their neighborhood. And in such items as furniture, their tastes run to light, expendable pieces either easily moved or discarded.

(4) Another large group, only recently city-dwellers, have moved out because they felt lost in the big metropolis. They are looking for a community where they can "belong." They attempt to conform to the patterns established in these older, once-rural towns; they join organizations and participate in community life. They are hungry for companionship and acceptance, for the satisfactions of a feeling of significance which they never could find in an overcrowded, impersonalized city.

The influence of these new suburbanites on style and taste is disproportionately greater than their population size. The vogue for station wagons, for a second car, for glamor pants, for ranch-style homes—all these and many more get their impetus from the suburbs.

The postwar industrial growth of major cities has created a flood-like migration of Negro workers and their families. Of all the babies born in Chicago in 1954, 25% were Negroes. But what do we know about the economic activity of the Negro consumer? Very little! Most of our stereotyped notions about Negro behavior in other areas have been revealed as fallacious, so we probably are equally wrong in our notions about the way he buys.

I have discussed this problem of selling the Negro market with countless sales executives, and no one had any more intelligent suggestions to offer than hiring a few Negro salesmen, and advertising in Negro periodicals with Negro models and Negro testimonials—same copy appeals but different models. Who knows if it is correct to use the same appeals that influence whites?

The Negro's economic gains have not kept pace with his political and legal advancement, but they are very considerable nonetheless. My guess is that his purchasing ability will become more important all the time. Therefore it is important to explore his preferences, motives, insecurities, and goals. Similarly there are other ethnic markets, such as the Puerto Ricans in New York, the Mexicans in Los Angeles, and the Orientals on the West Coast, which are enigmas to the sales manager.

Our studies would indicate that many of today's young married couples tend to have different ideas about the responsibilities each must assume to keep the family functioning. For one thing, there is a growing acceptance of the belief that the job of running the house is interchangeable. Servants have disappeared, and the young wife refuses to accept the role of a drudge as her life's work. So her husband often helps her bathe the babies, scrub floors, wash dishes, and shop at the supermarket.

These younger housewives will not accept the patriarchal, sternly dominant husband. They see no reason for definitions of sexuality and domesticity that establish deep cleavage between husband and wife. More and more married women want to work, not just for the feeling of independence and for added family income but for many other psychological reasons. The educated girl wants to feel that she is doing something much more useful than playing afternoon bridge. The urban wife wants to escape the loneliness of a long, long day with only cats and parakeets for companions. More and more "career women" want to succeed in the competitive world, just as do men.

In other words, there have been considerable upsets in the traditional roles of women in our society [10] Many of them have different aspirations, strivings, and conflicts from those of their

[10] See Margaret Mead, "What Women Want," in *Readings in Sociology*, edited by E. A. Schuler, et al. (New York, Thomas Y. Crowell Company, 1953), p. 125; also, Mirra Komarovsky, "Cultural Contradictions and Sex Roles," in *Readings in Sociology*, p. 133; and Clara Thompson, "The Role of Women in This Culture," in *Study of Interpersonal Relations* (New York, Hermitage House, Inc., 1949), p. 130.

mothers, all of which can become reflected in their behavior as consumers. Clothing styles represent wide departures from the "feminine role" conception of feminine dress. Dungarees, toreador pants, Bermuda shorts, three-quarter length wool socks, mannish-tailored shirts are all very obvious borrowings from the masculine costume.

True, this trend has reached only a part of the population; the traditional feminine market still exists. There are many women who fit the conventional pattern, and, more important, almost all women respond to an appeal to their domesticity as well as to their new-found freedom. But businessmen must consider the trend just the same.

In countless studies we have made, the crucial determinant in purchase and nonpurchase proves to be human personality types. The difference between the man who buys a heliotrope shirt and the man who doesn't, between the man who smokes a pipe and the one who doesn't, between the woman who loves to cook and the woman who dislikes all housework, between the woman with high brand loyalties and the one with almost none, all these apparently are personality differences. They definitely are not differences in race, income, family size, education, and so forth, the usual criteria in the market researcher's descriptive data.

Just look around your neighborhood. One of your neighbors is a very stodgy conservative who prefers brown suits and cars that last eight years. He never tries anything new, is very meticulous and fussy, and almost miserly in the way he bargains and schemes to save a few pennies. Next door is the exhibitionist, who makes a virtue of being different to attract attention. The test for most of his actions, for almost everything he buys, is whether or not it will create comment. And right across the street are the striver and his wife who are inordinately ambitious to move upward in the social scale. Each step they take is just as calculated as a move in a chess game. They pick their friends just as coldly as they choose their furniture, their vacation spots, their brands of liquor, and their children's schools. Everything must fit a grand design to facilitate their upward movement.

It is important to remember, however, that human traits are like the blocks in a child's toy box. They come in different sizes and shapes, and are put together in countless ways to make different structures: more of one kind will be used to make a tower, more of another kind will go into a wall, and so on; but there will always be some of every kind included. So when a businessman looks at the stodgy conservative, the exhibitionist, or the social climber, he has to remember that what he is seeing is an enlargement in one individual of a characteristic which is common to all individuals. Don't ignore the element of exhibitionism in the conservative!

The real trouble is that we make almost no effort to consider this kind of problem—the whole complex area of personality—in our business strategy. We have not explored its relation to buying patterns.

In many categories where there is clear brand differentiation, personality is a key factor in product choice. For instance, in the study we did on the automobile and its meanings,[11] it was very clear that the manufacturer in the final analysis is selling to a particular personality type. Income of course is a limiting factor, but within any price class there is a wide opportunity for choice. The Studebaker buyer is a very different person from the Chevrolet buyer, not in income or size of family but in personality. Consequently he responds to different advertising appeals.

Model, color, accessories, and make are used by different people to say different things about themselves. Even in such an area as shaving, the straight razor, the mug, the shaving brush are the distinguishing marks of the conservative. At the other pole, the sophisticate, the modern type, the attention-getter, the daring personality are reaching for the electric razor, the pressurized lathers, the highly scented aftershave lotions.

An excellent study in one outlying section of Chicago showed the relationship of housewife personality types to retail stores. The highly mobile woman who considered this neighborhood only a steppingstone to better things wanted to be very efficient about her shopping. She wanted a minimum of contact with store personnel, and she preferred the impersonality of the chain stores. On the other hand, the woman who had left her friends in other parts of the city, and had every reason to believe this would be

[11] Social Research, Inc., *AUTOMOBILES: What They Mean to Americans* (Chicago, Chicago Tribune, 1954).

the last stop in her moving, leaned very heavily on the acquaintance she established with the personnel of the independent store. She eagerly looked forward to this regular contact as a substitute for past friendships. The older families who resented the real or fancied deterioration of the neighborhood went out of their way to patronize the independent store. This was their way of rebuking the chain stores for their encroachment.[12]

The University of Michigan Survey Research Center has made a notable start in showing the importance of attitudes in economic behavior.[13] According to its study of consumer durable goods purchases, the family decision to buy is determined in large part by underlying attitudes about general economic conditions. A person may have sufficient money to buy, but if he is pessimistic about the immediate future, he holds back. Conversely, if he feels business is booming and employment and income will continue, he does not hesitate to go into debt to obtain what he wants.

In another study, it was found that shifts in consumer attitudes foretell general business conditions. The gloomy predictions of many economists and politicians for the 1954 recession never materialized because the consumer was not seriously infected with this pessimism. The Federal Reserve figures for department store sales in city after city showed little or no decline in the face of less employment and much less overtime pay. The family went right on buying under the impetus of favorable attitudes.

But these University of Michigan studies are barely a start. There is no broad systematized knowledge in this field with specific application for business—how attitudes are formed, how you can go about isolating the real attitudes, how you can modify negative attitudes, how attitudes preselect the audience for a product or an institution.

Quite apart from generalized behavioral attitudes, there are particular attitude problems applying to each product area. Every brand is the target of plus and minus attitudes, although usually the manufacturer is completely unaware of them. When the con-

[12] Gregory Stone, "City Shoppers and Urban Identification," *American Journal of Sociology,* July 1954, p. 36.
[13] See George Katona and Eva Mueller, "A Study of Purchase Decisions," in *Consumer Behavior,* p. 15.

sumer is faced with a buying choice, these attitudes play a highly significant role. Too often, when the product is struggling under a burden of unfavorable attitudes, the manufacturer is wandering around ineffectively with his advertising and consumer relations because he has never come to grips with his real problem.

The significance of attitudes applies with equal weight in any field: railroad travel, life insurance, investments, retail stores, to mention a few. The point about attitudes is that they may not be factual at all, but they exist, and they are highly important in buying action.

Though the largest part of consumer spending is done by women, it is fantastic how little the average businessman understands feminine psychological goals. We men spend a lifetime associating with women—our mothers, our sisters and teen-age companions, our wives, and even our own daughters—yet it never dawns on us that they have fundamentally different motives and interests. We never sense their passivity; their economic insecurity; their narrow world which deliberately shuts out the bigger, threatening outer world; the means whereby they try to support their self-esteem in the drudgery of housework and babies.

Our poor wives patiently and politely listen while we bore them to extinction with our profundities about politics, baseball, and the business scene. We drag them to mystery and western movies which they don't like because of the violence and aggression.

Just eavesdrop on some women to realize the wide gulf between their interests and ours. There is very little man-talk in their world. It's babies and beauty parlors, new clothes, parties, recipes, sickness. The pattern may nudge a little this way or that in time, but it still remains essentially the same. And it still is almost totally misunderstood by the masculine intellect.

To those firms that seek insight in this sphere by hiring brilliant women copy writers and executives, let me point out that the career woman is a personality extreme who is in no position to speak for the average housewife. In the eyes of the career woman, children, husbands, and housework are merely necessary nuisances that she has to abide to prove her feminine adequacy.

But they are strictly secondary to her career in her mind. Psychologically she is miles apart from the ordinary wife, whose central goals include pleasing and caring for her family.[14]

We constantly commit blunders in our sales strategies because our decisions about influencing the woman consumer proceed from these masculine misunderstandings. The automatic dishwasher is a case in point. Here is an excellent technical product which has not gone anywhere saleswise; you will find it in only 3% of wired homes. Why has it done so poorly? Several reasons, in all likelihood, account for these disappointing sales, but certainly one is a serious mistake in sales approach. The emphasis on convenience can have a negative effect on many women; some will conceive of this product as a threat to their position in the household, removing one of their traditional jobs and diluting their feeling of martyrdom (which most of us, men as well as women, are likely to glory in whether we realize it or not).

In a motivation study on soaps and chemical detergents, we found that women had below-average brand loyalties toward these products because the advertising too often labored impersonal technical claims and seldom recognized the emotional problems associated with house-cleaning.[15]

Motivation studies on the newer convenience food products like instant coffee show that most women feel guilty about the appeal of time-saving because it conflicts with their self-conceptions.[16] How can a woman look like a self-sacrificing mother devoted primarily to her family's welfare if she "cheats" on such important tasks as preparing the meals?

The primary form of human communication is word-of-mouth. The reputations or public images of products and institutions are determined in part by advertising and technical superiorities, but most of all by word-of-mouth judgments from our friends, neigh-

[14] See W. L. Warner and W. E. Henry, "The Radio Daytime Serial: A Symbolic Analysis," in *Reader in Public Opinion and Communication*, edited by Bernard Berelson and Morris Janowitz (Glencoe, Illinois, The Free Press, 1953), p. 423.
[15] Social Research, Inc., *Motivations Relating to SOAPS AND CHEMICAL DETERGENTS* (Chicago, Chicago Tribune, 1954).
[16] Maison Haire, "Projective Techniques in Marketing Research," *Journal of Marketing*, April 1950, p. 649.

bors, work associates, and certain authority figures whom we respect.[17]

Yet we know little about this process of creating favorable opinion about our products and institutions by a human chain reaction. The area of small group research is very active now at the academic level, exploring the establishment of group norms, the influence of leaders, and the rigidity of attitudes. But business virtually never utilizes this approach on a deliberate basis, singling out actual neighborhood leaders and using them to start chain reactions of favorable opinion.

Obviously, I have merely touched a scattered handful of areas where management could profit by the creation of a body of knowledge. My whole point is that there are any number of research fields which can offer tremendously significant insights and solutions to business.

It should be clear that if the individual firm does not feel in a position to underwrite research on a broad basis, there are areas which can meaningfully be explored even though confined to the problems of one industry or one firm. For instance, understanding the new suburbanites could be a primary objective for the bigger central city banks, since their desire for representation in the sprouting communities is cited as a major cause for the current wave of bank mergers.

I could keep on endlessly citing potential fields: social mobility and its drives and symbols, the middle-income group's wish for individualism within the limits of conformity (instead of Veblen's conspicuous consumption),[18] the mass emphasis on job security rather than on job opportunity, the completely different philosophy of the increasing elderly population, and so on.

I have not discussed motivation research as such because a great deal has already been written and said about it—actually more than is being done about it. The motivation research currently being undertaken (primarily by the larger advertising agencies) uses psychological and psychoanalytic approaches to

[17] W. H. Whyte, "The Web of Word of Mouth," *Fortune,* November 1954, p. 140.
[18] See Nelson Foote, "The Autonomy of the Consumer," in *Consumer Behavior,* p. 15.

study the motives, rationalizations, attitudes, and feelings associated with individual product areas, in order to produce more effective advertising. But virtually nothing is being done to synthesize and to use the material from sociology, social psychology, communications, and personality study.

Synthesis can mark out the "style of life" of the potential consumer for a particular product. We are not as much concerned with a woman as such, nor with a woman in a certain age bracket or income classification; we need to know her "style of life." Does she fall into the modern, active, League of Women Voters group, finding her satisfactions in her community achievements as much as in her housekeeping talents? If so, frozen foods, cake mixes, and instant coffee are just what she wants. Or is she the type who takes special pride in her skill as a wife and mother? If so, "quick and easy" desserts, time-saving floor waxes, and packaged salads are an object of disdain for her.

"Style of life" is made up of attitudes, emotions, traditions, and prejudices. Because such things do not fit neatly into his abacus-juggling, the market researcher angrily ignores them and ends up by inferring that they do not even exist. At best, he picks off stray pieces, but never fits them together in any coherent whole.

Yet this pattern that runs through all our behavior determines how we feel about education, liquor, modern furniture, owning our own homes, going to church, what we want our children to be, whether we are savers or spenders. There are substantial individual differences, of course, but all of us have a "style of life" into which we fit our decisions, including our buying choices. It seems obvious that business should want to use all the information and insight that it can get to do a better job of selling and advertising.

CAUSES OF FAILURE

How does it happen, then, that there is such a complete lack of awareness by business of what the social sciences can offer? There is available material on the consumer as a human being, and on techniques and approaches which can be adjusted to the problems business wants to solve. The social sciences have high intellectual status, certainly as high as the schools of business. Is there any college or university in this country which does not offer extensive courses in psychology and sociology? Why then does business ignore the accumulated knowledge and the potential help of these sciences, making its consumer decisions almost entirely on the basis of hunch, common sense, and trial-and-error—which demonstrably are pretty frail reeds to lean on.

Basically business fails to realize that social and psychological research are distinctly different from market research. Further, in view of what is happening to the current interest in motivation research, I would say there is even a greater failure: we are not appraising the function and limitations of the market researcher himself. Let me put the problem in extreme form so as to make my point; this is important enough to run the risk of doing injustice to individuals here and there.

The concept of market research has been captured by statistical technicians who are not qualified either by training or by temperament to study the consumer from the viewpoint I have indicated. Although they pretentiously assume the task of providing management with any and all business research, actually all they are providing is a form of accounting about production schedules, salesmen's territories and costs, broad potentials, and movements of merchandise. Although "Markets are People," these researchers offer only isolated bits and pieces of research about people.

Obsessed with the minutiae of methodologies and buried in their columns of figures, they completely fail to supply management with any sense of what is happening to the American consumer, what he wants, what he is worried about.

The very essence of scientific inquiry is to proceed from the particular to the general. We do not need people who run around measuring things and gathering little scattered facts. We need to universalize with broad laws, to construct hypotheses which will be predictive. But that is the last kind of material that the current breed of market researchers are able to offer about consumer behavior.

In the average company the market researcher is in a position to veto any inquiry into the perfectly legitimate areas of social and psychological research, although he has never had any exposure to the scientific disciplines involved in the study of human behavior and does not even know their procedures and assumptions.

The market researcher invariably comes from schools of business where he has absorbed economics and statistics, but very little of the humanistic sciences. How can he pass a competent judgment on something he knows so little about?

The study of human behavior today is an interdisciplinary one, involving several different sciences: anthropology, sociology, and psychology, plus various derivatives such as social psychology and psychoanalysis. But I don't think I ever met a market researcher who could even define "anthropology" adequately; even without knowing what the science is or where it applies, the typical market researcher contemptuously dismisses all anthropologists as "head-shrinkers."

Most of the procedures and assumptions in motivation research come from clinical psychology. (There are 24 hospitals in Chicago with psychiatric units.) Every form of psychiatry and clinical psychology in general practice is some variant of Freudian theory. The literature of all the behavioral sciences in some degree comes to terms with Freud. But again I don't suppose there are a handful of market researchers qualified to evaluate the various schools of psychoanalysis, or who are even well acquainted with its basic assumptions.

Instead of stepping aside, with a frank admission of his lack of familiarity with these sciences, the market researcher tries to jam these other disciplines into the only methods he knows. When they don't fit his particular rigidities, he solemnly vetoes them. This situation is as absurd as taking a chiropractor's judgment on a problem in surgery or in psychosomatic medicine.

Because management has turned consumer research over to the market researcher, it naturally assumes that the findings of market research represent all the help available in the area of consumer buying behavior. So the sales manager sighs and uses his intuition as his sole guide, just as if the social sciences did not exist.

Actually it is an odd state of affairs. For 35 years management and leading scientists from the fields I mentioned have cooperated to develop a very comprehensive approach to the problem of understanding the employee. Larger universities offer courses in industrial management which expose students to the best theories on personality, social class, communication, leadership, counseling, and so on.[19]

For years the personnel people have used multitudinous forms of psychological testing. I know any number of firms which use comprehensive executive personality evaluation studies stemming largely from dynamic psychology. Even National Sales Executives, Inc., is furnishing its members with a first-rate motivation guide to help the sales manager derive keen insight into the psychological drives and problems of each salesman.

Yet when the consumer is approached, the sales manager, the manufacturer of consumer goods, the big retailer, even the advertising agency whose function is to influence this consumer, all ignore these same sciences as a possible source of guidance and understanding.

What Can Be Done

In this discussion I have deliberately put man's humanness in sharp relief to make it very clear that the impersonal findings of market research view the consumer as a bloodless digit rather than a dynamic, emotional, living organism. Market research secures highly essential classified and descriptive statistics: how many people purchased which brands at what prices. But there is no valid research in such data as to why the consumer behaves as he does.

I suppose I have given the impression of disparaging market research. I don't mean to at all. Its achievements are very notable. At the *Chicago Tribune* we have always placed our principal emphasis on statistical research, and we probably always will. But I am pointing to a very regrettable lag in the wide application of social and psychological research for which I think market research must accept the blame. I think it is doing a serious disservice to business by cutting off inquiry into potentially valuable sources of understanding which can be both diagnostic and predictive about consumer behavior. These approaches offer access to "why" answers that market research does not even attempt to get at.

[19] See Chris Argyris, *Personality Fundamentals for Administrators: An Introduction for the Layman* (New Haven, Yale Labor and Management Center, 1953).

With literally no grounding in these areas, with no comprehension of the rationales which are used, market researchers have no business trying to pass judgment on them. The situation will only be improved by the development of researchers with a completely different background to handle the exploration of these other fields. Today's top-flight market researcher who has spent his life absorbed in sampling problems, interview costs, and the error in mail surveys probably does not have enough time left to acquire sufficient background in the social sciences.

Just as business has induced physicists, chemists, electronics engineers, and industrial psychologists to leave the universities, so it should develop specialists from the social sciences. Several of the largest advertising agencies have staffed departments with professional specialists from these fields without trying to use converted statistical researchers. A trained group that can adapt these humanistic sciences to the purposes and the uses of business is our great need. We have had competent scientists do our *Chicago Tribune* motivation studies—but we always face the task of adapting the findings to solve our problems.

Communicators are essential to bridge the gap between these sciences and the layman. Any executive can readily grasp the portent of statistical data. But obviously it is not so simple for the untrained person to accept conclusions based on the assumptions of dynamic psychology. The jargon must be translated so that management is not irritated with a morass of terminology which is meaningless to the uninitiated.

This inability to communicate easily with the different levels of management is a serious shortcoming of market research, and is one of the basic reasons why it is so seldom considered in planning the grand strategies of business. Too many market researchers are introverts by temperament, and unfortunately often lack the qualities of persuasive presentation. Because they communicate so poorly, they seldom convey significance and stature to top management. Major decisions on advertising copy themes, on sales strategies, on designs for new models are usually made without the counsel of the market research department.

A type of researcher is therefore necessary who can evaluate the possibilities of the various fields, appraise practitioners and their methods, direct the studies, and adapt the conclusions, and who then can communicate all this to management. A skilled researcher, synthesizer, and communicator who can bridge the various fields would be of inestimable value to executives. Only if we develop such specialists will market research measure up to its real possibilities.

6

COMPUTER SIMULATION OF CONSUMER BEHAVIOR

WILLIAM D. WELLS

Within the next few years it will become possible to pretest marketing strategies on electronic computers. When this happens, marketing managers will get a much greater return on the time and money they spend to try out market plans. They will be able to select the most promising strategies from a large number of alternatives in a matter of hours—with greater accuracy than is now possible and at a fraction of the present cost.

There are two current developments that support these promises: first is the advent of hardware which makes short work of massive computations; second is the rapid growth in understanding of how to use computing machines in the simulation of complex social systems.

WHAT IS SIMULATION?

Actually simulation is nothing new. The first cave drawing was a simulation, as are all maps, charts, and graphs today. Model airplanes and model trains are simulations. In fact, a simulation is any scaled-down or symbolic representation of anything at all.

What is new is that it is rapidly becoming possible to create working models of complex dynamic systems, such as markets, and to use them to pretest the outcome of some contemplated change.

104

A simulation is also an analogy. Because it is an analogy, and not really the object it represents, certain things can be done with a simulation that cannot be done with the real world. Because an architect's drawing simulates materials and space, he can "build" and "rebuild" the same structure over and over again to see which plan is best. Because airline and train schedules simulate time relationships, they permit travelers to decide on the best route and the best carrier available without taking all routes and all carriers themselves. Because a missile expert's formulas simulate an object's flight through space, he can predict just where a rocket shot will land.

These, and all other, simulations have one element in common. The critical parts of some real process have been reduced to symbols, and the symbols have been used to imitate the way these parts behave. The trick, of course, is to identify the critical parts of the system, and to figure out a method of symbolizing how they work.

Marketing theorists have tried this many times. Some have borrowed concepts from physics, and have talked in terms of "phases," "cycles," and "weights." Others have borrowed ideas from mathematics, and have attempted to describe marketing processes by means of functions, lines, and curves. In fact, students of marketing have always attempted to extract and symbolize the essence of the processes involved, even when the symbols they used were limited to words.

Until recently, attempts to simulate complex social systems have not met with much success. Analogies from physics prove to be too loose. Mathematical structures fail to represent the market with the fidelity required. And models couched only in words are much too vague.

IMPORTANT DIFFERENCES

Computer simulation differs from these previous attempts in two important ways. First, every unit in the simulated system is represented as a separate entity in the machine. Second, the units "behave"—they imitate the activities of the things they represent. Together these properties give computer simulation its unique power as a research tool.

In a computer simulation the units represent objects in the real world. In a simulation of a factory the units are men and/or machines. In a simulation of traffic system the units are pedestrians, trucks, buses, and cars. And in a simulation of a market, they are consuming units of some kind—households or individuals—depending on the intended use of the results.

When the number of units in the system being simulated is relatively small—as it would be in a simulation of a machine shop, for example—all the units in the system are matched one for one in the machine. When the number of units is large—as it would be in a simulation of a national market—the units in the machine represent a sample of the population. In this case the results of the simulation will be projected to the parent population, just as the findings of a store audit or an opinion survey are.

Representation of real-world objects as separate entities is a major departure from most previous attempts to symbolize the way a market works. Traditionally, changes in market behavior are attributed to changes in market-wide phenomena such as "disposable income," "demand," "distribution," or "advertising weight." As a consequence, interest has focused on relationships between these summary statistics and share-of-market or total sales.

In computer simulation, each unit in the system—each household, for example—is represented separately. But the units are made to "behave," and observations of their "behavior" constitute the output of the machine.

One advantage of this approach is that it makes it easier to build and verify large and complicated models, one part at a time. If the automobile market were being simulated, for instance, the simulation might proceed region by region, each region being worked out and tested before being added. Also, an automobile market simulation might well focus on private new car purchases first, leaving other purchases to be considered at a later date.

However, a more profound advantage of this approach is that it offers a way around a problem which so far has not been solved. The interrelations among marketing variables are bewilderingly complex. In fact, they are so complex that any serious attempt to represent them mathematically is quite likely to end either in an obvious oversimplification or in an incalculable mess. For those extremely complicated problems, simulation of a population of households or individuals and observation of their simulated behavior seem to offer the best present hope.

The objective of a computer simulation is to make the computer units imitate the behavior of the real-world objects which the units represent. In a market simulation, the units might be households. The objective of the simulation would be to make the "purchasing" behavior of the simulated households perform like the purchasing behavior of the real households for which they stand. The key to accomplishing this is the concept of probability.

The probability that a given household will purchase within a given product classification during a particular period of time depends on a variety of things:

Heavy users of a product are much more likely to buy it within a specified time interval than light users are.

Households in which the product is almost worn out or used up are more likely to buy within the time interval than are households where the product is new or in good supply.

Consumer attitudes define the range of brands the household will accept, as well as loyalties and tendencies to switch.[1]

Coupons, deals, premiums, and special advertising also influence purchase probabilities.

The problem in building a simulation is to assign these probabilities to the units in the most accurate way.

One of the safest bets a marketing manager can make is that different segments of the population will consume his product at different rates. Another good bet is that different segments of the population have varying consumption patterns for different brands. Indeed, a very large proportion of consumer research is intended to reveal just what these preference and consumption patterns are.

It takes only a slight shift in point of view to see that differences in preference and consumption patterns mean differences in purchase probabilities within any set span of time. The probability of buying Alpha Bits in two succeeding weeks is quite different in households with several small children than it is in households with no children at all. Also, the probability of buying new tires

---

[1] See Ross M. Cunningham, "Customer Loyalty to Store and Brand," *Harvard Business Review*, November–December 1961, p. 127.

after six months is one thing for the salesman who drives his car five days a week, but something quite different for the little old lady who drives her car only to church on Sunday.

But, of course, all families with young children do not spend their money in the same way. Neither do salesmen nor little old ladies. This variability in behavior can be reduced by cross-classifying segments into "household types." For example, the households in each income bracket can be subclassified by characteristics such as region of residence, education of the household head, occupation of the household head, stage in the life cycle, and other variables related to consumption of consumer goods. When this process is carried far enough and when enough different variables have been employed in the analysis, the result is a set of household types within each of which consuming behavior is much the same.

The information necessary for subclassification comes from consumer research. If surveys show that a specific household characteristic is significantly related to purchase probabilities, then the population must be divided until purchase probabilities are similar within each household type. But if surveys show that the characteristic is unrelated to probability of purchase, the characteristic can safely be ignored. For example, households would be divided into subgroups on the basis of local water hardness in any simulation of the detergent market, because water hardness is known to influence the rate of use and choice of brand. But in a simulation of the aspirin market this characteristic would not play a part.

In assigning purchase probabilities, data from any number of information sources can be employed as long as they can be subdivided in a useful way.

For instance, one marketing survey might supply estimates of seasonal variations in purchase rates, while another might supply information on rural-urban consumption differences, or breakdowns by geographic region, or race, or social class. Any data source is of potential value as long as the information it supplies can be related, even by inference, to the purchasing behavior of the household types.

This feature of computer simulation is important, for it permits use of much information which is relevant but often not utilized since it is incomplete. In fact, if it were not for this feature, simulation of national markets would probably be out of the question. Then the demand for data would be greater than any single survey could possibly supply.

How Simulation Works

Suppose that work has been completed on a set of household types and its associated purchase probabilities. The households included in the types would constitute a representative sample of the population, classified by variables known to be related to product use. Thus, the probability figures assigned to the households would represent varying likelihoods of purchasing the product within a specified span of time.

To simulate the first set of purchases, the computer would employ the initial purchase probabilities. Suppose, to give a specific, but hypothetical, example, that the product is coffee, and—for a certain household type—the purchase probabilities are .75 for any coffee, .35 for instant coffee, and .20 for brand Y instant coffee. This means that out of households of this type, 75% normally buy coffee within a given week; of those who buy coffee, 35% normally buy instant coffee; and of those who buy instant coffee, 20% normally buy brand Y.

By a process akin to spinning a roulette wheel with 75 "yes" and 25 "no" compartments, the computer would decide whether household 1 is going to buy coffee within the week. If the answer is "yes," it would spin a second wheel with 35 "instant" and 65 "ground" compartments to decide which form of coffee this household will buy. And, if the answer is "instant," it would spin a 20–80 wheel to decide whether the instant coffee will be brand Y.

After figuring out the simulated purchasing behavior of household 1, the computer would record the decision and set new purchase probabilities for use the next time around. If a purchase was "made," the probability of another purchase in a week would go down, because the simulated household would have a supply on hand. If a purchase was not made, the probability of a purchase the next week would increase.

The computer would repeat this process for each of the simulated households—deciding which ones made purchases and which did not, changing probabilities, and keeping track of the results. When all of the households have been treated in this fashion, the simulation for the first week would be complete.

Simulation of the second week would proceed in exactly the same way, with the important exception that the "events" of the preceding week would be taken into account. Households which had "made purchases" would then have new, lower purchase probabilities reflecting the increased supplies on hand. And households which had not "made purchases" would have new, higher purchase probabilities reflecting the fact that some of last week's supply had now been used. The nature and amount of these changes would be based on survey-research data relating rate of product use to household type. Repeated, these weekly purchase cycles could cover any period of time.

When the computer has cycled through a simulated quarter, it could be ordered to print out total purchases of coffee, total purchases of instant coffee, and total purchases of brand Y. These figures could then be compared with store audits or some other outside information sources. Good agreement between simulated sales and real sales would be at least a hopeful sign. But over-all agreement could be misleading; for compensating errors within the simulation could produce seemingly correct net results. The next step would, therefore, be to take the simulation apart and test it piece by piece. This could be done by rerunning those sections of it which correspond to independent information from the real world. For example, if store audits were available region by region, the simulation could be run one region at a time, and the results could be examined to determine where the simulation departed from the market it represented. Then, if errors concentrate in certain regions, real-world knowledge of what has been happening in those regions could be used to help correct the fault. Or a special survey may have been run within a limited group of cities. In this case, the simulation could be rerun, using only the relevant household types, and the results could be evaluated to determine whether the fault is within these types or somewhere else.

This checking process is much like hunting for trouble in a complex machine. Possible sources of trouble are checked successively until the trouble spots are found.

Marketing managers are always experimenting. Coupons, premiums, deals, added advertising—all these tactics, and others, are employed at various times in various places and in various ways. Since most of these tactics have some kind of impact on the market, a working market simulation must account for their effect.

In the simulation process just described, a "normal," or "standard," or "baseline" amount of advertising and promotion would be assumed. As soon as advertising and promotion change, the simulation must be amended to take new account of their effect.

Initially, this amendment may be based on information which is hardly more substantial than a hazy guess, but in many instances available information would be considerably better than that. Most marketing managers have reasonably clear ideas about what effect their moves will have, and these ideas would be used to make provisional changes in the purchase probabilities of the relevant household types. For example, a new campaign may have been executed in media which are presumed to have their strongest influence on middle-income groups. The effect of the campaign would be simulated by making provisional changes in the purchase probabilities of the types of households the media were known to reach.

When the market experiment has been executed in the real world and the results observed, the discrepancy between the simulated results, based on the provisional values, and the results which actually occurred can be used to correct the estimates that were wrong.

A market simulation of this type would, therefore, be a growing, evolving thing. By running it repeatedly in imitation of selected market events, by observing the "hits" and "misses" of the simulation results, by using these observations to make corrections, the simulation could be made to act more and more like the market itself. Through this continuous correction process, the simulation's congruence with the real-world market would continuously improve.

At some point in this correction process, the simulation will become a reasonably accurate model of the market it represents. At this point, when something is done to change the real market, and the market reacts, doing the same thing to the simulation will produce analogous results.

Then the observation process can be reversed. Various alternative strategies can be "tried out" on the simulated market, and the reactions of the simulated market can be used to forecast how the real market will behave. Kept in line and kept correct by periodic checks against real events, the simulated market can be used to answer a wide range of questions about "what would happen if . . . ?"

If this sounds visionary, consider the fact that today every marketing manager goes through a process somewhat similar to this himself. Using his own implicit model of the market—a model which he has developed through years of observation, trial, and error—the marketing manager "tries out" alternative marketing strategies in his head. Depending on the structure of his private model, one strategy wins out over the others and gets put into effect.

The major difference between current practice and the practices projected here is that the years of real-world experience are stored in the computer, and explicit formulation is given to the ways this experience is used.

THE STATE OF THE ART

A brief sketch of what has already been done in related fields will give some clues to what tomorrow's marketer might reasonably expect.

Probably the best-known computer simulation available is of the 1960 presidential election by Ithiel de Sola Pool of MIT and Robert Abelson of Yale.[2] In this study, stored data from opinion surveys were combined to forecast the effect of the candidates' religions on the election, and to make special forecasts of the impact of the Negro vote. When the simulated results were compared with the actual returns, agreement was quite good.

In a project somewhat closer to the marketing field, Pool and Abelson worked on a simulation of consumers' exposure to advertising media.[3] This project, which makes extensive use of the concept of consumer types, also capitalizes heavily on the capacity of simulation models to accept data from almost any valid source.

---

[2] "The Simulatics Project," *The Public Opinion Quarterly*, Summer 1961, p. 167.
[3] *Simulatics Media-Mix Technical Description* (New York, The Simulatics Corporation, 1962).

Another election simulation—this one focused on the Wisconsin presidential primary—has been constructed by William McPhee, a Columbia University sociologist, and Frank Scalora, a mathematician at IBM.[4] Because their model imitates the influences of messages on attitudes, major features of it have proved to be applicable to a simulation of the impact of recruitment advertising developed by Benton & Bowles and IBM.[5]

Simulation models of other large-scale and complex systems have been reported. R. M. Cyert, J. G. March, and C. G. Moore, of the Carnegie Institute of Technology, have described a model of department store ordering and pricing.[6] Alfred A. Kuehn and Michael J. Hamberger, of the same institution, have reported a simulation model for choosing warehouse sites.[7]

Perhaps the most ambitious, and certainly the most thoroughly reported, simulation model is described in a simulation study made by a team of scientists from the University of Wisconsin, The Brookings Institution, and MIT.[8] One segment of this model imitates the vital activities of a sample of the United States population. In it, simulated individuals are born, live their lives, and die. In the process of maturing, many of them meet and marry. Of those who marry, many have children and raise families. Some never marry. Some get divorced—all at the behest of probabilities obtained from census data and stored on computer tape. In the future, these investigators say that their simulated individuals will probably take "actions" of other kinds. They may take jobs, make purchases, take out loans, start businesses, or put money in the bank. In fact, the ultimate objective of this approach is nothing less than a working model of the way the economic system functions.

[4] "Note on a Campaign Simulator," *The Public Opinion Quarterly*, Summer 1961, p. 184.

[5] William McPhee, Frank Scalora, and Frank Stanton, "What Contribution Can Communication Theory Make to Constructing and Evaluating an Advertising Campaign?" in *Proceedings of the Eighth Annual Conference* (New York, Advertising Research Foundation, 1963).

[6] "A Model of Retail Ordering and Pricing by a Department Store," in *Quantitative Techniques in Marketing Analysis*, edited by Ronald E. Frank, Alfred A. Kuehn, and William F. Massey (Homewood, Illinois, Richard D. Irwin, Inc., 1962), pp. 502–522.

[7] "A Heuristic Program for Locating Warehouses," *ibid.*, pp. 523–546.

[8] Guy R. Orcutt, Martin Greenberger, John Korbel, and Alice Rivlin, *Microanalysis of Socioeconomic Systems: A Simulation Study* (New York, Harper & Brothers, 1961).

113

However, long before such an ambitious objective can be reached, more limited working market models will certainly be completed. At present many imaginations are being challenged by the uses to which such models might be put. At the very least, *they will provide a way to conduct test-market experiments at extraordinary speed and at a fraction of their present cost*. And, because they draw on such vast funds of information, computer simulations are certain to be much more accurate predictors than are the informal market simulations which now take place in human heads.

Second, the availability of working simulations is likely to have an even more profound effect. *Because they will reduce the costs and risks of experimenting, they will encourage the unusual, but brilliant, plan.* Present test-market experiments are time-consuming and costly; and, because they are likely to have share-of-market consequences, they are almost always conservative. The highly creative effort, the daring innovation, gets discouraged because it involves too much risk. But when an innovation can be tried out on a working model of the market, the consequences of a wrong guess will not be nearly so severe. Then bad guesses can be discarded, and good guesses can be put into operation with increased confidence that they will succeed.

Finally, and probably most important in the long run, *working models will bring the power of the controlled experiment to marketing research.* As usually conducted in the past, test-market experiments have been pseudoexperiments at best. Rarely if ever has it been possible to control all interference sources while the operation of a given set of factors is observed. A working market model will make a reality of experiments of this kind. Although the benefits of such a development cannot be guaranteed, experience in other fields has shown that the controlled experiment is one of the most productive research tools ever known.

Efforts at consumer behavior simulation are solving few, if any, practical marketing problems today, and simulation will never prove to be a panacea for such problems in the future. But impressive progress is now being made, progress which promises marketers a more insightful tomorrow in their attempts to assess the effect of marketing strategies on the way that consumers behave.

7

THE PRODUCT AND THE BRAND

BURLEIGH B. GARDNER AND SIDNEY J. LEVY

Basic to many of the problems of advertising and selling is the question of the consumers' attitude toward the product and particularly their conception of the brand.

Qualitative research, especially of the kind which has so recently come to the fore as "consumer motivation" research, promises to add substantially to our knowledge in this area.[1] The quantitative approach, which we used to have to rely on, only brings us part way to finding the kind of answers we need; now we can take a distinct step forward.

BLIND SPOTS

Inquiry has taken a direct route, in the past, oriented toward finding out the number of people who use the product, the main reasons they offer for doing so, the advantages and disadvantages they find in the brand, and so forth. The users have been counted; their reasons have been listed in order of frequency (and assumed to be the most potent); and their praises and complaints have been aired and duly registered.

This information is important and useful for many purposes.

[1] See Joseph W. Newman, "Looking Around: Consumer Motivation Research," *Harvard Business Review,* January–February 1955, p. 135.

But it leaves a great deal untouched and hence can be misleading.

For one thing, the reasons people usually give for using a product are inclined to be either strongly rationalized or related to the product's most obvious purposes. Thus, most surveys tend to show that consumers want products to be, in one form or another, effective: to get clothes white, groom the hair, quench thirst, prevent tooth decay, taste good, and so on.

When such goals as these are taken at their face value, and considered to be the end of the matter, they lead up many blind alleys. The belief that people are fretting over those minute differences, presumed to provide the best quality, results in such affairs as blindfold tests that try to find an otherwise indiscernible superiority on the part of one brand over other brands, in advertisements constantly claiming "more," and sometimes in a shrill focus on product merits beyond all proportion and sensible differentiation.

The consumer, who generally believes that well-known brands will quite adequately perform their intended functions, gets a glazed feeling at the scholarly astuteness required to distinguish between insistently repetitive claims.

A striking example of the stereotypes into which competitive brands can fall is this list of soap and detergent themes, each from a different brand's advertisement:

"No detergent under the sun gets clothes whiter, brighter."
"Washes more kinds of clothes whiter and brighter."
"Beats the sun for getting clothes whiter and brighter."
"Washes clothes whiter without a bleach."
"Gives you a whiter wash without bleaching than any other 'no rinse' suds with bleach added."
"Alone gets clothes whiter than bleach."[2]

Presumably little else can be done if the advertisers have the fixed idea that housewives are preoccupied solely with the whiteness of their laundry—because that is the most frequent, conscious, immediate notion women can muster up to explain their

---

[2] As noted in a study conducted by Social Research, Inc., *Motivations Relating to SOAPS AND CHEMICAL DETERGENTS* (Chicago, Chicago Tribune, 1954).

use of detergents and to justify the use of any preferred brand. But surely there is more to the matter than that.

What are some of the more fundamental issues a manufacturer and his advertising people should face in getting beyond such apparent aims, and what can they do about them?

NEW INSIGHTS

Answering this question calls for a greater awareness of the social and psychological nature of "products"—whether brands, media, companies, institutional figures, services, industries, or ideas. New conceptions and orientations are needed for a sensible understanding of the communication process that goes on in offering an object to the public.

Many current ideas about human psychology are overly simple and nonoperational in definition. Gross assumptions are made about what people want and what motivates their wanting. Quick generalizations are made and arbitrarily transferred from one situation to another, often inappropriately.

For example, two very common motives that are belabored (when specific product substances and effects are not made the main issue) are (a) the striving to be economical and (b) the desire to emulate people of higher status. Undoubtedly consumers do pursue bargains and many people do have social aspirations. In given instances these ideas may have to be given crucial consideration. Nevertheless, there is a tremendous range of other variables that may totally negate, or even reverse, the direction of these strivings—and the complications in any single situation should be specifically studied.

Thus, as far as economy is concerned, with many kinds of products low cost is not intently sought, or there may be a subtle assessment of "good value" being made. Indeed, consumers may have a definite figure in mind (arrived at in some curious way) which they believe is the price the object should cost. Hence elasticity of demand can vary in strange patterns.

Again, with the mobility of our society, millions of Americans do want to make progress, but not necessarily "upward." They simply may not want to be like, or to live like, people of diverse social status. While sometimes a "woman's point of view" may prevail in management councils, and the manufacturer's wife may then be a good source of information, all too often lower middle-class and upper lower-class housewives (the majority of the housewives) do not think like Mrs. Management, do not share many of her needs, her values, her esthetics, or her ways of solving problems.

Thus, one of the first things a manufacturer and his advertising people need to explore is the particular constellation of goals and attitudes most pertinent to their product and brand situation, rather than applying blindly the one that seemed so useful to Listerine nearly 25 years ago, and to Ford and Allsweet more recently.

Such explorations must take into account the character of the product (the human needs it serves and the particular way it does so), the dimensions employed in evaluating brands of such a product, and where the particular brand stands on these dimensions.

At the literal level, a newspaper, for example, is supposed to be "a printed publication issued at regular intervals, usually daily or weekly, and commonly containing news, comment, features, and advertisements" (according to the *American College Dictionary*). These are common expectations, and a newspaper will be measured as to how well or poorly it is printed, how regularly it appears, whether it distinguishes its news, comments, features, ads, and so on.

However, in our society other dimensions will emerge, perhaps of greater importance, to differentiate the papers in influential ways. The definition does not show (as qualitative research does) that the public tends to feel that a sense of public responsibility is a major ingredient in the character of a newspaper; and this factor will be very important to the image of any given paper, in itself and in how it compares with its competitors.

Furthermore, anyone can readily observe that different papers generally have what we can call different personalities. Thus, *The New York Times* is quite a different thing from the *New York Daily News*, or the *Chicago Tribune* is different from the *Chicago Sun-Times*. These differences appear in many ways: selection of news, handling of particular stories, choice of headlines, types of facts reported, and editorial content. Thus they represent complex systems of values and of judgments, applied to the daily process of getting out a paper.

In similar fashion, a brand name is more than the label employed to differentiate among the manufacturers of a product. It is a complex symbol that represents a variety of ideas and attributes. It tells the consumers many things, not only by the way it sounds (and its literal meaning if it has one) but, more important, via the body of associations it has built up and acquired as a public object over a period of time.

A well-chosen brand name may have a rhythmic quality (like Jell-O for desserts) or an apt air (like Bell for telephones). It will also convey meanings which advertising, merchandising, promotion, publicity, and even sheer length of existence have created.

The net result is a public image, a character or personality that may be more important for the over-all status (and sales) of the brand than many technical facts about the product. Conceiving of a brand in this way calls for a rethinking of brand advertising, and of the kinds of judgments that have to be made by an informed management about its communications to the public.

The image of a product associated with the brand may be clear-cut or relatively vague; it may be varied or simple; it may be intense or innocuous. Sometimes the notions people have about a brand do not even seem very sensible or relevant to those who know what the product is "really" like. But they all contribute to the customer's deciding whether or not the brand is the one "for me."

These sets of ideas, feelings, and attitudes that consumers have about brands are crucial to them in picking and sticking to ones that seem most appropriate. How else can they decide whether to smoke Camels or Lucky Strikes; to use Nescafé or Borden's instant coffee; to drive a Ford or a Chevrolet or a Plymouth?

Justifying choice is easier with the cars, there at least the products have clearly visible differences. But the reasons people give for choosing a brand of cigarettes (and soap and bread and laxatives) are pretty much the same. Thus you find drinkers of any brand of beer justifying their preference in identical terms: "Schlitz is better because it's dry." "I like a dry beer, so I prefer Bud to Schlitz."

Something must make a greater difference; the conceptions of the different brands must be compounded of subtle variations in feelings about them, not necessarily in product qualities. A big problem in this area, then, is what kind of symbol a given brand is to consumers.

RESEARCH IN DEPTH

Currently, a variety of concepts and methods are being taken from the armament of the social sciences and applied to this type of problem. Procedures first developed to explore the complex facets of attitudes and motives in clinical and academic research are finding new adaptations. They are especially useful for arriving at an understanding of the attitudes and feelings which make up the image of a product and a brand.

Rather than interviewing a large number of respondents in a terse, question-and-answer fashion, researchers take smaller samples and interview them at some length. The subjects are allowed to express themselves with a relatively large degree of individuality, to give their views in their own words. Hence, the interview usually proceeds in a conversational fashion rather than being held to a tightly circumscribed framework.

In addition, various kinds of more or less vague and ambiguous stimuli are introduced into the interview. They present an issue or a task which the respondent must handle in his or her own way, thereby "projecting" assumptions and evaluations that might not otherwise be made explicit. An example of one of these projective techniques is thematic analysis of storytelling. Interviewees are shown a picture that makes some reference to use of the product or a particular brand. Although respondents might not be willing to say, for instance, that they are relatively indifferent to the object, it may be apparent from their stories. Perhaps the stories are unusually brief, limited in variety of ideas, lacking in liveliness, or extremely repetitive. By contrast, another object being studied might elicit stories expressed enthusiastically and with a good deal of individuality of associations and experiences.

Where the various brands of a product are largely indistinguishable as to quality, cost, effectiveness, and so on—or, what is about the same thing, each user group claims that its brand is outstanding on the same points—how can the consumers' varying brand evaluations be discerned? Sometimes matching techniques show public views that consumers have difficulty in stating—or that they even deny.

When consumers are presented with a list of kinds of people and asked to name those most likely to choose each of the brands, many resist the task as meaningless, since presumably all the brands are basically comparable. Nevertheless, random patternings of these evaluations rarely emerge, as would be expected if consumers' responses were taken at their face value. Instead, definite dimensions do show up. In other words, consumers really believe there are differences among the brands.

For instance, on one device, brand A may turn out to be regarded as the most suitable for wives of doctors, lawyers, office managers, and company presidents, while brand B is attributed to the wives of electricians, carpenters, taxi drivers, and grocery clerks. Clearly, there is a social status differentiation between the two brands that helps a woman determine which is more suited for her own needs. (Remember, it does not mean that brand B will be rejected, either; many consumers do not want to emulate members of other social groups.)

It may also turn out that on another device brand A is named as especially used by home economists, stepmothers, professional women, and movie actresses, while brand B is regarded as suitable for motherly women, beginning housewives, practical cooks, and old-fashioned cooks. The image of brand A is more austere, less friendly; the consumers see it not only as of higher status but also somewhat remote. On the other hand, brand B has a warmer sound to it, a down-to-earth quality; it is regarded as a more ordinary brand, one for everyday people.

Exhibit I shows contrasting profiles for brands A and B.

By the use of such approaches, including incomplete sentences, word association, forced choices, and role playing, the main dimensions of a brand or product character can be drawn out. The important ideas may not be mysterious, or even profound psychological constructions; they are more likely to be similar in quality to the way human personalities show themselves. The techniques used are not the crux of the matter; they are only avenues to understanding.

The emphasis in such research must necessarily be given to

EXHIBIT I. CONTRASTING PROFILES OF COMPETING BRANDS

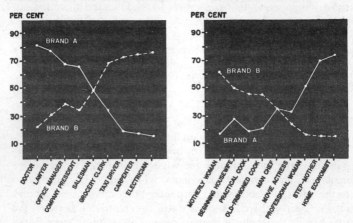

skill in interpretation and to reaching a coherent picture of the brand. The researchers must allow their respondents sufficient self-expression so that the data are rich in complex evaluations of the brand. In this way, the consumers' thoughts and feelings are given precedence rather than the preconceptions of the researchers, although these are present too in hypotheses and questions.

MANAGEMENT'S TASK

After having discovered how the product and brand are organized in consumers' minds, management's problem is what to do about it.

First of all, management must take into account these two basic points:

(1) A reputable brand persists as a stable image through time. The ideas people have about it are not completely malleable, not idly swayed by one communication and then another. If the public believes that a certain brand is of inferior quality, or that another is "on the skids," or that some other has all the latest improvements, these beliefs are not usually modified very rapidly. Such reputations are built through time, frequently in ways that management is not aware of.

122

(2) It is rarely possible for a product or brand to be all things to all people. It may be most desirable to sell to the most people, but hardly anyone can sell to everyone. Some brands have very skillfully built up reputations of being suitable for a wide variety of people, but in most areas audience groupings will differ, if only because there are deviants who refuse to consume the same way other people do. More significantly, there are different age, sex, social class, personality groupings, to say nothing of special-interest groups, ethnic groups, and occupational groups. It is not easy for a brand to appeal to stable lower middle-class people and at the same time to be interesting to sophisticated, intellectual upper middle-class buyers.

Accordingly, management has to determine what kind of brand it wants to present. Does it wish to be very dignified (and forego the teen-age, dime-store customers); does it want to be smart and individual (and latch onto *New Yorker* readers); or does it want to seem a bit daring and frivolous (and skip a lot of moral middle-class housewives)?

Basically, although advertising and research people can contribute a great deal toward making the judgment most realistic, this is a management decision. A great deal can stand or fall on the direction taken—such as whether the company stakes its success on winning a larger part of a smaller market, or moving more goods at a lower margin, or whatever the long-range strategy may be.

Knowingly or not, management makes this decision. Thus, some companies do it by refusing to sponsor certain radio or television shows because they believe they are undignified and (by making these and other such decisions) may wind up in the public eye as a rather stuffy outfit with a too-expensive product. Other managements insist on "hard sell," until they discover to their dismay that their market has become predominantly lower class.

Deciding about each campaign or action may not require a session on the razor's edge, but the most fruitful approach is one that involves an awareness of long-range goals for the character of the product as well as some attempt to be consistent with the chosen course.

It is not enough for management to say to itself, "Of course we

123

want a favorable brand image. So having decided that we want one which will appeal to all groups, which will have all good qualities and no negative ones, let's tell the world that this is what we are." The management which takes this approach to developing an effective brand image is no more likely to succeed than the management which tries to convince its employees it is benevolent and only concerned with their good by telling them loud and often about its benevolent intentions.

For management to be able to handle this problem effectively it should evaluate its brand's current public image, the differences seen by different important consumer groups, and the images of competitive brands. Otherwise it does not know just what it is working against, what limitations in image must be overcome, and what strengths it has to build on.

Basic attitudes toward products may set limits on the kind of image which might be developed or in the kinds of satisfactions which the product image may imply. Or a given brand may have such a strong image in some respects that it is more feasible to accept these than to change them. For example, if a product has a strong image of high quality and special-occasion use, it might be disastrous to try to reduce it rapidly to more prosaic everyday use.

By knowing the possible directions in which it might go, management is in a position to judge the specific moves or campaigns designed to reach the goals it has set.

THE AGENCY'S ROLE

Once the current public view of a brand has been explored and an image to be aimed at for the future has been determined, the major problems are assumed by the company's advertising agency. It is the business of advertising to assist in the creation of brand images, to give them structure and content, to develop a pattern of consumer attitudes likely to lead to brand purchase. How can the advertising agency go about this; what is its role?

As a profession, advertising is in the flux of transition. It is uncertain whether its image should be creative, businesslike, or sociable; whether it should nursemaid the client (and maybe his family) or strike out for independence and professional integrity.

Advertising has been subject to pressures from the whims and presumed knowledge of its clients in a way that well-established professions refuse to tolerate—and for several reasons:

Advertising has been an occupation of creativity and individual personalities.

The effects of advertising campaigns are often difficult to measure.

Single accounts can mean life or death to an agency.

Everyone believes he knows what an advertisement should be like.

However, as advertising builds up a body of principles, an increased understanding of audience composition and reactions, and a wide-ranging familiarity with procedures and techniques —plus a sense of responsibility and pride in good performance— management should recognize these developments and take advantage of them.

Having set the goals for its product, management ideally should leave to the skills and knowhow of the advertising people the job of implementing them. A layman (with reference to any profession) is frequently not in a position to understand how a particular process or step—or advertising layout—is conducive to the desired goals.

In creating, developing, or modifying a brand image, the advertising people must have a good understanding of the situation that confronts them. This includes a nuanced appreciation of the brand image as it already exists—with an awareness that the momentary sales position of the brand may be less important for its future than the danger that people may think of it as getting increasingly passé, perhaps.

Advertising men must think about such problems as:

In a lively product area, is the brand thought of as dull?

In a conservative product area, is the brand too frivolously presented?

Does it involve anxious connotations?

Does its use pattern seem increasingly circumscribed?

Is it an "unfriendly" brand, an overly masculine brand, a weak-seeming brand, and so on?

Understanding the brand problems and the manufacturer's goals (and remember that his objective is not always just to sell the most goods the quickest) is a basic requirement. Then a thorough knowledge of how to move ahead is needed. What are the kinds of variables that have to be dealt with? How can they be got across to the public?

The truly sophisticated advertising man realizes that communications are subtle, that many an advertisement says things about the product that were never intended by the copywriter. For example, some time ago a less sophisticated advertising man wanted to know why it was that instant coffee had come to be regarded as an inferior substitute when it was originally thought of as an expensive concentrate. It did not occur to him that his own agency had for a long time been instrumental in offering a brand of instant coffee with constant emphasis on savings, bargains, deals, economies.

Brand images do not grow in a vacuum. A newspaper advertisement that employed a heavy black border to demarcate it from its neighbors was noted by consumers as dead-looking, and the product was thought impure. An advertisement that showed the fine texture of the product under a microscope made people think of disease bacteria.

In themselves, such instances of individual advertisements may not be crucial; certainly a product image is the result of many varied experiences. They all make their contributions, for good or for bad, and will do so best when the long-range goals are kept in mind during their creation. Too many advertisements are built as individual units, with a conglomeration of elements to satisfy different agency and client tastes rather than with reference to a guiding, governing product and brand personality that is unified and coherently meaningful.

In many advertising conferences someone will ask: "Which of these campaigns will sell the most packages?" This is not an irrelevant question, certainly, since presumably advertising that does not sell is unproductive. Nevertheless, a single campaign is not the manufacturer's only salesman, and he usually intends to remain in business for many following years. From this point of view it is more profitable to think of an advertisement as a contribution to the complex symbol which is the brand image—as part of the long-term investment in the reputation of the brand.

This point of view has many implications. It means that:

Copy should be thought about in terms of its symbolic and indirect meanings as well as its literal communication.

Color and illustration are not merely esthetic problems since they also have social and psychological implications.

Media selection should be related to a brand image plan and not merely geared to circulation figures.

Research should seek out ideas and meanings as well as audience statistics.

Conclusion

We have sought to highlight some ideas that seem to be important in the thoughtful presentation of products and brands.

Products and brands have interwoven sets of characteristics and are complexly evaluated by consumers. Hence, advertising a product is not a matter of isolated messages. It calls for analyses of attitudes and motives. It also calls for a differentiated knowledge and judgment on the part of management and advertising people; in a sense, their tasks become richer, and the division of responsibility more meaningful.

With the findings of qualitative research, management can see its product in a clearer perspective. Advertising people can increase their awareness of the social-scientific nature of the communication process and the way in which their actions influence it. Those on the creative side of advertising, particularly, can find new sources of stimulation and inspiration in breaking away from the preconceptions and conventions that have fixed so much advertising in set molds.

8

BRAND LOYALTY—WHAT, WHERE, HOW MUCH?

ROSS M. CUNNINGHAM[*]

One of the important controversies among marketing executives today concerns the question of brand loyalty. How worthwhile is it for a company to spend hundreds of thousands of dollars in an effort to identify its products in buyers' minds with a brand label? Manufacturers of frequently purchased consumer products have necessarily had to act in reference to this question in planning their marketing strategy, but they have had little to go on in the way of factual information. There is no telling how many millions of dollars in promotion budgets have been predicated on one assumption or another which has never really been proved.

This paper discusses the results of a study of brand loyalty that develops new methods of measurement and investigates hitherto unexplored aspects of brand loyalty behavior. Interest in the general subject was stimulated in part by the important work of George H. Brown in a series of articles in *Advertising Age*.[1]

[*] This study was financed by the Sloan Research Fund of the School of Industrial Management, Massachusetts Institute of Technology. The *Chicago Tribune* has cooperated through Pierre Martineau, Director of Research, in permitting use of data from the *Tribune's* consumer purchase panel.

During the first part of the study, the author had the able assistance of Donald R. Sohn, then Instructor of Marketing at M.I.T., and more recently of Roger K. Olen and Charles Y. Chittick, Jr., Research Assistants.

[1] June 9, 1952 (margarine); June 30, 1952 (tooth paste); July 14, 1952 (coffee); July 28, 1952 (flour); August 11, 1952 (shampoo); September 1, 1952 (cereals); September 22, 1952 (headache tablets); October 6, 1952 (soaps and sudsers); December 1, 1952 (orange juice); and January 26, 1953 (a summary).

Here are the major questions and conclusions of the study, applying to low-price, frequently purchased items:

Is there really any such thing as brand loyalty? Some executives believe that the housewife distributes her purchases among the various brands of a product in a purely random fashion. They believe that the share of the market which a brand has depends primarily on such factors as the extent of retail distribution, the amount and location of retail display space obtained, product qualities, and the like. Other marketing executives believe that they have—or could have, with proper promotion efforts—a group of long-time loyal buyers for their products.

The study indicates that a significant amount of brand loyalty to individual products does exist—more, indeed, than has hitherto been realized by many marketing executives. There are many instances where 90% or more of a family's purchases have been concentrated on a single brand over three whole years.

Are there large numbers of housewives and families who are inclined to be brand loyal regardless of products purchased? "Loyalty-prone" purchasing behavior would be evidenced by consistent high loyalty to brands in a number of product classes. This is a matter of great concern to marketing men because many companies today produce several product lines. Their assumptions about the existence or nonexistence of important numbers of loyalty-prone families affect their basic sales strategy—for example, their decisions whether or not to promote each product line differently.

Understanding of loyalty proneness is also important to marketing research. We make assumptions about it when we decide to try to identify loyal families and analyze their behavior, or when we conduct field research product by product instead of by concentrating on a group of families of supposedly high loyalty.

This study shows that there is not a significant proportion of loyalty-prone families—housewives and other family purchasers who tend to have the same degree of brand loyalty in various product classes. Those who are highly loyal to a brand of one product may have very little loyalty to a brand of another product.

Do purchasers have any secondary loyalties? That is, if they are loyal in some degree to one brand, do they also have a lesser degree of loyalty to another brand of the same product and, if so, how much? Here is a matter of obvious concern to competing manufacturers.

The answer seems to be that they do have definite secondary loyalties which are of important magnitude for about half of the family buyers.

What effects do special price offers or deals have on brand loyalty? Since deals are often used in an effort to gain new users, their relationship to brand loyalty is of considerable significance.

It appears that deals have little impact on loyalty. Those loyal to a brand remain loyal; purchasing on deals tends to be concentrated among those with low brand loyalties.

How are store loyalty buying patterns related to brand loyalty behavior? Are families with high brand loyalty ratings also likely to rate high on store loyalty?

No truly significant correlation exists between high brand-loyal and high store-loyal families, but there is enough suggestion of some relationship that further analysis may be in order.

Are brand-loyal families typically large, small, or average users of a product? If consumption is randomly distributed over the brand loyalty scale, it can be ignored; but if it varies with the amount of loyalty, it is an important factor to consider.

The study indicates that there is no relationship between size of purchase and brand loyalty.

Are there certain economic or social characteristics associated with families who are high or low in brand loyalty? To the extent that such characteristics exist, the problem of identifying loyal purchasers of a product would be easier.

The evidence so far suggests that for low-price, frequently purchased items there are no socioeconomic characteristics associated with different degrees of brand loyalty. This conclusion is tentative; in fact, more refined analysis is planned which might reveal relationships not yet uncovered.

METHOD OF ANALYSIS

Because this study carries exploration forward into new territory, the description of the concepts and methods employed has more than usual significance. A description of the research should also serve to indicate the limits of applicability of the findings, and suggest where further research is needed.

The preliminary interviews conducted for the study revealed widespread differences of opinion and substantial confusion about the nature and significance of brand loyalty behavior.

It became apparent that the first step in clarifying concepts was to make a sharp distinction between the record of past consumer purchasing of product brands and the complex of forces which underlie and explain these purchases. This study has been purposely directed to detailed analysis of past buying behavior and has avoided becoming involved in complex motivational problems. The "why" of brand loyalty behavior can be effectively attacked by field interviewing only after we know its "what," "where," and "how much."

The second step was to find a helpful way of looking at brand loyalty. Should it be defined in terms of (1) customers lost and gained over specific time periods, (2) time sequences of individual purchases, or (3) share of the market?

(1) In the analysis of customers lost and new customers gained, the length of the periods chosen is usually one or two months. When the products are compared, the brand with a lower ratio of lost customers is presumed to have the higher loyalty.

This concept suffers the disadvantage or requiring an arbitrary time period, which may not reflect the natural purchasing cycle of the housewife for individual products. The number of lost and new customers tends to be overstated. If a housewife happens to be out of the market for the brand during one period but returns in the third period, she is classified as a lost customer in the second period and as a new customer for the third.

(2) The concept of time sequences of individual purchases usually involves the appraisal of various patterns of series or runs of given brands. Thus a family could purchase brand A six times in a row, then brand B once, then brand A five times; or brands A, B, and C one time each and then repeat them in succession several times; or brand A ten times and then brand B twice; and so on. Many families purchase five or more brands, and the time patterns can be very complex.

Some kind of judgment must be made as to which patterns are more or less indicative of brand loyalty, and an element of subjectivity is inevitably involved at this point. An essential part of the process is to distinguish between those patterns which could stem from random buying and those which represent truly loyal behavior on the part of the housewife. Methods must then be developed for applying these detailed criteria to individual families in a manner which eliminates personal discretion on the part of the analyst.

Also, for purposes of analyzing the many aspects of brand loyalty, it is desirable to have a quantitative measure of brand loyalty for each family, but the time pattern concept is more conducive to assigning families to several brand groupings, such as strongly loyal, loyal, weakly loyal, disloyal.

It is an intriguing concept, but the operational problems involved in applying it are so severe that they are likely to lessen its usefulness.

(3) In the case of the market share concept, attention is directed to the distribution of a family's purchases among the different brands in a product group—the proportion going to the largest single brand, the two largest brands, and so on. This concept assumes that the manufacturer is primarily concerned with how many of the dollars which Mrs. Housewife lays on the checkout stand for a given product class are spent on his brand rather than on the others.

The share of market concept provides an objective figure for brand loyalty on each family which can be compared with all the other families on a continuous scale of values. Such figures facilitate analysis of aspects of brand loyalty not hitherto investigated, such as loyalty proneness and relationships between brand loyalty and deals, store loyalty, consumption rates, and socioeconomic characteristics. Furthermore, this concept also happens to fit in better with the various ways in which information from consumer purchase panels is usually arranged, and therefore can make better use of such material.

The measure of brand loyalty chosen for this analysis was drawn from the third concept. The study uses both single-brand loyalty, or the proportion of total purchases represented by the largest single brand used, and dual-brand loyalty, or the proportion of total purchases represented by the two largest single brands used. In addition, variations of these two measures were developed: single brand minus deals, obtained by subtracting from total purchases all those sales made on special price inducements or deals and then calculating the percentage represented by the largest single brand among nondeal purchases, and similarly dual brand minus deals.

In order to measure brand loyalty behavior using past purchasing patterns, reasonably comprehensive and accurate records of family purchases were needed over a very substantial period of time. The limitations of human memory made it impossible to secure reliable information of this type by going out and asking questions, and data from a consumer purchase panel seemed the best solution.

The *Chicago Tribune* operates a consumer purchase panel in metropolitan Chicago which is favorably regarded by marketing research men. Moreover, the ability of the panel information to provide usable data on sales by brands for the metropolitan Chicago area is under constant check by companies that are in a position to know their own sales at retail in this area.

The *Tribune* was willing to cooperate in the study by furnishing at cost historical purchase records for the years 1950, 1951, and 1952 covering seven different products. These records consist of large books in which a separate line is printed for each purchase of each family. These lines contain the code number for the family, codes for socioeconomic characteristics of the family, brand name, size of package, number of units purchased, total price paid, and a code number of the store at which the purchase was made.

The Chicago metropolitan area has a large and diverse population and represents an important segment of the total United States market. Entirely apart from the matter of cost, a regional panel has a real advantage over a national panel. A good regional panel can be interpreted with more certainty, since it does not have a mixture of local brands from different areas as a national panel does.

The family purchasing information supplied by a consumer panel is not perfect. However, an evaluation of its limitations suggests that they do not significantly impair the validity of the data for an analysis of brand loyalty.

(1) Probably the most important limitation is that the purchases are for the total family and cannot be separated by individ-

ual family members. In order to partially offset this difficulty, the selection of products was weighted in favor of those in which the housewife played a major purchase role. The effect of analyzing family loyalties as opposed to individual loyalties is to understate the actual loyalties which may exist.

(2) Another difficulty is that the housewife may have different end uses in mind when she buys different brands. Thus, she might be completely loyal to one brand for one end use and to another for another end use, yet the purchasing record would indicate less than complete loyalty. The effect of this is also to understate true loyalty behavior.

(3) No consumer panel can be a probability sample in the strict sense of the term. The general population contains some portion of families who are not willing to take the trouble of completing purchase records. It can be said, however, that the families who comprise consumer panels appear to be reasonably representative of the total population in their purchasing of a wide range of products. If this were not so, panels could not provide the usable information in the areas they cover that experience has demonstrated they do.

(4) There may be problems of underreporting due to memory difficulty on the part of the housewife and failure of other members of the family to tell the housewife of their purchases, and possibly of overreporting in the case of prestige brands. But these are minimized by the fact that purchases are usually recorded daily and reported weekly by housewives who have become accustomed to doing it in a matter-of-fact way.

(5) Even though panels do provide purchase information which business finds very usable, they are sometimes criticized on the grounds that the participants are habit-ridden people, as evidenced by their willingness to prepare all of the necessary reports over long periods of time. Because this criticism strikes close to home on brand loyalty measurements, a special analysis was made comparing families who had been in the *Tribune* panel for many years with those who were relatively recent additions. No differences could be found in brand loyalty behavior between the two groups.

In sum, the above limitations do not introduce significant difficulties in measuring brand loyalty. Most of them lead to a degree of understatement of brand loyalty, and hence the results are essentially conservative. By the same token, positive findings take on added strength.

The selection of products for the study was based primarily on maximum housewife influence in brand determination and reasonably wide usage. In addition, variation in product type, extent of brand promotion, taste appeal, and newness to the market were taken into consideration. The products finally chosen were toilet soap, scouring cleanser, regular coffee (not instant), canned peas, margarine, frozen orange juice (concentrate), and headache tablets.

The three-year period of 1950–1952 was chosen in order to be entirely sure of having enough time to reveal complete patterns of buying behavior with respect to loyalty or disloyalty. It was recognized of course that the longer the time period, the more changes could occur both within the family itself and in the market—that brand loyalty would tend to be lower than it would be over a one-year or a two-year period, but that to the extent it did show up, it would represent a very positive finding.

Not all of the 402 families on the *Chicago Tribune* panel who reported continuously over the three-year period purchased normal quantities of the products studied. Consequently it was necessary to establish minimum thresholds of purchases, that is, a minimum figure which could be used to exclude light purchasers. The thresholds established and the number of families buying in amounts over thresholds were:

Minimum thresholds	*Number of families buying over thresholds*
Toilet soap—80 ounces (about 18 cakes)	390
Scouring cleanser—15 cans	319
Regular coffee—20 pounds	359
Canned peas—200 ounces (over 1 dozen cans)	325
Margarine—10 pounds	290
Frozen orange juice—10 cans	211
Headache tablets—4 purchases	208

The purpose of establishing such minimum thresholds was twofold. First, the manufacturer has only limited interest in very

EXHIBIT 1. 66 SEVEN-PRODUCT FAMILIES INDICATE THAT THEY HAVE VARYING DEGREES OF SINGLE-BRAND LOYALTY TO DIFFERENT PRODUCTS (Percentage of total product purchases represented by the most favored brand)

Family code number	Toilet soap	Scouring cleanser	Regular coffee	Canned peas	Margarine	Frozen orange juice	Headache tablets
1	58.7	88.2	73.8	43.7	44.9	47.2	54.2
2	40.5	58.8	56.2	12.8	37.2	26.7	40.2
18	68.0	47.9	64.8	34.3	53.6	63.2	100.0
37	72.8	52.7	50.7	48.9	77.3	50.0	100.0
57	74.5	79.5	82.8	44.3	33.1	50.6	34.2
71	30.3	45.9	50.0	57.6	73.3	97.5	60.0
119	49.5	92.1	64.2	44.7	36.0	98.0	75.7
123	42.4	50.0	74.3	73.5	53.8	59.2	100.0
148	24.2	45.4	88.9	39.7	93.2	35.7	72.9
163	24.3	57.1	70.2	84.4	48.6	67.9	49.4
183	42.1	73.4	91.0	42.4	98.9	85.4	98.1
193	61.7	33.3	45.5	24.9	35.7	23.1	43.0
205	37.5	57.1	56.5	27.6	57.1	44.5	42.1
206	58.4	57.6	78.2	93.2	72.9	36.6	68.1
212	55.0	100.0	37.0	25.8	44.4	53.1	65.8
233	37.6	51.0	30.6	34.7	72.0	46.6	65.6
244	76.1	92.5	98.7	24.9	35.3	76.4	69.1
266	26.7	45.7	52.1	31.2	48.9	59.4	84.3
273	90.4	36.5	61.4	38.0	75.0	19.1	47.4
276	38.3	55.8	62.0	59.2	57.1	50.5	70.8
282	17.2	39.5	88.0	45.2	40.0	35.3	64.1
307	45.9	74.7	63.0	27.1	67.6	87.9	23.8
321	38.9	40.9	55.7	34.3	41.0	46.3	90.9
322	69.7	51.8	76.1	43.6	98.3	32.8	59.8
327	51.6	35.3	84.8	38.2	50.0	35.8	50.7
342	86.1	46.1	61.5	47.5	83.3	91.8	48.5
345	48.0	59.3	55.4	23.2	49.3	38.1	28.6
349	29.9	35.9	33.0	46.9	69.2	77.0	70.8
350	35.3	58.3	76.1	86.4	76.9	84.7	87.3
354	40.1	61.9	72.3	54.3	37.9	47.2	93.0

355	**40.0**	48.8	90.2	55.9	50.4	28.4	50.0
356	**55.7**	38.5	24.2	38.8	77.3	30.5	46.7
359	**26.0**	60.5	56.7	27.5	27.1	43.2	77.2
363	**32.2**	46.3	36.1	26.1	50.0	83.2	87.9
377	**28.6**	50.7	51.8	40.9	26.6	30.0	51.4
381	**87.4**	91.7	39.3	50.3	100.0	50.0	84.6
383	**46.3**	84.6	66.2	82.4	94.9	34.4	98.2
385	**82.5**	40.0	88.2	57.4	54.5	80.4	47.6
390	**81.3**	42.0	43.6	84.0	57.6	83.8	40.3
406	**32.1**	33.3	38.9	33.8	69.2	45.6	59.8
424	**23.4**	29.3	38.2	29.5	23.1	62.4	76.4
431	**40.7**	39.5	53.0	64.6	29.9	43.2	49.5
441	**84.7**	97.0	40.9	71.5	34.9	32.1	100.0
489	**58.9**	31.7	85.4	44.6	47.2	88.5	100.0
496	**18.6**	46.3	17.5	48.6	65.1	74.3	53.2
521	**28.9**	94.2	26.1	80.2	100.0	81.8	33.0
530	**57.4**	70.7	89.8	53.9	70.9	63.6	62.7
583	**31.5**	80.0	44.4	61.4	70.0	46.7	78.5
600	**27.4**	51.7	61.7	60.9	79.2	59.3	55.2
631	**75.1**	60.0	29.0	65.4	71.1	88.9	75.7
632	**34.3**	39.1	50.0	57.7	61.4	56.4	44.2
636	**55.1**	63.2	28.0	73.1	45.5	30.0	93.2
639	**57.2**	100.0	83.2	34.6	80.8	30.8	100.0
642	**34.0**	32.6	28.8	21.6	27.7	23.2	71.1
819	**43.4**	70.6	37.1	21.0	63.7	59.3	40.0
823	**32.9**	22.0	34.3	34.6	29.1	73.1	47.6
825	**33.6**	62.2	90.4	48.4	38.9	68.4	91.0
828	**71.4**	50.0	31.1	25.5	26.8	39.4	85.5
831	**45.8**	81.2	30.4	35.5	31.6	25.0	39.4
838	**17.7**	33.3	43.7	32.7	49.2	46.4	73.5
846	**19.3**	33.3	24.3	51.9	40.3	41.2	98.0
850	**30.6**	50.0	31.2	80.1	75.0	75.0	76.6
918	**33.6**	70.4	29.4	41.2	42.9	28.9	87.1
931	**27.9**	40.0	51.5	21.4	87.1	57.9	77.7
939	**21.0**	46.2	33.9	35.3	22.5	52.8	34.6
950	**69.4**	64.0	77.5	24.8	90.9	38.6	98.0

137

small buyers, and there seemed to be no justification for including them in the analysis, for that would mean giving them an influence equivalent to purchasers of larger size. And second, the sheer fact of limited purchases tends to result in artificially high loyalty measurements. This can easily be seen in an assumed case where a family buying three pounds of margarine during the period cannot possibly have a single-brand loyalty measure of less than 33⅓% even if a different brand were bought on each of these purchases. If two of the purchases were of the same brand, the single-brand loyalty measure would be 66⅔%.

An analysis was made comparing the single-brand loyalty averages by deciles for below-threshold families and for the 66-family group which purchased all seven products in above-threshold amounts. As a result the below-threshold families did show up with apparent higher loyalty measurements for all of the product groups; so, if these below-threshold families had been included in the analysis, they would have raised brand loyalty ratings misleadingly.

The *Tribune* panel consisted of 691 available families in 1950, 634 families in 1951, and 629 families in 1952. In the various analyses undertaken in this study, samples were set up of 66 families buying all seven products, as noted above, and 244 families buying only toilet soap, scouring cleanser, regular coffee, and canned peas. How representative were these samples of the total panel?

The 66-family group is particularly important because it permits comparison of buying behavior for all seven products. Consequently, the purchases of this group were analyzed for all major brands of margarine, toilet soap, and scouring cleanser and compared to the purchase distribution by brands of the total panel. Correlation coefficients were calculated, and the values obtained were high enough (0.92, 0.94, and 0.99) to represent a very good fit between the two sets of data. These comparisons indicated that the 66-family group was generally representative of the total panel.

FINDINGS

This section reports the findings of the study, including loyalty proneness, effect of deals, store loyalty, size of purchase, and relation of socioeconomic factors.

The data indicate quite conclusively that a significant amount of brand loyalty does exist within individual product groups (this is not to be confused with brand loyalty across product groups, loyalty proneness, which will be treated later). Exhibits I–IV are pertinent to this point.

Exhibit I lists the brand loyalty to individual products of each of the 66 different families who purchased seven products in above-threshold quantities. The families are listed in order of their *Tribune* code number. This gives a detailed picture which is useful for what it does not show as well as for what it does show. Within these figures are plenty of instances of high brand loyalty, which show up better when the loyalty percentages are ranked separately for each product (as in the following exhibits). But only by looking at such an over-all picture as this one, demonstrating the absence of any uniform patterns among families as to their degrees of loyalty to the different products, can we see how definitely brand loyalty is tied to individual products.

Exhibit II dramatizes the presence of brand loyalty among the same 66 families more forcefully by presenting the data in deciles,

EXHIBIT II. 66 SEVEN-PRODUCT FAMILIES SHOW SIGNIFICANT SINGLE-BRAND LOYALTY WITHIN PRODUCT GROUPS

(Percentage averages for each decile for each product)

Decile	Toilet soap	Scouring cleanser	Regular coffee	Canned peas	Margarine	Frozen orange juice	Headache tablets
1	84.1	95.4	91.0	84.4	96.6	91.1	99.7
2	72.2	81.4	83.7	68.2	80.8	81.8	95.2
3	60.0	67.8	74.3	57.6	73.6	71.2	86.8
4	52.5	59.8	63.7	50.3	68.7	60.5	77.0
5	43.8	54.9	57.6	45.3	57.9	53.0	72.0
6	39.3	50.1	51.5	41.1	50.4	47.4	64.4
7	34.5	46.3	43.9	35.8	46.1	43.3	54.9
8	31.1	41.3	36.9	32.6	39.2	36.7	48.8
9	27.1	36.9	31.4	26.4	33.8	31.5	43.4
10	20.2	30.8	25.4	21.4	26.1	24.9	33.4

that is, the average loyalty to each product of the most loyal 10%, the second most loyal 10%, and so on. Naturally there are differences in brand loyalty ranges between product classes, but these differences are not striking. Loyalties are highest for headache tablets, margarine, and scouring cleanser, and lowest for canned peas and toilet soap. Note that the deciles for the various products will not contain the same families in each case.

Exhibit III follows the same pattern but broadens the coverage

EXHIBIT III. 244 FOUR-PRODUCT FAMILIES LIKEWISE SHOW HIGH SINGLE-BRAND LOYALTY WITHIN PRODUCT GROUPS

(Percentage averages for each decile for each product)

Decile	Toilet soap	Scouring cleanser	Regular coffee	Canned peas
1	90.0	97.8	95.1	86.4
2	75.7	89.2	85.5	70.8
3	63.2	79.4	75.4	59.4
4	55.3	68.1	64.6	51.7
5	48.1	61.4	55.1	45.4
6	40.0	54.5	48.7	38.1
7	35.6	48.9	41.8	32.8
8	31.2	43.3	35.9	28.4
9	26.6	37.1	29.8	25.0
10	20.8	29.3	23.1	19.2

to the 244 families who purchased four products in above-threshold quantities. Note that at both ends the range of percentages tends to be somewhat greater for this group, but only by about as much as would be expected for a larger sample. In general, the 244-family sample serves only to confirm and strengthen the findings from the 66-family sample.

Finally, Exhibit IV shows the dual-brand loyalty of the 66

EXHIBIT IV. DUAL-BRAND LOYALTY OF 66 FAMILIES IS DEFINITELY HIGHER THAN SINGLE-BRAND LOYALTY

(Percentage averages for each decile for each product)

Decile	Toilet soap	Scouring cleanser	Regular coffee	Canned peas	Margarine	Frozen orange juice	Headache tablets
1	94.8	100.0	95.8	92.2	99.8	98.9	100.0
2	87.2	96.9	93.4	82.3	98.5	93.1	100.0
3	81.0	90.9	89.3	76.6	91.7	89.3	100.0
4	75.6	86.4	85.1	72.2	85.3	84.0	100.0
5	70.2	80.6	80.2	66.2	82.0	77.7	97.8
6	62.0	76.4	71.6	61.0	74.2	71.6	93.6
7	57.2	72.7	66.9	51.1	69.3	67.0	84.0
8	48.9	66.8	59.1	50.2	61.5	60.4	79.1
9	44.5	61.2	51.2	47.6	54.2	55.7	72.5
10	37.0	53.6	42.6	38.8	44.8	45.2	57.2

seven-product families, the percentage of a family's total purchases in a product group represented by the two brands most heavily favored. Inevitably, the readings are higher than for single-brand loyalty. The interesting aspect of this exhibit is the fact that many families apparently have a "favorite second choice" —but that the more loyal they are to a single product, the less difference the second choice makes.

(Dual-brand analysis of the 244 four-product families showed the same general picture, though again with wider ranges than for the 66 seven-product families. Also, a trial run on the three leading brands for several products showed a significant fall-off in loyalty between the second and third brands, except where the top two brands already had no more than a low degree of loyalty.)

What about the possibility that the brand loyalty readings derived from the panel data could arise by chance, rather than represent positive loyalty?

To illustrate the possible dangers of this, take granulated sugar as an example. It is customary in some areas for food stores to carry not more than two brands of granulated sugar, and sometimes only one. If there were only one brand available in a store and a housewife traded entirely at that store, the purchasing record would show concentration on a single sugar brand, and the measurement would be 100% single-brand loyalty. If there were two brands, and again if the housewife did all her shopping in that store, a random choice of the two sugar brands would result in a loyalty reading of 50%.

Accordingly, it is necessary to calculate the expected values of brand loyalty measurements under conditions of random choice, the number of brands typically stocked, and number of purchases. A survey indicated that the average number of brands stocked by stores in metropolitan Chicago was: for coffee, 10 in chain stores and 9 in independents; for canned peas, 8 in chain stores and 4 in independents; for toilet soap, 14 in chain stores and 15 in independents; and for scouring cleanser, 7 in chain stores and 7 in independents.

Now, taking coffee as an example, let us say that only 8 brands are carried, to make the test more stringent, and that the number

141

of purchases is 10. When the probable values of brand loyalty calculated on a strictly random basis are compared with the actual reported data for the 244 four-commodity families in the panel, it is apparent that the brand loyalty measurements derived are far above expectations. Thus, the random data would predict that only about 3% of the families would be above 50% brand loyal, but the observed data show that about half of the families purchased their favorite brand more than 50% of the time.

Even if an extreme assumption were made that only three brands were available and nine purchases made, it is found that the probability of obtaining a brand loyalty greater than 80% is only about two chances in 100. Yet in reality more than 20% of the panel families fit into this category. The possibility that the readings could have arisen through chance alone is therefore ruled out.

Moreover, it has been assumed that all purchases of the family are made in one store and that therefore only the brands stocked by that store are available. Actually most housewives make purchases at more than one store. This buying practice increases substantially the number of brands available in different product categories. The effect of this, of course, is to make the brand loyalty readings even more significant than otherwise.

Another point of interest to manufacturers in planning their promotional strategy is the question of how brand loyalty is distributed within a product class. If there were a heavy concentration of highly loyal families at the top and a heavy concentration of low-loyalty families at the bottom, for example, then the selling and advertising effort could be better pointed up to accomplish specific objectives with one or the other of the concentrated groups.

Here the ranking of families into deciles, as in Exhibits II, III, and IV, throws light on the distribution of brand loyalties. In fact, the gradations from decile to decile are fairly even throughout. It looks as if, on this particular count at least, the manufacturer will have to address his promotion to the whole loyalty range of his market.

How many housewives and families are loyal to brands in different product groups—say, to one brand of margarine and one of coffee, and maybe one of canned peas or toilet soap?

Whether or not such loyalty-prone purchasers exist in numbers which are significant is a question of the utmost importance to marketing executives, especially executives of companies with a variety of frequently purchased product lines. What are the prospects of a good "return" on expenditures to secure a larger proportion of loyalty-prone families among the firm's customers? Should marketing strategy be planned around the concept of a substantial group of loyalty-prone families, or should individual product strategies be mapped out for each line in accordance with the type of loyalty behavior which consumers display for that line?

To measure the amount of loyalty proneness to the seven products covered in this study, the 66 seven-product families were analyzed statistically to determine the persistence of brand loyalty behavior between product groups. More specifically, the families were listed in order of brand loyalty for each of the seven products and assigned a rank (from 1 to 66). The resulting picture is presented in Exhibit V. Then the differences in rank were taken between every possible combination of two products (21 combinations in all). These differences were squared and totaled for all of the families, and Spearman's coefficient of rank correlation was then obtained for each pair of products. The resulting coefficients are listed in Exhibit VI. Note that a perfect correlation would be represented by a coefficient of 1.00.

In only two cases is the correlation of any statistical consequence; and even here it is quite possible that what appears as a slight relationship—between toilet soap and scouring cleanser, and between canned peas and margarine—could have occurred purely by chance. Looking at the exhibit as a whole—and that is the way it should be considered—the conclusion seems clear that loyalty proneness does not exist to a significant degree.

There is another and perhaps more striking way of demonstrating the absence of significant loyalty-prone purchasing behavior. This is to analyze the scatter of the 20 families comprising the three top deciles of one product among the decile groups of another product. This is shown in Exhibit VII for coffee versus mar-

(Ranking according to loyalty measurement for each individual product)

Family code number	Toilet soap	Scouring cleanser	Regular coffee	Canned peas	Margarine	Frozen orange juice	Headache tablets
1	17	8	18	33	44	36	43
2	34	25	31	66	52	62	59
18	14	40	22	47	34	21	3½
37	10	31	38	24	12½	33½	3½
57	9	12	12	32	57	31	63
71	51	45	39½	17	17	2	39
119	25	6	23	30	53	1	26½
123	31	37	17	8	33	26	3½
148	60	47	6	38	6	51	29
163	59	28½	20	3	41	19	49
183	32	14	2	35	3	7	8
193	15	60½	41	59	54	65	56
205	40	28½	30	53	30½	42	57
206	18	27	13	1	18	49	34
212	23	1½	50	57	45	29	35
233	39	34	57	44	19	38	36
244	7	5	1	60	55	14	33
266	57	46	35	51	40	23	20
273	1	56	28	41	15½	66	53
276	38	30	25	15	30½	32	32
282	66	53	8	29	49	52	37
307	28	13	24	55	25	6	66
321	37	49	32	48	47	40	14
322	12	32	15	34	4	54	40½
327	24	58	10	40	36½	50	46
342	3	44	27	27	9	3	50
345	26	24	33	62	38	48	65
349	52	57	54	28	23½	13	31
350	41	26	16	2	14	8	16
354	35	21	19	20	51	35	12

355	36	39	4	19	35	61	47
356	21	55	65	39	12½	57	54
359	58	22	29	54	62	43	23
363	47	41	51	56	36½	10	15
377	54	35	36	37	64	59	45
381	2	7	48	23	1½	33½	19
383	27	9	21	5	5	53	7
385	5	50½	7	18	32	12	51½
390	6	48	44	4	29	9	58
406	48	60½	47	49	23½	41	40½
424	61	65	48	52	65	22	25
431	33	52	34	12	59	44	48
441	4	3	45	10	56	55	3½
489	16	64	9	31	42	5	3½
498	64	42	68	25	26	16	44
521	53	4	63	6	1½	11	64
530	19	15	5	21	21	20	38
583	49	11	42	13	22	37	21
600	56	33	23	14	11	24	42
631	8	23	60	11	20	4	26½
632	42	54	39½	16	28	28	55
636	22	19	62	9	43	58	11
639	20	1½	11	46	10	56	3½
642	43	63	61	63	61	64	30
819	30	16	49	65	27	25	60
823	46	66	52	45	60	17	51½
825	44	20	3	26	50	18	13
828	11	37	56	58	63	46	18
831	29	10	58	42	58	63	61
838	65	60½	43	50	39	39	28
846	63	60½	64	22	48	45	9
850	50	37	55	7	15½	15	24
918	45	17	59	36	46	60	17
931	55	50½	37	64	8	27	22
939	62	43	53	43	66	30	62
950	13	18	14	61	7	47	10

Note: Fractions result from ties in rank.

garine, coffee versus toilet soap, and toilet soap versus margarine, in the 66-family sample. (Analyses were also made reversing the order of these pairs, and similar results were obtained. As an additional check, the bottom 20 families in brand loyalty were tabulated, and again very comparable distributions were found.)

EXHIBIT VI. COEFFICIENTS OF RANK CORRELATION BETWEEN PAIRS OF PRODUCTS FOR 66 SEVEN-PRODUCT FAMILIES SHOW THAT LOYALTY PRONENESS IS NOT SIGNIFICANT

Products	Correlation coefficient
Toilet soap vs. scouring cleanser	0.30
Canned peas vs. margarine	0.27
Coffee vs. toilet soap	0.23
Frozen orange juice vs. canned peas	0.22
Margarine vs. frozen orange juice	0.19
Scouring cleanser vs. coffee	0.17
Margaine vs. toilet soap	0.14
Margarine vs. scouring cleanser	0.13
Headache tablets vs. canned peas	0.13
Coffee vs. margarine	0.12
Scouring cleanser vs. canned peas	0.12
Scouring cleanser vs. headache tablets	0.10
Coffee vs. headache tablets	0.09
Margarine vs. headache tablets	0.08
Canned peas vs. coffee	0.07
Coffee vs. frozen orange juice	0.06
Frozen orange juice vs. scouring cleanser	0.02
Frozen orange juice vs. headache tablets	0.02
Toilet soap vs. canned peas	0.02
Toilet soap vs. headache tablets	0.002
Toilet soap vs. frozen orange juice	−0.06

Are special price offers powerful incentives to switch brands? To answer this, the purchases made on manufacturers' special price inducements were deducted and favorite-brand percentages calculated on the remainder of the purchases. The decile averages are shown in Exhibit VIII in terms of single-brand loyalty for the 66-family group. (When the dual-brand measurements were recalculated with deals omitted, and also when the same procedures were applied to the 244 four-product families, very much

EXHIBIT VII. THE 20 TOP-LOYALTY FAMILIES IN ONE PRODUCT SCATTER WIDELY IN LOYALTY DECILES OF OTHER PRODUCTS (66 SEVEN-PRODUCT GROUP)

Deciles	Distribution of top 20 families in coffee loyalty among the 10 margarine deciles.	Distribution of top 20 families in coffee loyalty among the 10 toilet soap deciles.	Distribution of top 20 families in toilet soap loyalty among the 10 margarine deciles.
1	4	2	3
2	1	3	3
3	2	5	3
4	1	2	1
5	2	1	2
6	2	2	1
7	3	2	2
8	3	–	–
9	2	1	4
10	–	2	1
Total	20	20	20

the same patterns were found as in Exhibit VIII—and the same slightly different characteristics between the two samples as appeared before.)

Comparing Exhibit VIII with Exhibit II we find that:

(1) The readings for toilet soap are uniformly from 2 to 5 percentage points higher than in Exhibit II. Since toilet soap is a field in which special price inducements are very common, it is of considerable interest that the differences are no greater than they are.

(2) A much more marked difference is found in the scouring cleanser group. Here are jumps which in five of the deciles range from 10 to 17 points.

(3) Coffee shows little change, which is explained in part by the fact that, during the period studied at least, there was little special dealing in the regular coffee field.

(4) Canned peas, likewise, show little change.

(5) The upward shift in margarine is roughly equivalent to that of toilet soap, with increases of 1 to 6 percentage points.

(6) Because the frozen orange juice had very little dealing during the period covered, the measurements are almost identical.

(7) Headache tablets show identical figures.

EXHIBIT VIII. SINGLE-BRAND LOYALTY FIGURES FOR 66 SEVEN-PRODUCT FAMILIES ARE LARGELY THE SAME AFTER SPECIAL-OFFER PURCHASES ARE DEDUCTED

(Percentile averages for each decile for each product)

Decile	Toilet soap	Scouring cleanser	Regular coffee	Canned peas	Margarine	Frozen orange juice	Headache tablets
1	86.5	100.0	91.9	84.5	98.5	91.1	99.7
2	76.1	97.8	84.2	68.4	87.1	81.3	95.2
3	65.6	85.4	76.8	58.5	76.3	71.4	86.8
4	55.0	76.9	65.6	51.5	70.0	60.4	77.0
5	47.3	69.1	57.9	47.1	61.0	52.9	72.0
6	42.5	60.1	52.1	42.3	54.0	47.4	64.4
7	38.0	51.5	44.3	36.3	49.3	42.3	54.9
8	34.1	47.9	37.3	32.7	42.8	36.7	48.8
9	30.0	43.8	31.6	26.8	36.0	31.5	43.4
10	23.5	29.1	25.7	21.5	27.4	25.0	33.4

Certainly deals and special offers lead to purchases. But when these special purchases are subtracted from the various families' total purchases for the period, brand loyalty patterns remain much the same as before (with the possible exception of scouring cleanser).

A special analysis of the 244 four-product families did show that a high percentage of purchasing on deals tends to be correlated with low brand loyalties (the evidence on this was considerably stronger for toilet soap and scouring cleanser than for margarine and coffee).[2] But this only highlights further the steadfastness of the top-loyalty families in the product groups.

In order to examine the store purchasing patterns of the families studied, two measures of store loyalty were devised, based on the same general concept as the brand loyalty measures: (1) single-store loyalty consisted of the percentage of total purchases within each product class made at a single store: (2) dual-

---

[2] Marvin Caplan, *A Measure of the Effect of Special Price Inducements on Loyalty Behavior*, B.S. Thesis, School of Industrial Management, Massachusetts Institute of Technology, June 1954 (unpublished).

store loyalties were calculated for the percentage of purchases made at the two largest stores. Decile averages for each of these measures are presented in Exhibit IX.

EXHIBIT IX. 66 SEVEN-PRODUCT FAMILIES SHOW SIGNIFICANT STORE LOYALTY

(Percentile averages for each decile for each product)

Decile	Toilet soap	Scouring cleanser	Regular coffee	Canned peas	Margarine	Frozen orange juice	Headache tablets
			A. Single-store loyalty				
1	95.2	99.0	93.4	97.8	96.5	97.6	96.0
2	88.7	91.7	88.4	92.0	87.2	93.3	87.1
3	77.8	80.9	80.4	85.7	81.1	87.4	79.6
4	68.4	72.3	73.6	81.1	71.7	78.6	70.7
5	56.6	61.9	65.2	64.9	65.9	66.0	66.4
6	49.3	55.2	59.0	65.9	57.2	61.4	61.5
7	45.5	55.1	49.3	57.2	52.7	56.7	57.4
8	41.6	47.0	41.8	50.7	49.9	52.3	51.5
9	36.8	43.6	38.2	44.9	42.6	44.7	40.5
10	32.6	37.1	32.0	35.6	34.4	35.6	33.2
			B. Dual-store loyalty				
1	100.0	100.0	99.0	100.0	100.0	100.0	100.0
2	95.6	100.0	96.7	99.6	97.4	100.0	100.0
3	90.4	96.8	92.7	97.3	94.3	98.1	98.7
4	86.0	92.0	89.0	94.8	91.0	95.1	96.6
5	81.6	88.8	86.0	92.0	88.5	91.9	93.8
6	75.7	85.4	82.1	87.6	84.4	88.5	90.8
7	71.8	79.8	77.0	83.2	78.7	84.7	84.5
8	67.2	74.7	70.5	79.9	74.3	79.9	79.8
9	62.4	68.9	64.1	72.4	69.6	75.7	69.2
10	53.8	58.0	56.3	62.5	59.8	64.3	58.2

It will be noted that the figures for single-store loyalty have somewhat the same general configuration as the single-brand loyalty decile averages shown in Exhibit II, with the exception that they tend to start at a considerably higher level and do not drop as low at the bottom of the decile scale. These higher readings probably reflect, in part, some overstatement of store loyalty due to the fact that the coding of the historical purchase record is in terms of ownership of stores rather than individual store locations.

Are the families who are particularly loyal in brand purchasing also loyal in store purchasing? In order to answer this, the null hypothesis was set up that there was no relationship between brand purchasing and store purchasing. The data were then analyzed by rank correlation, and the results are shown in Exhibit X.

EXHIBIT X. BUT SUMMARY OF RANK CORRELATIONS BETWEEN SINGLE-BRAND LOYALTY AND SINGLE-STORE LOYALTY FOR 66 SEVEN-PRODUCT FAMILIES INDICATES THAT THERE IS LITTLE RELATIONSHIP BETWEEN THE TWO

Product	Correlation coefficient
Scouring cleanser	−0.050
Headache tablets	0.050
Toilet soap	0.198
Margarine	0.305
Frozen orange juice	0.391
Canned peas	0.418
Regular coffee	0.428

The statistical evidence suggests that this hypothesis is correct —that no meaningful relation exists. However, there is discernible in the data enough of a tendency toward a very minor degree of correlation so that this question may deserve further investigation.

The total purchases of the families in the *Chicago Tribune* panel varied over a wide range (even when purchases below the minimum threshold were excluded). Taking the 66-family group as an example, scouring cleanser purchases over the three-year period ranged from a low of 15 cans to a high of 173 cans, or slightly more than an eleven to one ratio. For coffee, the range was from 34 pounds to 390 pounds, also an eleven to one relationship. In canned peas, 216 ounces was the minimum amount purchased as compared to a high of 4,395 ounces or a twenty to one ratio.

In view of these wide differences, it is clearly of great interest and significance to inquire whether the families who measure in the higher ranges of brand loyalty have high, average, or low rates of consumption. Marketing executives would be particularly interested in such loyal families if they should turn out to be very large consumers, but would not have much interest in them as very small consumers.

In order to measure the relationship between size of purchase and degree of brand loyalty or disloyalty among the families, the 66 families were arranged in order of brand loyalty from highest to lowest. The three-year consumption of the families was then determined and ranked. The ranks in brand loyalty and consumption were then compared, and correlation coefficients derived as shown in Exhibit XI.

EXHIBIT XI. SUMMARY OF RANK CORRELATIONS BETWEEN SINGLE-BRAND LOYALTY AND SIZE OF PURCHASE FOR 66 SEVEN-PRODUCT FAMILIES SHOWS THERE IS LITTLE RELATIONSHIP BETWEEN THE TWO

Product	Correlation coefficient
Toilet soap	0.109
Scouring cleanser	0.089
Regular coffee	0.003
Canned peas	0.195
Margarine	0.133
Frozen orange juice	0.028
Headache tablets	0.102

The resulting correlation coefficients suggest that there is little relationship between consumption and brand loyalty in these product groups. In other words, a family which is highly brand-loyal apparently is no more or no less desirable from the size-of-purchase point of view than is a family in the middle or lower ranges of brand loyalty.

Is it possible to identify families who are unusually loyal by means of various socioeconomic factors such as age, income, size of family, and so on? This question was not an integral part of the research program, but a limited analysis was undertaken as a thesis project, using the same basic data from the *Tribune* panel that were used in the study.[3] The thesis work related primarily to the top and bottom 15 families in the 66-family group ranked

[3] Gerald Perlstein, *A Study of the Economic Characteristics of Loyal and Disloyal Buyers*, B.S. Thesis, School of Industrial Management, Massachusetts Institute of Technology, August 1954 (unpublished).

by average loyalties for the seven products. (Because loyalty proneness tendencies were very weak, this particular ranking has distinct limitations for correlation analysis purposes.)

In the usual presentation of family information in the panel reports, codes for the four major socioeconomic characteristics of race, tenure, family size, and total family income are shown. In addition to these, the *Tribune* collects information on a number of other characteristics, and these data were also examined. It was thus possible to check the characteristics against the average high-loyalty and average low-loyalty groups.

The hypothesis tested was that buyers with high brand loyalty have socioeconomic characteristics which differ significantly from those of buyers with low brand loyalty. The distribution of various socioeconomic characteristics in the group of high-loyalty families was compared with the distribution of these characteristics in the low-loyalty group, and the resulting differences were put to the chi-square test.

The values obtained from this test suggest that the distribution found could have been caused by chance alone. This disproves the hypothesis and indicates that socioeconomic factors are not correlated with loyalty behavior, at least so far as the ranking of families based on the average loyalty for all seven products is concerned.

But would similarly negative results be found if families were ranked by loyalty in a particular product group? Some work on this has been begun, and the first indications suggest tentatively that very little relationship is to be found. However, this conclusion must be viewed with caution because a number of other analyses are planned which may well lead to some change in the finding.

The one definite lesson that can be drawn is that, in the absence of positive evidence to the contrary, manufacturers had better check carefully before they make the assumption that their products are different from those studied here (because of price range or consumption characteristics, for instance), and that they can distinguish between high-loyalty and low-loyalty families in their particular market by certain socioeconomic characteristics.

Looking Forward

If significant numbers of loyalty-prone housewives and families do not exist, as this research shows for low-price, frequently purchased products, then management would do well to put less emphasis on blanket marketing strategy and more on strategies developed individually for each product. In a phrase, it is "every brand for itself." This situation raises some interesting questions about the role and effectiveness of advertising, especially that of an institutional character. For example, if housewives do not carry over their brand loyalty from one product to another, how likely are they to be swayed by advertising that does not emphasize the merits of a particular product?

Market strategy, promotion, and advertising alike can probably be improved in many companies by new kinds of market research. For example, if, as has been concluded, there are both high-loyalty and low-loyalty families within each product class, learning more about these groups ought to be very helpful in making better sales decisions.

This research program was directed to the analysis of brand loyalty as revealed by detailed records of past purchases. The single-brand and dual-brand measurements using consumer purchase panel data proved to be extremely useful for the purposes. The study, however, did not attempt to uncover the reasons underlying the different behavior patterns. The next step would be to take selected groups of high-loyalty and low-loyalty families in a product class and conduct intensive field interviews in an effort to discover the reasons why purchasers act as they do. Comparisons between high-loyalty groups in different product classes might also be rewarding.

Such a program would require highly skilled field personnel and the use of various types of psychomotric techniques, and it would have to be conducted with great care and sophistication. But if it revealed ways of identifying families with different degrees of brand loyalty for different products and pointed to the kinds of approaches most likely to interest them, it should be worth its cost many times over.

Other work should also be done with existing panel data. The need for more investigation of the socioeconomic characteristics of brand loyalty was mentioned earlier; so also there is need for more studies showing how different price ranges affect brand loyalty, and how distributors' brands compare with manufacturers' brands as subjects of loyalty.

It is hoped that from this study businessmen will draw three main conclusions for themselves: (1) that brand loyalty is a very substantial asset; (2) that in their promotional planning they should consider brand loyalty carefully and in terms of each individual product; and (3) that the very fact that brand loyalty can be so strong is all the more reason for not taking its "what," "where," and "how much" for granted. If this study has opened the way to new and sounder ideas, it has also indicated that the still-to-be-realized potentials of further research are even richer.

9

FUNCTIONAL FEATURES IN PRODUCT STRATEGY

JOHN B. STEWART

In recent years styling and brand image have come to occupy a prominent spot in marketing managers' concern for creating and maintaining brand preference. Meanwhile, marketing strategists continue to employ functional product features as a means of achieving differentiation, just as they have over the years. Advertisers vigorously promote the features to the public, whether they be filters and flip-top boxes, razor blade dispensers that change with a "push-pull, click-click," or push-button gear shifts.

But for all their getting and using of features, does management have an understanding of the role of product features in the over-all marketing plan? Actually, in spite of their continued use, surprisingly little attention has been devoted to refining the art and strategy of using these features in the marketing effort.

This paper presents some findings from a study of approximately 5,000 functional claims made by 206 companies over a period of some 26 years. Some of these features were trivial product modifications, while others were basic improvements; but they all represent attempts by businessmen to gain preference for their brand through functional product differentiation.

The study not only sheds light on the marketing use of functional features but also points up some of their advantages over such other kinds of product differentiation as styling and brand image. There is also the suggestion that the use of this and other kinds of differentiation, either collectively or individually, may raise the problem of limiting rather than building markets and the concomitant challenge to marketing managers to make the best strategic use of their preference-building elements.

RANGE OF PRODUCTS

It is not always easy to draw a clear distinction between functional product features and other differentiating devices. For the purposes of this study, however, a feature is *a physical and functional characteristic or component of the basic product that may be used to distinguish it from competing products of similar quality.* For example, the basis of a feature may be:

1. Material of construction (e.g., the glass-lined water heater).
2. Method of construction (e.g., the "unitized" automobile chassis).
3. Kind of performance (e.g., the television console combined with radio).
4. Method of performance (e.g., the refrigerator working on gas rather than electricity).
5. Construction or performance of one part (e.g., power steering).
6. Arrangement of component parts (e.g., the freezer at the bottom of the refrigerator).

To get a perspective on how the manufacturers of consumer durable goods can employ functional features, this study sought to learn what kinds of features have actually been used in the past, by whom, and when. It also examined general patterns of relationship, such as:

How many features has the typical firm used, and have the manufacturers of some product types found it advantageous to use more features than other firms have?

Have increased research expenditures raised the number of new features introduced in the market each year?

And, most important, when a firm succeeds in developing a successful feature, how long will it be able to enjoy the benefits of its research expenditure and the risk it has sustained?

In order to answer these and similar questions about use of features, an examination was made of magazine advertisements of eight types of consumer durable goods selling for $50 or more.

EXHIBIT I. AVERAGE NUMBER OF FEATURES ADVERTISED PER COMPANY

Year	Auto-mobiles*	Cameras	Refrig-erators	Rotary mowers	Television sets	Vacuum cleaners	Water heaters	Wrist watches	Average for all 8 industries
1930	4.3	3.0	0†	—‡	—	0	0	0	3.6
1932	5.4	8.0	3.3	—	—	4.2	1.7	0	4.5
1934	5.3	4.2	5.2	—	—	4.5	0	0	4.8
1936	6.9	2.7	6.8	—	—	4.3	0	0	5.2
1938	7.5	—	4.0	—	—	2.6	2.8	1.7	3.7
1940	4.9	0	4.6	—	—	6.7	3.0	4.0	4.6
1941	4.3	—	5.2	—	—	4.4	2.7	2.8	3.9
1946	2.2	3.6	3.2	—	—	5.0	1.5	2.2	3.0
1947	3.0	4.6	2.2	—	—	3.6	3.0	1.4	3.1
1948	16	5.3	4.7	0	2.7	6.3	1.9	2.3	3.5
1949	2.8	6.8	3.7	5.0	2.1	2.0	2.9	2.6	3.5
1950	4.8	7.4	3.5	5.0	2.8	1.7	2.1	2.1	3.7
1951	4.6	6.6	5.6	3.2	3.3	3.8	1.9	2.9	4.0
1952	4.8	5.5	5.2	4.0	3.1	4.2	2.4	2.8	4.0
1953	6.4	6.4	6.4	4.9	2.8	4.8	2.8	3.2	4.7
1954	4.0	5.1	8.3	4.4	3.1	5.4	2.8	4.7	4.8
1955	6.3	6.4	9.1	5.1	3.1	6.0	3.7	3.4	5.4
1956	6.1	5.3	9.6	4.6	4.5	4.6	1.7	2.8	4.9
Average	4.9	5.4	5.4	4.5	3.1	4.4	2.5	2.8	4.9

* In 1957 the average was 8.8 for automobiles.
† The figure zero indicates that less than two companies advertised.
‡ The dash indicates insufficient data available.

157

Studied were automobiles, 35-millimeter cameras, domestic refrigerators, television sets, gasoline-powered rotary lawn mowers, vacuum cleaners, electric water heaters, and jeweled wrist watches. These range from relatively mature products (wrist watches) to young products (television sets, rotary mowers); from highly personal products (cameras) to products of low individual interest (water heaters); from a broad market (refrigerators) to a more specialized market (cameras); and from the $50 price range (some watches, cameras, rotary mowers) to several thousand dollars (automobiles).

INDIVIDUAL PATTERNS

Some interesting differences in the average number of features claimed per company among the various product types are shown in Exhibit I. Advertisements for wrist watches and water heaters contained, on the average, only half as many features as did those for cameras and refrigerators. What accounts for these differences? The statistics themselves cannot reveal the reasons, but by comparing the nature of the products it becomes possible to suggest some logical reasons.

For the products included in this study there appear to be two particularly important characteristics that influenced the profitable number of features a company could use. One is the amount of operational effort that is required to use the product in terms of skill, work, and frequency, as shown in the following examples.

The smallest number of features were utilized by manufacturers of water heaters and wrist watches in their advertising. Water heaters require the least work to operate of any of the products studied. Wrist watches require little more operation.

Television sets require more varied operation and have had a few more features advertised.

Vacuum cleaners and rotary lawn mowers require still more operation, and their advertisers have found it advantageous to utilize substantially more features.

Automobiles not only require a great deal of skill and effort in operation, but the circumstances of operation vary widely. They have had still more features advertised.

The largest number of features were employed by the advertisers of cameras and of refrigerators. The correct use of a good, flexible 35-millimeter camera requires precise operation to match the circumstances of use. As for refrigerators, although the range of service is limited to storing various types and sizes of food, the high frequency of use by the housewife makes operation important; also, there are few good alternative methods of obtaining differentiation.

Another factor which appears to have been a pertinent determinant of the number of features used is the degree of interest consumers have in the "output" of the various products. While few people get excited about hot water (unless they do not have it), nearly every amateur photographer takes a keen interest in the quality of his pictures. His pictures are an expression of his ability—almost an extension of his personality. Advertising managers have been well aware of this and have taken advantage of the photographer's willingness to notice and to remember specific differentiating features.

In view of the expanded research budgets of manufacturers in recent years, it would be logical to expect both more new features and an improvement in feature quality. Figures published by the Resources Division, Office of the Secretary of Defense, show a fourfold increase in total United States research expenditures from 1941 to 1952.[1] While a large part of that rise was accounted for by government-sponsored projects, the same figures indicate that company-financed research by industry tripled from 1945 to 1952. And after the Korean War—from 1953 to 1957—business research expenditures nearly doubled.[2]

Did a rash of new features result from these research dollars? Apparently not. Exhibit II shows the cumulative number of new features advertised each year for the eight consumer durables studied. While there are significant differences between the rates at which the various product types adopted new features, there are almost no differences between their prewar and postwar rates of adoption. Indeed, the rates of feature development appear to be so constant that they suggest an inherent feature adoption rate

[1] From Howard S. Turner, "How Much Should a Company Spend on Research?" *Harvard Business Review*, May–June 1954, p. 102.
[2] Robert P. Ulin, "Thinking Ahead: What Will Research Bring About?" *Harvard Business Review*, January–February 1958, p. 27.

EXHIBIT II. CUMULATIVE NUMBER OF NEW FEATURES INTRODUCED TO THE MARKET

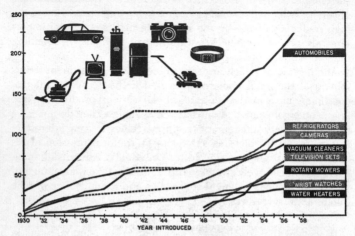

for each of the separate industries, perhaps determined by the nature of the product itself.

The study reveals that the automotive industry was by far the most prolific innovator during the period studied, averaging 10 new features per year. The closest rival was the television industry, averaging seven and a half new features per year. The averages for all the industries were:

	New features per year	
	1932–1956	1948–1956
Automobiles	10.5	8.8
Television sets	—°	7.6
Rotary mowers	—°	6.9
35-mm cameras	6.0	6.2
Refrigerators	5.8	4.7
Vacuum cleaners	5.1	2.7
Wrist watches	2.4	2.0
Water heaters	1.9	1.2

° Not comparable

It is interesting to note that the number of new features advertised each year in the various industries does not correspond to the number of competing firms within the same industry. One might suspect that in an industry characterized by a number of small producers, such as the camera industry, the large number of separate organizations and viewpoints would result in a wider variety and larger number of product developments. The figures above do not support this hypothesis.

Nor can it be said that those industries with a few large firms will necessarily have a high rate of feature development. Many of the same large firms that produced television sets and refrigerators, with a fairly high rate of new feature adoption, also produced electric water heaters, with very few new features. Again, the nature of the product itself would appear to have been one of the major determinants of the rate of product development.

The two newest products, television sets and rotary power mowers, both had relatively rapid rates of functional feature innovation. Did this result from a greater need for functional differentiation, or from more opportunity for improvements? New products generally have been accompanied by numerous consumer dissatisfactions, and this creates an initial opportunity for rapid improvements. In addition, new products have tended to be accompanied by vague and flexible demand specifications. In the field of rotary power lawn mowers, for instance, consumers have been willing to accept an extremely broad variety of product configurations. For example, in 1956 rotary mowers were being offered with one, two, or three cutting blades; with gasoline engines or electric motors; with two-cycle engines or four-cycle engines; with dozens of different transmissions and clutches. Some had to be pushed by the user, some were self-propelled, and others were built to be ridden on. Of the riding mowers, some had steering wheels, some had handle-bar steering, and one used a joy stick like an airplane's. Judging from these variations the producers did not feel limited to a narrow array of product specifications. The product was so young that consumers had not developed rigid conceptions of what they wanted. This flexibility in the nature of demand presented mower manufacturers with many opportunities for functional product variation—far more, for instance, than the wrist watch industry had during the period under study or is ever likely to have in the future; it went through the innovation stage earlier. Thus, it would seem that the maturity of a product has had an important influence on the number of new features brought to the market by manufacturers.

Turning now to the question of how many features a company should advertise, we find that there are conflicting opinions about the proper number of features to advertise at one time. One school of thought has held it best to concentrate attention on one or two product features and thereby make a definite and lasting reader-impression. An opposing school has suggested the virtues of scattering the shots—reasoning that if enough features are pointed out, at least one will appeal to almost everyone. How many in fact have been used?

The survey results show that within each industry there were strong differences of opinion as to the optimum number of features to use. It is not possible to say that after 25 years of experience all companies selling vacuum cleaners found it most advantageous to use x number of features simultaneously. It is possible, however, to show that most industries had certain central tendencies.

The distribution of the average number of features used by the individual companies is shown in Exhibit III, and it is apparent that the strength of these central tendencies varies. Apparently the individual manufacturers of automobiles, cameras, and rotary

EXHIBIT III. DISTRIBUTION OF THE AVERAGE NUMBER OF FEATURES USED PER ADVERTISEMENT BY COMPANIES IN THE VARIOUS INDUSTRIES

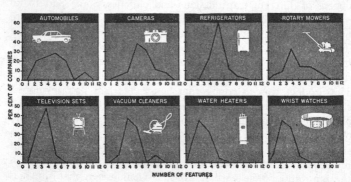

mowers found it desirable to deviate considerably from the average of their industry. The nature of those products enabled a large number of features to be used effectively, and yet there were many companies that chose to use only a few. This would suggest that specific companies within each of the industries had their own peculiarities which played an important part in determining the best strategy for them to follow.

In contrast, companies producing refrigerators tended to follow quite similar paths, as did television manufacturers. Apparently the nature of the product itself was a large determinant in selecting the best number of features to use; or, perhaps equally likely, even though the character of the companies themselves was important, they were so similar in size, goals, and customers that what was best for one company was best for all.

It is interesting to compare the strategy followed (in regard to the number of features used simultaneously) by some of the well-known companies. One might suspect that in an established industry, such as automobiles, the largest number of features would be employed by the smaller, struggling firms, while the older, more sedate firms such as Cadillac would use few features and concentrate on prestige building—institutional selling. As Exhibit IV demonstrates, the established firms did tend to use more, but the reverse was not true. For instance, Buick used more features per advertisement than any other make of automobile, and did so almost continuously throughout the ten years its advertisements were studied. Likewise, Chrysler maintained a high average during the twelve-year survey period. Neither company could be described as being new or struggling, at least not relative to the small independent firms.

It is difficult to make any safe correlations between the number of features used and company characteristics. For instance, it would be hard to find two companies more similar in size, age, product, price level, and method of distribution than the Oldsmobile and Buick divisions of General Motors. Yet their strategies concerning the number of functional features to use were at opposite ends of the spectrum. Buick, with an average of 10.3 features per advertisement, used more than two and a half times the 3.9 features averaged by Oldsmobile.

Which company was more successful? Apparently each com-

EXHIBIT IV. NUMBER OF AUTOMOBILE FEATURES ADVERTISED IN MEDIA SURVEYED

Company	1930	1932	1934	1936	1938	1940	1941	1946	1947	1948
Auburn	2		2							
Buick	6	12	9	15						
Cadillac	6	1		2		1				
Chevrolet	6		4			8	6			
Chrysler	6		5	8	17	3	3			
Franklin	1	2								
Hupmobile	8			10						
La Salle	6			2	2					
Lincoln	1									
Nash	8		8	9	3	7	10	4	3	1
Oldsmobile	4		3	14	10	3	3	1	2	1
Packard	1	4		1	8					2
Plymouth	1	8	5	6	14	6	4			3
Pontiac	8			6	3		1			
Reo	1			6						
De Soto		3	3	6	6	4	3			
Hudson		8		8	4	2				
Dodge			9	5	1		2			
Studebaker				4	14	5	8		2	
Ford				9		6	2	2	5	1
Mercury						9	5	2		
Henry J. Kaiser										
Kaiser										
Imperial										
Rambler										
Total features advertised	65	38	48	111	82	54	47	9	12	8
Number of companies	15	7	9	16	11	11	11	4	4	5
Average number of features per company	4.3	5.4	5.3	6.9	7.5	4.9	4.3	2.2	3.0	1.6

pany believed its strategy to be successful, for each continued its practices. Their averages for the period from 1950 to 1957 were 10.2 and 3.3 features, respectively—almost the same as their over-all averages from 1930 to 1957. The only hint of dissatisfaction came from Oldsmobile, when in advertising its 1957 models it jumped to 10 features.

However, while Oldsmobile's sudden shift in the number of features used was unusual for it, sudden changes were common among most of the companies studied. As Exhibit IV shows,

1949	1950	1951	1952	1953	1954	1955	1956	1957	Total features	Total years	Average per year
									4	2	2.0
		12	13	8		5	11	12	103	10	10.3
						2	4	4	20	7	2.9
	3	9	7			16	2	4	68	10	6.8
			6	6	5	8	6	12	85	12	7.1
									3	2	1.5
									18	2	9.0
									10	3	3.3
						3	11	6	21	4	5.2
4	8	6	7	1	10	2	11	13	115	18	6.4
1		1	1	3		3	2	10	62	16	3.9
			3	1		7			27	8	3.4
5		8		7	3	13	4	9	96	15	6.4
	5		3			4	1	4	35	9	3.9
									7	2	3.5
	3		7	6	5	10	3	17	76	13	5.8
		4		6	4		6	12	54	9	6.0
	2	6	2	8	4	6		10	55	11	5.0
	1	10	3			14			53	11	4.8
2	7		5	8	3	8	6	5	69	14	4.9
4	4	3			2	7	10	10	56	10	5.6
		5	3						8	2	4.0
2					2				4	2	2.0
						1	3		4	2	2.0
		1				7		9	17	3	5.7
17	38	46	57	58	48	95	97	140	1,070		
6	8	10	12	9	12	15	16	16		197	
2.8	4.8	4.6	4.8	6.4	4.0	6.3	6.1	8.8			5.4

Chevrolet dropped from 16 features in 1955 to 2 in 1956; Plymouth dropped from 13 in 1955 to 4 in 1956; De Soto dropped from 10 in 1955 to 3 in 1956, and then jumped to 17 features in 1957. Such large changes indicate that there were not only wide variations between the different companies' opinions as to the best number of features to employ, but also equally large variations within a given company over a short period of time.

It is possible that the nature of the particular features available each year plays an important part in determining how many features are advertised. For example, it might be assumed that during those years when a company had more new features it would be inclined to advertise more features in general. As it turns out, the data do not support any such conclusion; there were simply too few new features to account for much of the fluctuation discussed above.

The companies either did not know what was best and made changes to experiment, or the determinants that guided their decisions were so complex as to defy visual correlation.

COMPETITIVE RATIOS

One of the problems the use of functional features raises for management is the ease of duplication by the competition. How quickly in fact do competitors follow in adopting new product features? The answers to this question are summarized in Exhibit V, both in terms of all features (the lower curve) and of successful features (the upper curve). For example, the lower curve

EXHIBIT V. AVERAGE NUMBER OF COMPETITIVE ADVERTISERS FOL-
LOWING A FEATURE'S INTRODUCTION

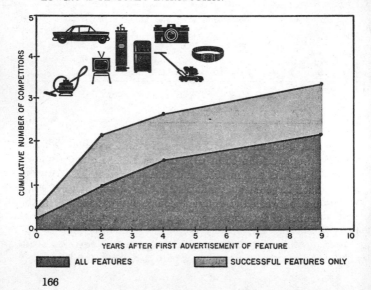

shows that when the typical company included in this study brought out a new feature—any feature at all—it was advertised at least once by an average of one competing company within two years after its introduction. After the new feature had been on the market four years, an average of 1.5 competitors had advertised or were advertising it; and after nine years an average of 2 competitors had used it.

Many of the features were not followed by any competitors simply because they were not judged to be worth duplicating. In fact, in each of the product types, almost half of all the features introduced to the market were not followed. The percentages of features not followed at all were: automobiles, 54%; 35-millimeter cameras, 46%; refrigerators, 49%; television sets, 47%; rotary lawn mowers, 48%; vacuum cleaners, 48%; electric water heaters, 47%; and wrist watches, 50%. Furthermore, the vast majority of these unimitated features were quickly dropped by the originating company.

Since the more pertinent question is, "How quickly will competitors follow the better features?" separate analysis is needed of the follow rate on features which appeared to be "successful." This analysis excludes all features that were not advertised a second year (not necessarily a successive year) by some company —either the originator or a competitor. By examining the upper curve in Exhibit V, it may be seen that the number of competitors duplicating these features each year is one and a half to two times the over-all average.

For each of the product types there was a slightly different pattern of competitive behavior, as shown in Exhibit VI. The exhibit brings out the following observations.

Among automotive manufacturers nearly all the competitors who were destined to follow had done so by the time the feature was two years old.

Among refrigerator manufacturers the number of followers increased at a uniform rate through the fourth year of use.

In the case of both electric water heaters and wrist watches, even during the tenth year of use a substantial number of new competitors were giving the feature a try.

In the television industry not only was the number of followers

EXHIBIT VI. COMPETITIVE FOLLOW RATES IN THE VARIOUS INDUSTRIES

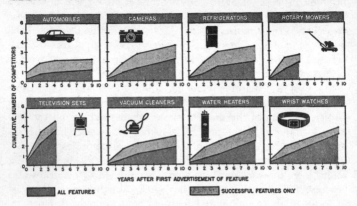

YEARS AFTER FIRST ADVERTISEMENT OF FEATURE

ALL FEATURES   SUCCESSFUL FEATURES ONLY

greater than in any of the other industries, but the competition followed more quickly. In fact, the typical company in the television industry which innovated a feature had as many competitors duplicating its feature after two years as an innovating company in the automobile industry usually had after ten years. While it may have been easier for the television set producers to initiate

EXHIBIT VII. COMPETITIVE FOLLOW RATES ON SELECTED AUTOMOTIVE FEATURES

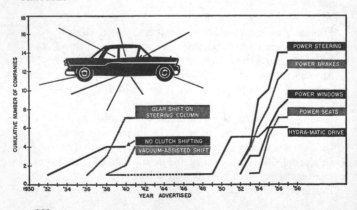

new features (because of technological progress and lower tooling costs), it was apparently more difficult for them to maintain whatever functional differentiation they achieved.

To give some idea of the patterns of competitive following on individual features, several examples are presented in Exhibits VII and VIII. The features selected are not necessarily typical, though most were eventually adopted by the majority of producers. The curve for each feature gives the cumulative number of companies (including the originator) that had advertised the feature, and the line was continued as long as at least one company advertised it.

Exhibit VII covers certain automotive features that are designed to reduce driving effort. It is particularly interesting to note how rapidly power-assist features were adopted by automobile manufacturers. Exhibit VIII shows the behavior of competitors following several wrist watch features. As may be seen

EXHIBIT VIII. COMPETITIVE FOLLOW RATES ON SELECTED WRIST WATCH FEATURES

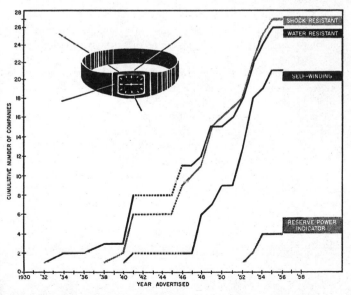

from both the watch and automotive features, it is not uncommon for two or more additional competitors to adopt a feature each year when the feature is of general interest to consumers. In short, out of all 715 features studied, no more than half a dozen appeared to have succeeded in keeping exclusive use of a general interest feature. One of these was Crosley's "Shelvador" feature, wherein a patent was granted on the idea of storage shelves built into the refrigerator door. But within two years after the patent expired, 15 competing companies adopted the feature.

STRATEGIC ADVANTAGES

In view of the high probability that competitors will quickly follow a firm's better features, why is so much money still spent developing new features? Why is so much emphasis put on features in selling and in advertising? One does not have to look very far to find marketers who advocate placing the major selling effort elsewhere. Writing on the virtues of a strong and clear company image to boost sales, Pierre Martineau recently said: "It is taken for granted that all products will perform their functions. But in my experience there are far too many mental 'DP's' at the management level who cannot shift their perspective from the long-gone days when there were distinctive product differences to dramatize."[3]

Is this kind of thinking really justified? What can be said in defense of relying heavily on functional features to gain consumer preference?

First, it would seem reasonable that the development of new functional features is one of the most effective means of building a company image of progressiveness and leadership. Further, the aura of leadership so established is apt to last long after competitors have duplicated the feature. But the most outstanding virtues of functional features in the strategy of achieving product superiority are more direct: (1) functional features are an extremely flexible competitive tool, and (2) they can gain the intense preference of a preselected market segment.

Features are a flexible tool because they can be adapted quickly,

[3] "Sharper Focus for the Corporate Image," *Harvard Business Review*, November–December 1958, p. 56.

dropped quickly, and often can be made optional at very little expense. In contrast, trying to obtain an equal amount of brand preference on the basis of a distinctive company image usually takes years to accomplish. Once established, moreover, the image is expensive and time-consuming to change. These characteristics make differentiation through an image almost useless for a new company just entering the market. They also make it dangerous for the company to develop a distinctive image which may have to be changed as market conditions change.

Probably the safest image that a company can cultivate is one that is "good" in general—"You can be sure if it's Westinghouse." No one can argue against the desirability of having such a good-in-general image, but it should be recognized that intense consumer preference is not likely to result.

Distinctive product styling is a great deal more flexible than an image is, but it is usually not as flexible as functional features. Styling can be adopted or dropped quickly, but it usually cannot be made optional as easily as functional features. It was impossible to buy an Edsel without the distinctive grill! Extreme styling variations are dangerous when they cannot be made optional.

Also, more often than not, it is difficult to predict the degree of acceptance a new styling will obtain, and it is still more difficult to predict what kind of people will prefer the style. Will the group preferring the style be the kind you wish to sell? With functional features, in contrast, it is often easy to fit features to segments with some degree of sureness. For example, a refrigerator without a freezing compartment appeals specifically to what, in this instance, turns out to be two distinct markets: (1) high-income families that already have a deep freeze as a separate unit, and (2) large families of lower income that need maximum storage space at minimum cost.

The fact that functional features can be used to develop an intense preference within a preselected market segment may or may not be important to a company. It is certainly not important if the strategy is to try to be all things to all people. On the other hand, it is rarely possible to produce a product that is better in the eyes of all consumers. If you are only going to capture 5% or 10% of the market anyway, why not recognize it and produce a product that *is* better to one or more segments of the market?

MARKET SEGMENTATION

Let us consider this matter of segmentation at greater length because of the implications it bears for marketing planning. As a market grows in size, it becomes increasingly feasible for manufacturers to specialize the appeal of their product. Wendell R. Smith has noted the value of market segmentation and offered additional explanations for the increasing interest in this type of specialization:

> There appear to be many reasons why formal recognition of market segmentation as a strategy is beginning to emerge. One of the most important of these is decrease in the size of the minimum efficient producing or manufacturing unit required in some product areas.
>
> . . . Present emphasis upon the minimizing of marketing costs through self-service and similar developments tends to impose a requirement for better adjustment of products to consumer demand.
>
> . . . It has been suggested that the present level of discretionary buying power is productive of sharper shopping comparisons, particularly for items that are above the need level. General prosperity also creates increased willingness "to pay a little more" to get "just what I wanted."
>
> . . . Many companies are reaching the stage in their development where attention to market segmentation may be regarded as a condition or cost of growth. Their *core* markets have already been developed on a generalized basis to the point where additional advertising and selling expenditures are yielding diminishing returns. Attention to smaller or *fringe* market segments, which may have small potentials individually but are of crucial importance in the aggregate, may be indicated.[4]

Still another reason for the increasing interest in market segmentation may stem from the development of more sophisticated market research techniques. Marketing research may reveal that management has unintentionally brought out a product which has appeal only to a specialized market. For instance, a company may learn that most of the customers preferring its product are elderly people, yet it may have been spreading the selling effort equally over a market composed of many age groups. Thus the company may have been suffering from the disadvantages of a limited market size while undertaking the expense of promoting

---

[4] "Product Differentiation and Market Segmentation as Alternative Market Strategies," *Journal of Marketing*, July 1956, pp. 6–7.

a product of general appeal. The other side of this coin is that the company is not taking advantage of the potential benefits of a specialized appeal to a specialized market—the market economies of reaching a homogeneous group of consumers.

If management decides to pursue a course of market segmentation as a means of improving efficiency, there are several dimensions which provide specialization. For instance:

> Geographical segmentation—such as northern, southern, and western markets; urban and rural markets; and similar divisions according to climatic differentiations.
> Cultural segmentation—according to race, language, or cultural mores.
> Socioeconomic differences—income, occupation, education, or family size.
> Personal differences—including sex, age, interests, and various psychological differences (introverts or extroverts, for example).

Although there may be many potential dimensions for market segmentation, not all of them are equally useful. One rather obvious limitation is the size of the segment. Many possible segments are simply too small to warrant the design of products to match their individual needs. Other segments may be large enough in size, but their particular needs are not acute enough to make possible the development of an intense preference. As an example of the latter effect, consider this: in 1950 a television manufacturer promoted a product feature which consisted of a switch that would instantly magnify what was on the screen, so that if the viewer wished to view a particular scene in greater detail, by turning this switch the center portion of the picture would be magnified to full-screen size. Now while most people might occasionally make use of such a feature, it is not one that is used often enough to promote any compelling preferences. As a result, the feature was dropped after one year.

Much less obvious, but of extreme importance, is the "accessibility" of the segment. Can the segment be reached efficiently through existing channels of distribution and through existing advertising media? For instance, if a product were differentiated to appeal strongly to left-handed customers, how could it be advertised efficiently through existing media? For every potential customer covered, there would be multitudes who were not potential customers.

In contrast, specialization which is based on geographical segmentation can be much more efficient. If a product can be developed to do an unusually good job of meeting the needs of a given area, all of the local channels of distribution and advertising media may be used without covering market segments which have no advantage to be gained from the product specialization.

In short, the more efficiently the selected segment can be reached, the greater the specialization can be and still yield an acceptable volume of sales.

Once an attractive market segment has been selected, management may proceed to formulate a product with characteristics that will meet the needs of the segment. Although this formulation should not be difficult, it is surprising how often management needlessly overspecializes the product.

All too frequently management (1) selects a group of functional features which "are rated highly by consumers" when tested individually; (2) combines these with a style which is not too expensive to produce and is thought to be preferred by the largest number of consumers; (3) sells the product under a brand that has an image which has been built up over a period of years —partly without conscious guidance and partly according to what an advertising agency thought the image should be. And yet when these three elements—each of them strong—are combined in the strategy, the result, as often as not, is a product with rather low over-all consumer preference. The problem is this: the group of consumers that liked the features may be different from the group that liked the style, and the group that liked the image may have been different from either of the first two groups!

The problem becomes increasingly acute as more distinctive— and hence possibly more market-limiting—characteristics of the product are combined. Accordingly it is highly essential that great care be used in coordinating the means of differentiation.

Distinctions may be made between the alternative means of differentiation on the basis of their effect on the market. Aside from whether the means of differentiation happens to be quality, style, brand image, or functional feature, is the effect a general increase in preference or is it only a specialized increase in preference, that is, does only a part of the market consider the differentiation to be preferable?

Combining general preference changes is not dangerous. They may not be efficient to use—either because of high development costs or because all competitors can advantageously follow them —but they cannot limit the breadth of preference for a brand.

In contrast, combining specializing means of differentiation may be dangerous, depending upon their specific effects. Some consumers will be enthusiastic and others will be indifferent or show an active dislike. For example, electronic flash synchronization on a camera appeals strongly to some customers but is not apt to bother or please those who do not need it. In another instance, a reflex type of view finder is preferred by some camera purchasers, while others insist on having an eye-level view finder. The latter type—potentially market-limiting—may in some case be made optional in order to add value for some consumers yet not detract value for any consumers.

Still other market-limiting feature types cannot be made optional at reasonable costs, and hence are inherently market-limiting.

Despite the danger of using inherently limiting means of differentiation, it is sometimes desirable or necessary to do so. It may well be the least expensive method of achieving an intense preference within a smaller part of the market. Because of their market-limiting effect, such features may be less attractive for large competitors to follow. It may also be necessary for management to accept an existing market-limiting characteristic of its product (or its brand image) and to build additional differentiation around this existing characteristic.

For purposes of discussing the problem of combining two or more market-limiting means of differentiation, two terms may be helpful, defined as follows:

Parallel means of differentiation refers to any and all distinguishing characteristics of the product which appeal to the same market segment.

Divergent means of differentiation refers to any and all distinguishing characteristics of the product which appeal to segments of the market that bear no clear relationship to one another, that is, only by sheer chance are the members of one segment also members of another segment, which usually means that those who belong to both segments are few.

To illustrate, take a hypothetical manufacturer of automobiles. Suppose that this manufacturer is one of the smaller producers and decides it would be advantageous for him to specialize his brand to avoid direct competition from the larger firms. To do this, the manufacturer may develop a small, lightweight automobile with an engine of small displacement. These characteristics are limiting, but they parallel one another in building an appeal to the economy-minded segment of the market. But then suppose the brand is also given a divergent "distinctive" styling. Now note what may result: if only 10% of potential automobile purchasers are economy-minded enough to prefer this type of automobile over larger, more powerful, and softer-riding makes, and if also only 10% of the total market is willing to accept the "distinctive" styling, the result is apt to be an over-all preference by only 1% (0.10×0.10) of the market.

When there is no reason to believe that the market segment preferring one type of differentiation also tends to prefer a second type of differentiation, then the two characteristics will be cross-dimensional or completely divergent. In the above example, the 10% of the market preferring an economy automobile is no more likely to prefer the brand's styling than any other segment of the market taken at random. If a styling cannot be developed which will appeal to economy-minded consumers, then care should be taken to ensure that the style is not market-limiting. And if additional means of differentiation are used which are also market-limiting in nature, the size of the remaining group that prefers the brand continues to drop at a geometric rate.

In practice, most differentiating devices are neither exactly parallel nor completely divergent. There probably is some degree of overlap between the segments being appealed to. However, management is hardly safe in assuming that the segments will overlap enough to eliminate the dangers of overspecialization. To ensure that a product is not overspecialized, management must know who the consumers are that prefer certain characteristics of their brand—not just how many consumers prefer each of the characteristics.

The rapid rate at which a product may become overspecialized puts a heavy premium on those means of differentiation which are not inherently market-limiting or which can be made optional. Considerable emphasis must also be placed on those means which —if they are limiting by nature—can be focused to parallel the existing dimensions of a product's specialization. Finally, the geometric rate at which a product can become overspecialized sets particular value on those means of differentiation which can be changed rapidly if the need arises. The use of functional features as a means of differentiation can meet all of these requirements.

CONCLUSION

Besides directly bolstering consumer preference, new features often bring the innovator undreamed-of free publicity, step up the enthusiasm of salesmen, and do more toward building an outstanding brand image than words alone can ever do. Moreover, they offer management freedom and flexibility to a degree that images and styling can never match. But, unfortunately, all of this is a two-way street. A poorly engineered "improvement" rushed into production can quickly destroy a reputation for product quality or undermine sales enthusiasm.

As a higher level of sophistication develops in the art of product strategy, it is not going to be enough for management to simply sort out the "good" feature ideas for development and adoption. Managements will be forced to pick features appropriate to their company's size and goals.

For instance, small companies should think twice before pouring research and development funds into features of general interest to consumers. They rarely have sufficient advertising funds or retail distribution to capitalize fully on the value of such features. Further, these general interest features are the very ones which are most likely to be rapidly duplicated by large companies.

As for large companies, when they introduce new general interest features, the managements must have enough market research information available to recognize in advance the potential of the features and be prepared to make the most of them quickly.

Features which are of intense interest to only a segment of the market can do wonders for a company—especially a small company. The high consumer interest makes advertising dollars go further and will help to draw consumers to sparsely scattered retail outlets. At the same time, more planning is needed here also. Market research must have identified those who now prefer your product and who will prefer it with the new feature. Will the feature build up loyalty among existing customers or shift it to a new segment? The identification of this new segment is vital for efficient advertising, selling, and distribution.

This, then, is the role of functional features in marketing strategy:

In the struggle for the creation and preservation of brand preference, the product features are a potent, flexible element offering greater maneuverability to management than the more stable or general dimensions of style and image.

Successful features are most likely to be followed in the absence of strong patent protection, but again the flexible nature of functional features continually presents new opportunities.

When employed in combination with style and image, or with other features, management must combine with care lest the net effect be a dilution of the market.

As the economy and the total market grow, and as management seeks to serve specialized segments more efficiently, the characteristics of functional features make them an especially powerful ingredient in the marketing mix.

Management must recognize, however, that intelligent use of the advantages depends to a large extent on how well it knows its market, both present and potential, and how well it can deliver products that really are better . . . if not to all of the people all of the time, at least to a lot of the people a lot of the time.

10

THE STRATEGY OF PRODUCT POLICY

CHARLES H. KLINE

The first concern of most businessmen is the content of their product lines. No other problem of management affects profits more directly. Few problems require more constant attention from management.

Active executives make decisions almost every day that affect the product line in such matters as allocations of manpower, factory space, or sales effort. Frequently they must also decide major product questions—whether to undertake a new development project, to introduce a new product, or to eliminate an old one. Mistakes in any of these are usually costly, and may even be ruinous.

To help get better and faster decisions on problems of product-line content, executives in a number of manufacturing companies have developed formal product policies. These policies summarize the business characteristics which experience has shown successful products must have. In effect, each policy is a statement of long-range strategy that defines the means for a particular company to make the greatest over-all profits.

Experience has shown that a product policy serves these three main functions:

(1) A product policy helps to provide the information required for decisions on the product line. It tells lower management and professional staffs of market analysts, research workers, and in-

dustrial engineers what top management needs to know. Furthermore, it provides a convenient framework around which this information can be organized.

(2) Also, a product policy gives executives a supplementary check on the usual estimates of profit and loss. Even though modern techniques of market research, sales forecasting, and cost estimating are often surprisingly good, the data they provide are still only approximations.

It is often impossible to make any realistic financial estimates at all—for example, at the start of a long-range research program. At other times available sales and profit data may not be significant. An unsatisfactory record for an existing product may reflect a basic mistake in product policy, but it may also be the result of poor organization, unsuitable sales and promotion, faulty design, or inadequate plant facilities.

An analysis in terms of a basic product policy shows up weak spots in the financial estimates and indicates imponderable factors that cannot easily be reduced to numbers.

(3) Most important of all, a product policy guides and directs the activities of the whole organization toward a single goal. Only rarely are product decisions made solely by top executives. More often such decisions require the specialized knowledge of experts in many fields—research, development, engineering, manufacturing, marketing, law, finance, and even personnel. The original idea for a new product may occur to an engineer at the laboratory bench, a copy writer in the advertising department, or a salesman in the field. Between the first concept and the final decision by top management to introduce the new product there comes a long series of investigations, analyses, research and development studies, pilot production runs, and marketing tests. This work is expensive and time-consuming, and it involves a great many people in the organization. To complete these indispensable steps as quickly and thoroughly as possible requires good teamwork and a clear idea of management's over-all policy.

A sound product policy, well prepared and well taught to all professional and supervisory employees, is thus an important tool for coordination and direction. It applies not only to those major decisions which are the ultimate responsibility of presidents and general managers but also to the many day-to-day decisions by which lower-level employees shape the course of a business.

ANALYZING RESOURCES

The first step in developing a product policy is to make a careful inventory of a company's resources along the lines suggested in Exhibit I. Every company is unique. As a result of its history, experience, and personnel it has certain strengths and certain weaknesses that distinguish it from other business organizations. The ideal product policy makes the best use of a company's strong points and avoids its weak points.

In this sense every business enterprise is specialized, so that it is best suited to perform only certain services or to produce only

EXHIBIT I. INVENTORY OF COMPANY RESOURCES

Financial strength	Money available or obtainable for financing research and development, plant construction, inventory, receivables, working capital, and operating losses in the early stages of commercial operation.
Raw material reserves	Ownership of, or preferential access to, natural resources such as minerals and ores, brine deposits, natural gas, forests.
Physical plant	Manufacturing plant, research and testing facilities, warehouses, branch offices, trucks, tankers, etc.
Location	Situation of plant or other physical facilities with relation to markets, raw materials, or utilities.
Patents	Ownership or control of a technical monopoly through patents.
Public acceptance	Brand preference, market contracts, and other public support built up by successful performance in the past.
Specialized experience	Unique or uncommon knowledge of manufacturing, distribution, scientific fields, or managerial techniques.
Personnel	Payroll of skilled labor, salesmen, engineers, or other workers with definite specialized abilities.
Management	Professional skill, experience, ambition, and will for growth of the company's leadership.

certain types of product. The product lines of many large and successful corporations are so extremely varied that this point is often missed. One well-known company makes everything from light bulbs to jet engines, and another has a product line ranging from flashlight batteries to synthetic fibers. Although at first glance it may seem difficult to relate such diverse products to a single product policy, closer analysis shows that they all have in common certain strategic business characteristics which are related to company resources.

DEVELOPING THE POLICY

It is these business characteristics that make up the elements of product policy. Individually they are all well known. Every business executive deals with one or another of them daily. But in developing a product policy he must look at all these strategic points together. Let us see how they fit into an over-all policy.

Financial strength. In many respects the most important characteristic of any business is the investment required to enter it. This investment includes the land, buildings, and equipment needed for the business; the required inventories of raw material, work in process, and finished stock; and the funds necessary to carry accounts receivable and provide cash for working capital.

These components of the total investment are all related to the volume of sales. Investment in inventories, receivables, and cash varies almost directly with sales. Even the investment in such fixed assets as land, buildings, and equipment must be scaled to the volume of product to be sold. Thus a given operation may require a high capital investment merely because the volume of sales will be large. Many merchandising ventures are of this type.

In manufacturing industries, however, capital requirements usually depend on process economics. Some products inherently require manufacture on a larger scale than others. Exhibit II compares the size of plant, as measured by the number of employees, in four types of establishment in the chemical process industries. As the exhibit shows, synthetic rubber and synthetic fiber plants are always large, soya oil mills are usually of moderate size, and plants producing cleaning and polishing compounds are generally small. The typical synthetic fiber plant has a thousand times more employees than the typical cleaning and polishing compound plant. The difference in fixed plant investment is probably much greater.

EXHIBIT II. SIZE OF MANUFACTURING ESTABLISHMENTS FOR VARIOUS PRODUCTS

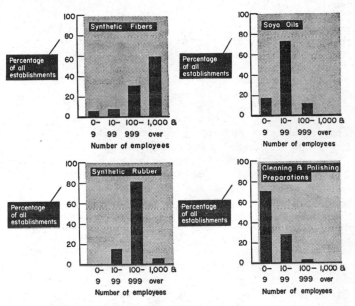

Source: U.S. Census of Manufactures, 1947.

Small companies with limited financial resources are restricted to businesses that require a relatively low investment. On the other hand, large and wealthy corporations have the choice of entering either high-investment or low-investment businesses—though experience has shown that such companies are most successful (indeed, sometimes only successful) in high-investment businesses, where large-scale operations do give them a competitive advantage.

In these connections, the observation made by Crawford II. Greenewalt, president of Du Pont, is significant:

There is much misconception also about the relationship between big and little businesses. . . . No little business could compete with us in nylon for the reason that no such business could bring together the capital and technical resources required for an efficient producing unit. We, on the other hand, have no interest in competing in spheres where we can make no substantial technical contribution, and there are many activities, particularly in the fields of marketing and distribution, that small businesses can do better than we . . .

Let me cite an example. We make nylon yarn and sell it to whoever will buy. Your wife buys, let us say, a nylon blouse. Between the sale of that yarn and that blouse are the throwster who twists the yarn, the weaver who weaves it, the finisher who finishes and dyes it, the cutter who makes the garment, and the retail store that sells it. For the most part these are small businesses.[1]

As a general rule, the smallest economic unit that has the facilities to undertake a given operation performs it most efficiently. That is why, when large companies enter low-investment businesses, they very often run into difficulties.

For example, the breakeven charts shown in Exhibit III summarize the findings of a cost analysis of the manufacture and sale

EXHIBIT III. BREAKEVEN CHARTS FOR MANUFACTURE OF SPECIALTY SEMIFABRICATED PRODUCT IN LARGE AND SMALL COMPANIES

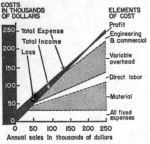
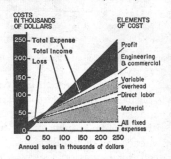

of a specialty product under two sets of conditions: (a) actual operating results in one of the largest corporations in the United

[1] From a speech reported in *Chemical and Engineering News*, October 10, 1949, p. 2896.

States; and (b) the estimated results in a small independent business. The product in question was a semifabricated material with a small but assured market potential of about $200,000 annually. The investment in plant equipment necessary for this volume of sales was about $25,000.

As the left-hand chart shows, the large corporation needed a sales volume of $216,000 per year to break even on this product. The small company, however, could make money anywhere above the breakeven point of $55,000 in annual sales shown in the right-hand chart. At the breakeven volume of $216,000 for the large company, the small company would net $72,000 before taxes.

Comparison of the two charts shows that the lower costs in the small company would come partly from lower fixed charges, raw material and direct-labor costs, and commercial, administrative, and engineering expenses. An operating manager primarily concerned with this one product could reasonably be expected to make small savings in these items. But the principal advantage of the small company would be its far lower variable overhead costs, estimated at less than half those of the large company.

Actually this analysis was made by the large corporation after several years of poor operating results. When this cost study became available, the product was dropped.

Sales volume. The financial strength of a company also influences the desirable level of sales for its products. A large volume of sales requires a large investment. For the reasons already mentioned, large companies are generally most successful in products with a large annual volume of sales, and small companies in low-volume specialty items. However, the acceptable range in dollars will obviously vary from one type of business to another.

Sales volume depends partly on the number of potential applications of a product, the number of potential customers, and the size of the area in which it will be distributed. These factors also determine the degree of stability in the sales volume. A product with only one application and relatively few customers is liable to sudden obsolescence and violent fluctuations in sales. Therefore most large companies seek products with broad markets and avoid items salable only to one or two customers, the government, or the armed forces. The small company can sometimes afford to take more chances, for it has more flexibility to turn around and adjust to changing circumstances.

Distribution channels. Channels of distribution consist largely of intangibles. There may be some investment in warehouses, trucks, and offices, but these facilities may also be rented. In any case the fixed investment is generally small. Perhaps for this reason business executives sometimes overrate the flexibility of their distribution channels.

Engineers and production men are particularly apt to assume that a salesforce can always handle "just one more" product, regardless of its market. Even sales managers sometimes say that a product will "sell itself" or "take no effort." As a result, one of the commonest problems in business today is that of the single salesforce trying to cover too many markets.

Professor Melvin T. Copeland summarizes the problem this way: "Early in my research work in the field of marketing, I found that when a company was catering to two different markets, such as the consumer market and the industrial market, for example, better results typically were secured by segregating the salesforce into two groups, one for each type of market. It appeared that ordinarily a salesman could not be continually shifting back and forth between different types of buyers without having his effectiveness materially impaired. The buying habits and the buying motives of the two types of buyers were so different as to involve difficult mental shifts by the salesman."[2]

Any new product has a great advantage when it can be sold to the same consuming groups as existing products. The new product benefits from the company's accumulated knowledge of the markets, close relationships with customers, and public acceptance which the salesforce has built up over the years.

On the other hand, a new product is at some disadvantage when it must be sold in entirely new markets. In this case the company must build entirely new distribution channels for the product. Sales executives must develop new sales and promotional concepts, hire and train a new salesforce, perhaps select

[2] *The Executive at Work* (Cambridge, Harvard University Press, 1951), p. 85.

new distributors, and ultimately win new customers. These steps are costly and time-consuming, and they may prove a steady drain on executive effort that could be better spent elsewhere.

Accordingly a product intended for an entirely new market should generally have other advantages strong enough to justify the risks involved in distribution.

Effect on present products. A going concern cannot forget the products which are already earning assets.

Ideally every addition to the line should improve the profitability of present products. When a company such as Westinghouse develops a new electrical appliance, it increases the overall demand for electricity and thus increases the market for its turbines, generators, transformers, and other power equipment.

Unfortunately situations of this sort are rather rare. For practical purposes a proposed new product will be satisfactory as long as it does not hurt the sale of present products. Of course, the situation is different when a new product makes an old one obsolete. It is obviously better for a company to replace its own products than to let a competitor do so.

Competition. In entering a new market a company should usually have some advantage over present and potential competitors in the field. At the least it should have no disadvantage.

The number and type of competitors a company will have to face in a new business generally depend on the capital investment required to enter the business. Where the investment is high, the number of competitors is fairly small, but they are usually strong, well entrenched, and difficult to dislodge. On the other hand, where the investment is low, there may be so many small, relatively weak companies in the field that poor pricing practices prevent any one from making a reasonable profit.

Executives in some companies with national distribution make it a policy not to enter any new market unless they believe they have enough advantages over competition to capture at least 20% of the market on a sound pricing basis.

Cyclical stability. Steady, nonseasonal demand is nearly always desirable in a product. It is desirable also to have a product that is relatively independent of fluctuations in the business cycle.

Capital goods and some consumer durable goods are particularly vulnerable to periods of depression. Some companies in these fields lay special stress on new products that go into consumer nondurable markets. These products include not only items sold to the ultimate consumer, such as paints, drugs, lubricants, or antifreeze, but also industrial materials sold to fabricators or processors of consumer goods—for example, tetraethyl lead to gasoline refiners or tin cans to food packers.

Research and patents. Research brings profitable new products and leads to strong patent positions. It can also be very expensive. Products which offer the opportunity for important technical achievement are generally most attractive to financially strong companies, especially those which already have large research staffs as corporate resources. Smaller companies tend to avoid businesses requiring much development. Many small companies operate in highly technical fields, but these are usually rather specialized.

The attitude toward research and development also varies from one company to another on purely strategic grounds, regardless of size. Some companies specialize in very technical products. They carry on as much research as they can afford, continually seek out new technical fields for development, and even abandon older products that have reached a fairly stable technology and are no longer protected by patents. Joel Dean describes one such company in these terms: "It is a fairly conscious policy of one of the large chemical companies to choose only those new products that have been developed by its product research organization and that are distinctive enough in both chemical and manufacturing requirements to be protected for some time to come. The counterpart of this policy is to abandon products when they have degenerated to the status of commonly produced commodities. The company advances to new monopoly positions as fast as economic progress wears down the walls of the old."[3]

In a company like the one just described any product that does not offer much opportunity for technical advances is not very attractive.

On the other hand, some companies concentrate on making old

[3] *Managerial Economics* (New York, Prentice-Hall, Inc., 1951), p. 130.

or relatively nontechnical products better and cheaper than any one else. Here the emphasis is usually on expert low-cost production or aggressive merchandising. The company resources are primarily the production or sales staff, and the need for much research is an unfavorable factor.

Raw materials. In the event a company owns or controls a source of raw material, it has a resource which it should obviously use whenever possible. However, most companies must buy all or the greater part of their raw materials. These preferably should be basic commodities that are readily available in constant supply from several sources. They should also be free of any restrictive competitive control. Any raw material available from only one source is vulnerable to interruption by strikes, fires, bankruptcy, or other disasters—and even, on occasion, to the supplier's flat refusal to sell.

Distant and unreliable sources are also dangerous. For example, one large company is a heavy consumer of Indian mica. Because of unsettled conditions in India and throughout the world, this company always keeps a protective inventory of about one year's supply. Since the total expense of maintaining an inventory for a year (including interest, taxes, insurance, warehousing, and losses) is about 20% to 25% of its cost, this company pays a heavy penalty for its unavoidable dependence on an unreliable source.

Freedom from competitive control is especially important for raw materials used in large quantities. Thus, after World War II several chemical companies developed methods for polymerizing styrene to polystyrene. After spending considerable sums on technical developments, the companies all eventually abandoned these projects. Executives realized that they would have to buy styrene from the basic producers, who also made and sold polystyrene. As converters of a material under the control of competitors, they would be at the mercy of more integrated companies both as to supply and in regard to the relative price level of the two materials.

Value added. The fate of those styrene projects calls attention to the strategic value of highly integrated businesses. The best measure of integration is the value added by manufacture—that is, the spread between the cost of raw materials and the total cost

189

of making the product, expressed as a percentage of total cost. Where distribution costs are high, the value added by manufacture and distribution is a more appropriate measure.

A high value added means that the product demands a high plant investment or considerable expense in engineering, labor, or supplies. These requirements give producers greater scope for improving efficiency, reducing costs, and developing a superior product. Furthermore, all these factors represent capital requirements. For this reason a high value added by manufacture is usually more desirable for the large company and less important for the small one.

Manufacturing load. In many types of manufacturing, executives have some freedom of choice in deciding whether to produce standard products that can be sold from stock or custom products made to the individual customer's order. Standard products sold in large volume can be made most economically with equipment specially designed for mass production. The heavy capital investment and high volume of sales make such products particularly suitable for large companies.

On the other hand, the smaller company with limited capital may find it more profitable to make custom products or to supply standard products in a larger number of grades, sizes, and finishes. This type of manufacture substitutes labor for expensive and inflexible plant equipment. Operating costs are higher but can sometimes be offset by higher prices. Furthermore, since the investment is smaller, lower margins may still give a satisfactory return.

The job-shop processing of industrial goods—for example, custom molding of plastics—is an example of diversified manufacturing load where the small company has a great advantage over the large. The production of fashion goods is another. Professor Copeland describes this situation:

From an administrative standpoint, style merchandising calls for rapid adjustment to continual and frequent changes in demand. Designing, purchasing, production, pricing, and sales have to be adjusted quickly to each change in a volatile market, and the various activities are so closely interdependent that they must all be adjusted almost simultaneously. Under these circumstances the activities of an enterprise manufacturing style merchandise are not sufficiently standardized or stable to permit the delegation of much decision-making to lieutenants. Hence, the small manufacturer who can constantly feel the pulse of the market and who can transmit his instructions directly and immediately to the operating forces is in a strategic competitive position. In such an industry the advantages of quick decision-making and speedy transmittal of decisions to operatives more than offset the economies which might otherwise be gained from large-scale manufacture.[4]

STATING THE POLICY

Even this brief review shows that different companies may take diametrically opposite positions on each of a dozen or more points of product strategy. The contrast in over-all policy between two hypothetical companies is illustrated in Exhibit IV. Both companies are assumed to be manufacturers of synthetic organic chemicals and similar in all respects except one—size. In size they are assumed to differ by a factor of 1,000 as measured by their net worths. As the exhibit shows, this one difference is reflected in almost every aspect of their product policies.

In practice the differences between companies are never so simple and pronounced. Consequently the differences between product policies are often more elusive, though nonetheless real.

Whatever policy is adopted, it must generally be reduced to written form if executives and employees are to use it throughout a company. The statement of policy may be a series of short definitions, as in these excerpts paraphrased from the instructions of a large manufacturer of industrial goods:

Sales volume—Each product line should have a large potential volume of sales. It should be useful in a number of different applications and salable to a large number of customers.

Patent protection—Each line should be well protected by patents arising from the company's own discoveries or acquired by purchase or other means.

Effect on present products—Each line should improve the company's over-all sales and profit position. It should preferably help to promote the sale of the company's other products. If, however, it would hinder the sale of other company prod-

[4] *The Executive at Work*, p. 149.

EXHIBIT IV. EXAMPLES OF PRODUCT STRATEGY IN LARGE AND SMALL COMPANIES

Product requirements	Company A Net worth $500,000,000	Company B Net worth $500,000
Capital investment	High	Low
Sales volume	Large volume	Small volume
	Mass markets	Specialized markets
	Many applications	Many to few applications
	National distribution	Local or specialized distribution
Similarity to present distribution channels	High to moderate	High
Effect on going products	Good to fair	Good
Competition	Relatively few companies	Few to many companies
	Sound pricing	Sound pricing
	Good possibility of securing a large percentage of the market	Desirable market position variable
Cyclical stability	High	High
Technical opportunity	Great	Moderate to small
Patent protection	Great	Great to none
Raw materials	Basic materials	Intermediate or basic materials
	Many suppliers	Many to few suppliers
	Standard products	Standard or custom products
Manufacturing load	Mass production	Specialized production
	Few grades and sizes	Few to many grades or sizes
Value added	High	High to moderate

ucts, it should have a greater potential long-range profit than the products in conflict with it.

The statement may also be written up as a series of questions arranged as a check list. The following excerpts are paraphrased from such a statement developed by a well-known manufacturer of consumer goods, whose strategy was "to serve the market for nondurable household goods bought by large numbers of families with a fairly high frequency of purchase":

Customer advantage—Does the proposed product offer the customer an advantage?

Is it superior to competition in a major property?

If equal to competitive products in use properties, can it be sold profitably at a lower price?

Mass market—Is there a mass market for the product?

Stability—Will the product be free of undue breakage or deterioration from normal handling in distribution?

Permissibility—Will the product conform to applicable government regulations?

To summarize the appraisal of actual products against the product policy, one large materials processor supplements the formal statement with a simple check form. Exhibit V shows this company's summary appraisals of two proposed new businesses. In case A, although the proposed business was quite different from the company's present lines, it did represent a favorable over-all pattern. In case B, on the other hand, the over-all pattern was poor even though there were several favorable points, such as general similarity to the present operations. The company in question developed case A into a major new business but did not consider case B further.

Applying the Policy

A product policy is especially helpful as a supplement and check on the usual estimates of profitability in three types of product activity: (a) development of new products; (b) vertical integration in manufacturing; and (c) elimination of old products.

New products. Research and development programs usually proceed stepwise, and in a completed project executives must make at least four major decisions:

EXHIBIT V. EXAMPLES OF SUMMARY PRODUCT APPRAISALS BY A LARGE
MATERIAL PROCESSOR

Case A: A generally favorable pattern

	Rating				
	Very good	Good	Fair	Poor	Very poor
Sales volumes	x				
Type and number of competitors	x				
Technical opportunity	x				
Patent protection		x			
Raw materials		x			
Production load		x			
Value added		x			
Similarity to major business				x	
Effect on present products			x		

Case B: A generally unfavorable pattern

	Rating				
	Very good	Good	Fair	Poor	Very poor
Sales volume	x				
Type and number of competitors					x
Technical opportunity				x	
Patent protection					x
Raw materials		x			
Production load			x		
Value added		x			
Similarity to major business	x				
Effect on present products	x				

1. To undertake preliminary exploratory research, either technical or commercial.
2. To launch a full-scale development program.
3. To build a pilot plant and conduct pilot market tests.
4. To build a commercial plant and put the product on the market.

If the development does not satisfactorily meet the requirements of the company's over-all product policy at each of these check points, it should be dropped or seriously changed.

Of course, at the start of an exploratory research program there will not be enough information for a complete analysis of the project. An important part of the development will be to obtain the needed information through marketing research, product research, and engineering studies. Nevertheless, early analysis of the information that is available can help prevent such wasted projects as those on the conversion of styrene already mentioned.

Executives can ensure proper consideration of product policy in development work by requiring a brief analysis of each project whenever they must authorize major operating expenditures. One company that controls research and development work by formal "development authorizations" has incorporated such an analysis in its standard authorization form. Despite some initial protests from the research department, the system has worked well for several years now.

Integration. Should a company make or buy a component part or raw material? Captive production gives certainty of supply control of quality, and the possibility of substantial cost savings. It may also divert capital from more profitable end products and lead a company into unrelated fields in which it cannot operate efficiently. Furthermore a captive production unit lacks the spur of competition. It may produce only at high cost and lag behind in technological development.[5]

Analysis in terms of a company's product policy helps to indicate these dangers. In general, a company should produce its own parts or materials only when all three of these conditions are met:

(1) The raw material considered as a product by itself meets the requirements of the company's product strategy.

(2) Internal consumption is large relative to the output of a plant of economic size—say, over 50%. (Otherwise the company is adding a new product, not primarily integrating.)

(3) Production will give substantial savings—or profits, if the material is to be sold externally as well.

[5] See Carter C. Higgins, "Make-or-Buy Re-Examined," *Harvard Business Review*, March–April 1955, p. 109.

Somewhat similar considerations apply when a company decides whether to sell an intermediate product or to process it further toward the form in which it will finally be used. Each additional step in manufacture eliminates the cost of intermediate distribution, increases the value added by manufacture, and adds to total profits. However, further processing can also lead a company into fields where it cannot function as efficiently as its customers.

Here again an analysis in terms of product policy is useful. As a general rule, further processing is justified only when all three of these requirements are satisfied:

(1) The new end product resulting from further processing meets the requirements of the company's product strategy.

(2) The cost of the present product is large relative to the total cost of the new end product—say, over 50%.

(3) The new processing step will improve the profitability of the over-all operation.

Old Products. The analysis of unsatisfactory products already made and sold is a less common but widely needed application of product policy. Some executives periodically review all product lines to eliminate obsolescent items and to prevent the diversion of effort on low-volume, relatively unprofitable products. For example, after such a survey one company with annual sales of $40,000,000 eliminated sixteen different products with a total volume of $3,300,000. It also made a number of improvements in methods of handling the products retained. Over the next three years the company's total sales increased by one-half and its profits by some twenty times. Among the many factors contributing to these spectacular increases, top executives have stated that dropping unsatisfactory products was one of the most important.

BUILDING FOR THE FUTURE

Besides helping the executive himself make better decisions on product questions such as those just discussed, a good product policy helps to build teamwork throughout the organization. If soundly conceived, clearly stated, and thoroughly understood by all supervisory and professional employees, the policy can be an important tool for control and coordination.

Finally, this approach to product strategy can also have a very dynamic effect in shaping the future development of a company. There is no need to take the present weaknesses for granted. If different resources and a different product strategy show greater promise for the future, then the analysis will indicate where the company must change and strengthen itself. On this basis management can take the constructive steps that are needed.

11

STRATEGY OF PRODUCT QUALITY

ALFRED A. KUEHN AND RALPH L. DAY

If marketing executives are truly "consumer-oriented," they know
that their marketing efforts face an uphill climb when the physical attributes of their product do not fit the preferences of a
substantial group of consumers better than competing brands do.
Certainly the physical product is not the only important factor.
The consumer purchases a "bundle of satisfactions" that includes
a variety of other considerations, such as convenience of purchase, design of the package, manufacturer's reputation, and style
of advertising. But it is nevertheless a bad mistake to become so
preoccupied with packaging, distribution, and promotional activities as to forget the importance of the contents of the package.
The marketing manager cannot afford to think that his responsibility for the nature of the product is fulfilled when he has as-
certained that his product is "just as good" as competing products
are.

In all fairness, it must be recognized that the problem of determining exactly what the attributes of a product ought to be is
extremely difficult. We believe, however, that the approach to the
measurement and evaluation of consumer preferences presented
in this article will make the task much easier for many products.
After making some general observations about product quality
we shall outline new procedures for (a) matching product features to consumer preferences, and (b) developing measures of

the consumer's ability to recognize differences in products. These procedures should help management to recognize what levels of product quality and other characteristics appeal to what proportions of the market; decide whether or not it is desirable to aim for parts of the market not covered by the "most popular" brands; and ascertain the most promising directions for new products or improvements in existing products.

WHAT IS "PRODUCT QUALITY"?

When considering the physical product apart from the additional attributes, real or fancied, bestowed on it by an effective marketing program, the manufacturer's attention is usually centered on "product quality." In this context, product quality is often measured in terms of the purity or grade of materials used, the technical perfection of design, and exacting standards of production. The level of quality is usually set in terms of either meeting or beating competition. Once a level of product quality, in this sense, has been determined, most firms carry out rigorous programs of quality control and product testing to ensure that technical standards of product quality are upheld.

The quest for this kind of product quality on the part of technically trained and oriented people is understandable and, within limits, highly laudable. However, thinking of product quality simply as a function of the commercial grade of materials used or the technical perfection of design and manufacture is a denial of "consumer orientation." Consumers do not make chemical or physical analyses of the goods they buy. They use a product and react to its ability to satisfy their wants. They have little knowledge of, or concern for, the technical standards established by chemists, physicists, and engineers in its manufacture. In fact, they may prefer products made with certain lower cost ingredients while management is equating higher cost with higher quality.

This is not to say that product quality in the technical sense is unimportant. Consumers generally wish to be reassured that they are not getting inferior materials or shoddy workmanship. They can be alienated by lack of consistency in the product characteristics which they regard as important. And they are not as gullible and manipulatable as they are apparently believed to be by some

199

critics of advertising. To be sure, given only minor product differences, or differences in unimportant attributes, advertising can precondition the consumer's feelings and attitudes toward a particular manufacturer or brand and thereby influence his evaluation of and reactions to a product. Thus, preferences can be established largely through marketing efforts. The job is much simpler, however, if actual perceivable differences (preferably important differences) can be demonstrated to the consumer.

The manufacturer should also realize that consumer preferences for physical aspects of the product may or may not be closely related to currently established technical measures of product quality. Consumers, for example, may judge such a quality as "softness" of paper products on different grounds than laboratory testing devices do. Laboratory test values, in such a case, may even misdirect research efforts aimed at developing products with greater consumer appeal. In the final analysis of the marketplace, the "quality" of a product depends on how well it fits patterns of consumer preferences.

Unfortunately, giving the consumer what he wants is easier in the saying than in the doing. Standards for measuring certain technical aspects of product quality may be well established in most companies, but how does one establish measures of consumer preferences across the broad ranges of possible product characteristics? That is the question we shall turn to now. The approach we shall describe is not a "drawing board" idea. It is finding acceptance by manufacturers of consumer nondurables and seems to hold promise for an even broader spectrum of products.

PREFERENCE TESTING

Especially in the period since World War II, manufacturers have become increasingly aware of the need to learn more about what consumers like and dislike in the products they buy. Consequently, large sums of money have been spent on consumer research. Many methods have been used to gather information. In addition to the traditional "nose counting" survey, continuous consumer panels have been established on a national basis, a variety of motivational research methods have been used, and extensive field testing of products has been done.

In general, these kinds of research have provided useful information to marketing management, but at times it has been difficult to interpret and apply the results. There have been many cases where the results of costly research have not been used, and also other cases where the results were misinterpreted, leading to ill-advised actions.

The approach to be described was developed in the belief that field research is likely to be worth more than it costs only when it is designed and interpreted within an analytical framework which relates it directly to specific managerial problems. This approach, which might be called "preference distribution analysis," involves no new field research technique. Rather, it provides a meaningful structure for the use and interpretation of an accepted procedure, the "blind," forced-choice, paired-comparison test, in a way that sheds new light on what consumers want and facilitates development of effective market-segmentation policies.

The nature of the paired-comparison test is basically simple. Here are the main features. Samples of two brands of a product, or proposed products which differ in some way, are prepared in identical containers and are given to a representative group of consumers to use. After they have used the samples, the consumers are asked to pick the one they prefer. Every effort is made to eliminate any influences other than the features of the products in the packages. For instance, to eliminate "position bias," the order in which they are asked to use the two products is alternated among the members of the test group. Again, the boxes are identified with psychologically neutral symbols, such as three-digit numbers which contain no 7's. It has been found that different colors, single letters, single numbers, or "magic numbers" may introduce biases among those consumers who do not have strong preferences for one of the samples. Occasionally, the tests are repeated with the same consumers and the same products but with different numbers on the boxes to test the consumers' consistency in choosing between the two products. After all members of the test group have used the samples and stated their preferences, the results are carefully analyzed to determine the percentages of the test group which preferred each product.

While the paired-comparison test is a very useful method for testing consumer preferences for products, free from any associations created by advertising, its results frequently lead to misinterpretations. That is why we must go several steps further than companies generally do to get the results that we want.

The danger of testing in the conventional way can be illustrated by a hypothetical example.

Suppose there is no chocolate cake mix on the market. A company decides to produce a chocolate cake mix and does extensive testing to find the degree of "chocolaty-ness" which consumers prefer. It tests with various levels and finds the degree of chocolaty-ness which the largest number of people prefer—a medium level. It introduces the product with success.

Then another company decides to enter the market and tests various levels of chocolaty-ness against the first company's product. When it tries any other level, either a lighter or darker chocolate, it finds that any such level is less preferred than the medium level.

As more companies enter the industry and test proposed products, the medium level always is preferred by a higher percentage of consumers. So each company enters the market with a medium-level chocolate cake mix, and the consumer has no choice between the brands in terms of physical characteristics. Consumers who like light chocolate and who like dark chocolate are out of luck.

If there were five companies marketing a chocolate cake mix and all their products were at the same level of chocolaty-ness, each company might be expected to get 20% of the chocolate cake-mix market if all other factors were equal.

Suppose now that a sixth company wants to enter the market. It decides to test two proposed levels of chocolaty-ness against the existing brands. It tests a considerably lighter chocolate cake mix against each of the established brands and finds that 65% of consumers prefer the other brand in each test. It tests a considerably darker chocolate against the established brands and again finds that 65% of all consumers prefer the brands against which it is tested. Both proposed products have failed in the preference tests.

This company then tests a product at the medium level and finds that 50% of all consumers prefer it when it is tested against any of the present brands. Now the comparison tests indicate that the new company has a product "just as good" as any of the competing brands. This product will be indistinguishable from the established brands and, if it can overcome the disadvantage of being a latecomer in the market, it might eventually be expected to attain a 17% share of the market.

This situation illustrates what is sometimes called the "majority fallacy," that is, assuming that every product must be acceptable to a majority of all consumers if it is to be successful. A little reflection suggests that a substantial number of consumers might strongly prefer a considerably lighter chocolate cake, and another segment of the market might strongly prefer a much darker chocolate. It is certainly conceivable that each of these groups would amount to a larger segment of the entire market than the one-sixth share that our hypothetical new company might eventually expect to attain with a cake mix just like all the others (if it can overcome the handicap of being last in entering the market). For a picture of the majority fallacy, see Exhibit I.

EXHIBIT I. ILLUSTRATION OF THE MAJORITY FALLACY

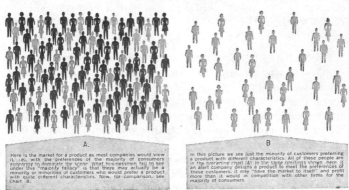

A.

Here is the market for a product as most companies would view it, i.e., with the preferences of the majority of consumers appearing to dominate the scene. What businessmen fail to see under this "majority fallacy" is that there may actually be a minority or minorities of customers who would prefer a product with quite different characteristics. Now, for comparison, see Chart B.

B

In this picture we see just the minority of customers preferring a product with different characteristics. All of these people are in the preceding chart (A) in the same positions shown here. If an alert company designs a product to meet the preferences of these customers, it may "have the market to itself" and profit more than it would in competition with other firms for the majority of consumers.

Unfortunately, conventional product testing sheds little light on the existence of such submarkets. However, this failure does not imply that the two-product comparison test is worthless. Rather, it suggests the need for a more meaningful way of planning product tests and interpreting the results. Preference-distribution analysis fills this need when the important characteristics of a product can be meaningfully "scaled" over a range of values.

STEPS IN ANALYSIS

Just as the cake-mix producers in the foregoing example could vary the level of chocolaty-ness of their products, many manufacturers must choose a product characteristic or feature from a wide range of possible characteristics. Awareness of the significance of such characteristics and the ability to vary their levels is not enough, as illustrated in the cake-mix example. In order to choose the level which will suit the preferences of the largest segment of the market, management must be able to: (a) relate the various levels of the characteristic directly to the preferences of consumers, and (b) determine the proportions of all consumers who prefer each level. Preference-distribution analysis provides such a means by establishing a scale of feasible values for a product characteristic, estimating the percentage of all consumers who prefer each value on the scale, and providing a probabilistic measure of consumers' ability to distinguish between different values on the scale.

The first step is to devise a scale of feasible values for each significant characteristic. The limits of the scale are the lowest value and the highest value preferred by any appreciable number of consumers. Between the extreme values, the scale is divided into a number of equal increments in ascending order. The width of the steps depends primarily on the consumer's ability to perceive differences.

Examples of easily scalable characteristics are the sweetness of cola drinks, the quantity of suds produced by soaps and detergents, and the saltiness of margarine. However, some product characteristics have not as yet been scaled in a way which will permit this form of analysis. For example, no satisfactory techniques have been developed for scaling colors, flavors, and odors in a way amenable to preference analysis. (Although psychologists have developed multidimensional scales for such variables, these scales are not suitable for determining distributions of consumer preferences. For example, orange and red appear close together on most color scales while red and blue are far apart. Yet, in terms of consumer preferences, red and blue might be more interchangeable, or "closer together," than red and orange. Undoubtedly, further research into the nature of human behavior will yield methods for scaling currently intractable characteristics.)

Once a "product attribute scale" is established, otherwise identical samples of the product are made up with each level of the particular characteristic. Each of the values on the scale is then tested in paired-comparison tests against every other value on the scale, using a representative sample of consumers for each test. The results of all these tests are analyzed simultaneously using a computer program which estimates the percentage of consumers who prefer each level, weights these percentages according to rates of use of the product, and provides a measure of the consumer's ability to discriminate among the various levels on the scale. (More will be said about consumer preferences and discrimination presently.)

When the preference distribution for a particular product characteristic has been estimated, a company's existing product or products and all competing products can be analyzed to determine their level on the scale. This will indicate the degree to which existing products match consumer preferences and will reveal any market segments which have been neglected. Thus, the analysis of the distribution of consumer preferences over a product-attribute scale will provide a highly meaningful frame of reference for the development of product strategies that are truly consumer-oriented.

The patterns of consumer preferences over a scale may take a variety of forms. Several types of distributions are shown in Exhibit II. Although the scales must be divided into discrete steps for testing purposes, actual preferences probably follow a smooth curve, as indicated by the dotted lines.

"Normal distribution." As one might expect, the distribution of

EXHIBIT II. DIFFERENT PATTERNS OF CONSUMER PREFERENCES OVER
LEVELS OF A PRODUCT CHARACTERISTIC

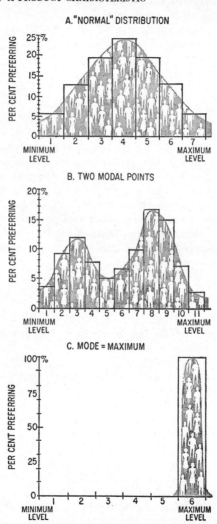

A. "NORMAL" DISTRIBUTION

B. TWO MODAL POINTS

C. MODE = MAXIMUM

preferences over many product characteristics is roughly similar to the "normal" probability distribution, as in Chart A. Preferences are distributed around a more-or-less central value on the scale, tapering off to a low level at both ends of the scale. If preferences for levels of a particular characteristic fit this pattern, would the key question for a firm be the exact level which is the central point of the distribution? It is not clear that this would be the optimal value, even if the company markets only one brand of the product. If several competitors are marketing products with the characteristic at the most popular level (4 in Chart A) or at higher levels, then the optimum point for our firm would most likely be well below the peak point—say, at level 2. The product would then be better suited to the tastes of a sizable segment of the market than is any competing product.

As we saw in the hypothetical chocolate cake-mix example used earlier, traditional methods of interpreting the results of preference testing lead to the "majority fallacy" whereby all companies tend to introduce products at a "medium" level of a significant product characteristic. Let us assume that the preference distribution for chocolaty-ness looks much like Chart A. Then, if the original five brands in the cake-mix example were at level 4 on the scale shown in that chart, it seems clear that a new brand at level 2 would be preferred by a considerably larger portion of the market than it would at level 4, where all the competing brands are clustered. It could expect to be strongly preferred over all the old brands by consumers with preferences at levels 1 and 2, and would be equally as attractive as the old brands to consumers at level 3. A new product at level 6 would enjoy a similar "preference share" without detracting to any significant degree from the market for the product at level 2.

Thus, an alert company which knew the preference distribution could bring out two new products which would be preferred over other brands by perhaps 40% of consumers (and maybe more), leaving the other five brands each with "preference shares" of about 12% (maybe less) of the market.

Even if a new brand could not be expected to obtain a preference share greater than the average for existing brands, it might still be advantageous to introduce it at a level of the characteristic appealing to a submarket neglected by other brands. It would appear to be much easier to attract consumers to a new product which better matches their preferences than to shift consumers from existing brands to another brand which has the same characteristics. In this way, a similar share of market probably could be obtained with much lower promotional costs.

Other preference distributions. Chart B in Exhibit II illustrates another fairly common pattern of preferences. Preferences tend to cluster around more than one modal point. An example might be preferences for the level of sweetness of a beverage with the peaks representing those who prefer a dry beverage and those who prefer a sweet drink. This kind of distribution will be discussed more fully later.

Chart C shows a concentration of preferences at the highest level on the scale. That is, all consumers prefer a level as high or higher than the highest level now available. This may indicate that there is a technical limitation on the achievement of the characteristic, assuming that level 6 is the highest commercially available level. (For example, almost every housewife would probably like the lightest possible vacuum cleaner, without loss of power or efficiency.) If consumers would prefer an even higher level of the characteristic, an opportunity for further technical development is suggested.

Changing preference patterns. Distribution of consumer preferences may change over time as the result of changes in patterns of end use and shifts in consumer attitudes. The existence of such trends can be established by periodic retesting of consumer preferences.

To what extent can a manufacturer alter basic patterns of consumer preferences for product characteristics through its advertising efforts? This is a more complicated problem. In general, it would appear less difficult for manufacturers to adapt their products to consumer preferences than to alter those preferences —but this depends on one's view of advertising effectiveness as well as on the role of fashions, fads, and changing tastes in the particular market being served.

How does management obtain a measure of the consumer's ability to recognize the level of a product characteristic that he actually prefers? This step is an important part of consumer-preference analysis. Marketing researchers have long recognized that consumers are not perfectly consistent in their behavior. The consumer will not appear to "prefer" the same value on a product-characteristic scale every time in repeated trials. It is not at all uncommon for a housewife to choose one of two products in a paired-comparison test only to choose the other if the test is repeated. Yet extensive testing suggests that most of the time an individual will choose the product which is on, or is closest to, a particular value on the preference scale.

It is useful to think of the particular value of a product characteristic which a person would choose most often if exposed to repeated trials as his or her "true" preference. Of course, ability to recognize this preferred value when compared with neighboring values varies with the nature of the characteristic, the width of the steps in the scale, the stability of the conditions under which the product is used, and the importance of the characteristic with respect to the use being made of the product. Nevertheless, when choosing between his preferred level and an adjacent value on the scale, the individual will be likely to choose the preferred level more than one-half of the time. The greater the distance of the alternative from the preferred value, the more likely he is to recognize his true preference. For instance, if the alternative product is two steps away on the scale, he will choose his preferred product a greater portion of the time than if it is one step away.

The foregoing observations suggest that it is appropriate to think of consumer choice as a probabilistic process. It is obviously a mistake to assume that consumers are perfectly consistent in their behavior. But it would also be a mistake to assume that it is useless to attempt to analyze consumer behavior because of this inconsistency. The approach used in preference-distribution analysis is to estimate the probability that a consumer will recognize his or her "true" preference, or the product closest to it, when faced with a choice. A "discrimination parameter," developed in the analysis of the results of forced-choice, paired-comparison tests for all possible combinations of values on a preference scale, provides a probability measure of the ability of consumers to discriminate among values on a preference scale.

Once a company knows the distribution of consumer preferences over a product-characteristic scale and has a measure of the consumer's ability to discriminate among levels of the characteristic, it can approximate the preference share for any product, existing or proposed, with regard to that characteristic. When all significant characteristics are studied in this way, the company is provided with valuable new information on which to base its product strategy. The implications are great for the design of new products, improvements in existing products, and the development of marketing strategies to exploit preference advantages.

USING THE NEW METHOD

In recent years, several manufacturers of consumer nondurables have attempted to devise techniques for establishing the distributions of consumer preferences for individual characteristics of products. The method outlined in this article is one such approach which, although still in a development stage, is now in use. Practical results have been obtained from it and are being applied by management in product evaluation and planning.

Although the results obtained in specific applications cannot be disclosed, we can give the essence of the approach by referring to a fictitious example. Let us take a product for which consumer preferences have been extensively studied by many firms—detergents for household use. For purposes of illustration we can draw on knowledge previously reported in the marketing and advertising trade press.

To begin, how do we ascertain what consumers' preferences are? We could proceed along the following lines.

Extensive consumer research of all types, ranging from traditional interviewing techniques to complex motivational studies, has revealed that there are several basic attributes of the contents of a detergent package which are significant in determining consumer preferences. These include the "washing power" of the detergent, the quantity of suds it produces, and how gentle it is to human skin.

The extent to which a particular detergent formula possesses these properties can be measured in the laboratory. The levels of these properties can be related to the chemical composition of detergents so that a formula can be developed to have any desired level of a given characteristic within the limits of technical feasibility. Thus, the significant product characteristics can be "scaled" over the total range of values which are both technically feasible and within the limits of consumer acceptability. For example, a "sudsy-ness" scale can be developed to cover the range from completely sudsless detergents up to the maximum amount of suds compatible with ordinary usage. Since the quantity of sudsing agents added to detergents is readily controllable, it is possible to consider a large number of levels, or "steps," in sudsy-ness. However, on any preference scale the steps should be large enough to enable the consumers to distinguish between products at adjacent levels on the scale with better than a 50–50 "pure" chance" probability.

Once a preference scale is established, the next task is to estimate the distribution of consumer preferences over the various values on the scale. The usual approach is to prepare product samples with otherwise uniform features for each level of the pertinent characteristic. Then forced-choice, paired-comparison tests are made for each possible pair of samples possessing different levels of the characteristic, using a representative sample of housewives for each combination. That is, the housewives in each of the groups are given samples of detergents with differing sudsy-ness values in identical plain packages. After they have used both packages of the detergent, the subjects are asked to choose the one they prefer.

When the results of the tests are formally analyzed, using a computer program which requires only a few minutes for computation on a high-speed machine, the distribution of consumers' preferences over the various levels of sudsy-ness can be estimated and a measure of the housewife's ability to discriminate between levels of sudsy-ness is obtained.

When the distribution of preferences is obtained, the pattern might be very much like that shown in Chart B of Exhibit II (where level 1 is no suds and level 11 is maximum suds). A substantial proportion of detergent usage centers about low sudsing products, but the heaviest concentration of usage is around a much higher level of sudsy-ness.

The next step is to look for an explanation of the observed pattern of preferences. Often it can be explained by different end uses for the product; that is, those who use detergents in one way want such-and-such a level of "washing power," suds, and so forth, while women using detergents in another manner have different preferences. In other cases the pattern of preferences can be explained in terms of cultural and climatic differences. At times, "there is no accounting for tastes." But, even in the latter situation, knowing the pattern of tastes is of great value in developing product strategies.

In the case of sudsy-ness, the preferred level is clearly related to the end use of the product. Extensive consumer research has shown that housewives tend to prefer a somewhat sudsy detergent in spite of the fact that suds have little to do with cleaning ability. But to the housewife the presence of suds seems to provide reassurance that the product is doing its job. However, high sudsy-ness interferes with the operation of automatic washing machines, especially the front-loading type.

With this information about the major end uses of detergents, we can relate observed preferences to the purpose for which the product is used. Housewives who use automatic washers account for most of the peak toward the lower end of the sudsy-ness scale. (See the left section of the top line in Exhibit III.) The higher and broader peak at a considerably higher level of sudsy-ness (right-hand section of the top line) represents the level of suds desired for several other end uses, such as dishwashing, which is sufficiently unique to be considered separately. Other end uses include wringer washers, hand laundry, car washing, household cleaning, and some top-loading automatic washers. Since sudsy-ness preferences for these uses are relatively similar, they can be conveniently considered together as a "general purpose" group.

By relating patterns of preferences to the end use of the product, analytically convenient "submarkets" are defined. A company's own products and those of its competitors can then be evaluated in terms of how well their sudsyness levels fit the pattern of preferences in each such submarket. Changes in the sudsing level of existing products or opportunities for new products can be considered, and possibilities may be seen for improving advertising, promotion, package design, and so forth.

EXHIBIT III. PREFERENCES FOR THE SUDSING LEVEL OF A HOUSEHOLD
   DETERGENT

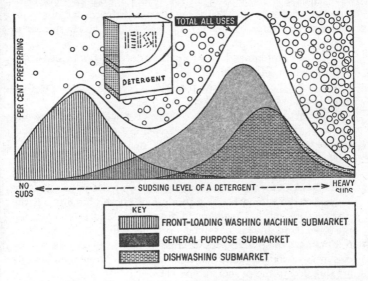

The preference distributions for other product characteristics
such as washing power and gentleness can also be related to the
end-use submarkets. This step can provide the basis for the development of an optimal "portfolio" of product features to conform with consumer preferences while taking advantage of any
failures by competitors to gear their product characteristics to
market needs.

CONCLUSION

To summarize the major steps in consumer-preference-distribu-
tion analysis:

1. Determine the physical characteristics of a product that appear to be significant to consumers.

2. Establish a scale of values, in equal increments, from a minimum level up to a maximum level for each characteristic.

3. Test consumer preferences for products located at approxi-

mately equal-increment levels on the scale in a series of paired-comparison tests, using representative samples of consumers.

4. Analyze the results of all the tests for each product characteristic simultaneously, so as to estimate the percentages of consumers who prefer each level and the ability of consumers to recognize their true preferences.

5. Relate preference levels to patterns of end use or other significant actions of consumers.

6. Locate the value on the preference scale possessed by each product already on the market.

7. Estimate the preference shares of existing products and evaluate opportunities for product changes or new product entries in all "neglected" segments of the market.

The physical characteristics of products are not, of course, the only determinants of consumer demand. A product with ideal characteristics for a particular submarket may not obtain as large a share of the submarket as a product of poorer "quality," if the superior product has inadequate distribution and promotion. On the other hand, the job of selling a product will certainly be easier if it matches the preferences of large numbers of consumers more closely than competing products do, and if its promotional efforts are directed to the proper submarket.

The approach to product testing outlined here does not attempt to estimate directly the effects of price on consumer choice. The products being compared are presented to the consumers participating in the test as being identical in price. Price has not been incorporated into this approach to consumer product testing because of the difficulties encountered in obtaining realistic price responses from subjects in the test environment. If a method of product testing capable of eliciting realistic price responses could be devised, however, a simple extension to the technique outlined here would make it possible to estimate the interbrand price elasticities directly from such data.[1]

The preference-scale approach to consumer-preference analysis adds new dimensions to the manufacturer's concept of product

[1] Another approach to evaluating the influences of price on consumer brand choice has been outlined in an earlier article: Alfred A. Kuehn, "A Model for Budgeting Advertising," in *Mathematical Models and Methods in Marketing*, edited by Frank M. Bass et al. (Homewood, Illinois, Richard D. Irwin, Inc., 1961).

quality. Product-development decisions can be consumer-oriented in a highly meaningful way for the first time with respect to many types of products. Better knowledge of preferences and of how they are related to end uses of the product can provide the basis for better marketing planning and more effective utilization of marketing resources. For the consumer, preference analysis promises a more satisfactory range of product choices as the significant characteristics of products are more closely adjusted to preferences.

The distribution of the product-preferences approach has not actually been applied to products other than frequently purchased consumer nondurables. Insofar as paired-comparison tests can be used to ascertain consumer preferences for other types of products, however, the methods outlined would be applicable to the analysis of such test data. For example, it might be possible to conduct similar tests to determine the distribution of consumer preferences with respect to the size of freezer compartments in refrigerators, of portable camp stoves, and of electric wall clocks, the width of lawnmowers and men's belts, and the weight of kitchen utensils and fabrics used in clothing.

While the basic concept of the preference-scale approach is quite simple, its implementation is both difficult and expensive. It requires extensive consumer testing, and a proper analysis of the results is too complex to be done without a high-speed computer. This is because the approach calls for testing of consumer preferences for an entire product class rather than a mere comparison of two existing brands (in the latter case, the majority fallacy is a likely result). Making the adjustments in products indicated by new knowledge of consumer preferences can also lead to costly changes in product design and methods of manufacture.

Nevertheless, preference-distribution analysis is a most promising new approach for companies that want to give more than lip service to the concept of consumer orientation. Handsome rewards await the company which offers products that fit the preferences of sizable segments of the market better than competing products do, and then supports these products with promotional efforts directed to the proper target.

Appendix. Analytical Procedure for Estimating the Distribution of Consumer Preferences Using Paired-Comparison Tests

Let us consider the most simple case, that of estimating the distribution of consumer preferences for a single product characteristic (C). All other product characteristics of the test products will be identical (controlled at some arbitrary value). The analytical procedure outlined below* will then provide an estimate of the distribution of consumer preferences for the product characteristic being studied if we can assume that there is no interaction between consumer preferences for product characteristic C and the other characteristics being held constant at some arbitrary value. (If interactions do exist, the problem becomes much more complicated as separate distributions of preferences for characteristic C would be required at the various levels of the other characteristics.)

We first divide the likely or possible range of consumer preference, with respect to the product characteristic under study, into n segments. Associated with each segment is an unknown, w_i, the proportion of consumers (weighted by volume of the product they are likely to consume) having a preference for the product characteristic value specified by the segment i. The figure

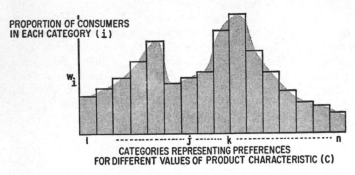

PROPORTION OF CONSUMERS IN EACH CATEGORY (i)

w_i

CATEGORIES REPRESENTING PREFERENCES FOR DIFFERENT VALUES OF PRODUCT CHARACTERISTIC (C)

illustrates how a distribution of consumer preferences for a product characteristic might be represented within the framework of this model.

The authors wish to acknowledge the contribution of Bruce Becker, Yuji Ijiri, and Jon Zoler to the development and programing of the parameter estimation procedures required for the analysis of consumer preference distributions.

Let p_{jk} be the probability that a consumer whose preference falls into the category specified by segment i would prefer brand A to brand B, where the product characteristics of brands A and B fall into the categories specified by segments j and k, respectively. Then, p_{kj}^{i} represents the probability that consumers in the ith category would choose brand B in preference to brand A on a "blind," forced-choice, paired-comparison test.

The consumer's ability to choose (that is, discriminate) "correctly" between pairs of products depends on a number of factors including the variability of conditions under which the product is used, the importance of the differences to the consumer, and the difference between the two products with respect to how well they match the true preference of the consumer. These factors are taken into account in the following formula representing the probability of a consumer with true preference i preferring a product with characteristic value j to a second product with characteristic value k in a paired-comparison test:

$$p_{jk}^{i} = \frac{(1 - d_c)^{|j - i|}}{(1 - d_c)^{|j - i|} + (1 - d_c)^{|k - i|}} \tag{1}$$

The parameter d is a measure of the consumer's ability to discriminate with respect to the product attribute in question, reflecting both variability in test conditions and the importance of the characteristic to the consumer. If consumers cannot discriminate between products with different values of a characteristic, $d_c = 0$. If consumers can discriminate between very minor differences, d_c approaches 1. The exponents $|j - i|$ and $|k - i|$ represent the degree to which each of the two test products is consistent with the true preference of the consumer.

The $n + 1$ parameters to be estimated in this model are a set of w_i $(i = 1, 2, \ldots, n)$ to establish the over-all distribution of preferences and the discrimination parameter d_c.

By a single forced-choice, paired-comparison test of two brands, A and B, we get an estimate of the proportion of consumers preferring brand A (P_{jk}) and an estimate of the proportion of consumers preferring brand B (P_{kj}), where

$$P_{jk} + P_{kj} = 1.$$

The expected value of P_{jk} is given by the following formula, assuming that the consumers participating in the test were chosen randomly:

$$E(P_{jk}) = \sum_{i=1}^{n} w_i p_{jk}{}^i = \sum_{i=1}^{n} w_i \; \frac{(1 - d_c)^{|j - i|}}{(1 - d_c)^{|j - i|} + (1 - d_c)^{|k - i|}}. \quad (2)$$

Each single comparison test provides one equation. In addition, we obtain one equation from the fact that

$$\sum_{i=1}^{n} w_i = 1. \quad (3)$$

Therefore, given n single comparison tests, the parameters w_i ($i = 1, 2, \ldots, n$) and d_c can be estimated. The actual P_{jk} obtained from comparison tests (observed proportions) are used as estimates of the $E(P_{jk})$ in the second equation.

To establish the full range of the distribution of consumer preferences, we need one brand whose characteristic falls into segment 1 and one which falls into segment n, the two extremes, since for all i less than j, p_{jk} is a constant given by

$$p_{jk}{}^i = \frac{1}{1 + (1 - d_c)^{|j - k|}}, \text{ where } i < j < k. \quad (4)$$

Similarly, for all i greater than k, $p_{jk}{}^i$ is a constant given by

$$p_{jk}{}^i = \frac{(1 - d_c)^{|j - k|}}{1 + (1 - d_c)^{|j - k|}}, \text{ where } i < k < j. \quad (5)$$

To minimize the effects of sampling variation on the estimates of d_c and the w_i, the products tested should be spaced at equal intervals. The number of segments (w_i) into which the consumer population can be subdivided is then equal to the number of independent, single, paired-comparison tests performed. The maximum number of subdivisions possible with single paired-comparison testing of N brands is then $\frac{N!}{(N-2)! \, 2!}$, the maximum number of pairs which can be formed from N brands each having a different characteristic value.

12

PHASING RESEARCH INTO THE MARKETING PLAN

LEE ADLER

Because of its preoccupation with gathering unrelated facts, the pressures of day-to-day business, and other unfortunate tendencies, marketing research today tends to be out of phase with other marketing operations.

The key to a larger and more important role for research is a systematic effort to design individual studies so that they not only contribute useful knowledge for short-term marketing needs but also help in the development of a long-range departmental program.

In making research planning effective, it is important to set up the work so that a series of studies can "feed in" to the needs of the marketing department as a whole.

Firms that have successfully used research planning have discovered in it a variety of important advantages, ranging from more sophistication and economy in the design of studies to better anticipation of marketing problems.

In the past few years there has been much talk about the creation of a unified concept of marketing research that would make it possible for researchers to grapple with marketing problems as seen by top management. Unfortunately, to date, this idea has remained talk more often than it has become action. As a consequence, marketing research is not helping to solve management's problems as it might.

If research executives want to assume more responsible positions in the corporate structure, they will have to find ways of increasing the contribution of their groups to the successful implementation of the marketing concept. By "marketing concept" I refer, of course, to the idea of customer rather than factory orientation, and to the idea of making integrated use of all the tools of marketing.

OBSTACLES TO PROGRESS

Success for the research executive is not likely to come easily. He inherits a legacy of practical difficulties. In company after company a gap exists between marketing research needs and fulfillment. Breakdowns of communication occur between researchers and marketing management. And many researchers' studies—prettily bound and lavishly illustrated with charts— gather dust.

Why? One reason looms large. The problems that marketing management must deal with are broad-scale and complex. But the problems that are defined for investigation by researchers are so delimited that the findings made either deal with too small a piece of the total problem or cannot be easily related to other aspects of the total problem. They lose their link with reality as the top marketing executive sees it.

What accounts for marketing research being out of phase with marketing in so many firms? There are, I believe, five principal reasons.

Preoccupation with the gathering of unrelated facts—On the whole, American marketing researchers are busy collectors of isolated bits and pieces of information, but they pay scant attention to constructing bodies of knowledge. In part, this tendency derives from the history of research in the United States. Still in its formative years—50 years old altogether—the marketing research function has enjoyed substantial growth only since World War II. As a result, expectations from research have been modest. Many a corporate executive, if he authorizes research at all, has not looked for—and still does not look for—more than a mechanical assemblage of "facts" which he may or may not apply to the problem at hand. Accompanying this limited role for research have been limited budgets, staff, and time for doing a job thoroughly.

It is not surprising, then, that it is only accident when several studies in a field can be related to each other so that the whole is greater than the sum of the parts, or even as great as the sum of the parts.

Pressures of day-to-day business—The competitive pressures of American business result in a demand for concentration on urgent, immediate problems to the exclusion of the more leisurely contemplation of broad problems. Of course, it is understandable that some short-range assignments of applied research cannot be readily integrated into any larger scheme. But to the extent that today's frantic drive to solve short-range problems deflects attention from the more fundamental and thornier problems of the long term, the urgencies of the market place do disservice to broader scale research.

This failing is not entirely the responsibility of researchers themselves. If pressing problems need solution, they must be solved, whether or not they contribute to a system of hypotheses for longer range study.

Insistence on rigorous methodology—Robert K. Merton has noted that "the American [researcher] raises aloft the standards of affirming adequacy of empirical data at any price, even at the price of surrendering the problem which first led to the inquiry."[1]

A case in point is the work of David Riesman. His studies have appeared to many to offer significantly new ways of looking at the American way of life, with important consequences for marketing management in his analysis of our consumption-oriented economy.[2] Yet the ardent defenders of rigorous methodology have criticized Riesman for his relaxed, impressionistic approach to his studies. The trouble is that the socio-psychological well-springs of our culture do not readily lend themselves to multiple correlation analysis. How can Riesman possibly cite levels of significance in his discussion of the "other-directed" personality?

Our culture is so complex and the forces prevailing on Amer-

[1] *Social Theory and Social Structure* (Glencoe, Illinois, The Free Press, 1949), pp. 205–206.
[2] See *The Lonely Crowd* (New Haven, Yale University Press, 1950), and *Faces in the Crowd* (New Haven, Yale University Press, 1950).

ican consumers so numerous and subtle that a technician has trouble getting at them. By contrast, an approach which permits a freer play to imagination and a broader sweep to an investigation than statistical designs will allow stands a better chance of showing a more complete view of our society.

Tendency to specialize—Applied research also mirrors the specialization of knowledge and function that characterizes American civilization. To a certain extent, the researcher and his work exemplify the popular observation that excesses of specialization result in "knowing more and more about less and less."

Recurring love affairs with new techniques—In a curious way, the very advances made in marketing research contribute to the trend toward specialization by leading to a preoccupation with technique instead of content.

For example, during the past decade more and more behavioral scientists have joined the ranks of business researchers. And these men have had a healthy effect in broadening the horizons of applied research; they have made available entirely new dimensions and tools for solving problems. But instead of these welcome additions to the armory of researchers being integrated into a battery of weapons designed to combat problems in their totality, they have helped fragment research even more. The spotlight has played around on the methods, leaving the problems themselves partly in the dark.

Again, the injustice of pointing accusing fingers only at the researchers must be emphasized. As marketing management has become increasingly enamored of the new disciplines, it has created a demand for applied sociological and psychological research. And in research, too, the customer is always right.

Take motivation research. From being virtually unknown in the 1940's, the technique blossomed into the research giant of the late 1950's. Rightfully, the behavioral scientists insisted on documenting William I. Thomas' observation that if men define situations as real, they are real in their consequences.[3] So the psychologists proceeded to demonstrate that products have not only rational meaning and serve utilitarian purposes for consumers, but also have symbolic and emotional meanings. Then,

---

[3] William I. Thomas and Florian Znaniechi, *The Polish Peasant in Europe and America* (New York, Alfred A. Knopf, Inc., 1927).

not so long ago, when there was great fascination with the discovery that men unconsciously regarded their cars as surrogates for the mistresses they enjoy in their fantasy lives, it was almost forgotten in Detroit that a more basic *raison d'être* for the automobile is to get people from one place to another at fairly reasonable cost. The stage was set for sexless and inexpensive foreign cars to have a field day.

The foregoing is, of course, oversimplified, and it is not intended as an attack on motivation research, already much maligned. I simply want to stress that new methods have succeeded too well in making American researchers and their clients technique-oriented instead of problem-oriented. A few years ago, probability samples were all the rage. Today it is fashionable to use the semantic differential technique. Preoccupation with any one method hurts marketing.

MEETING THE CHALLENGE

All this puts the research director in a tough spot. If, bowing to the needs and pressures just outlined, he designs and carries out studies dealing with very narrow problem areas, his findings will not fully meet the needs of marketing management. But if he goes to the other extreme and examines general, abstract questions, his data may have no validity at all for a particular firm in a particular situation. Somehow he must define his problems concretely enough to be manageable.

Is there a way out of this dilemma? I believe that there is. It seems to me that the solution lies in the formulation of an over-all, long-range research program for each firm and for each market. This program would be used to guide the design of individual studies so that they not only contribute knowledge for the short term but also contribute to the evolution of a unified body of information needed to implement the marketing concept over the long term.

There is a common expression among advertising men about the need to "see the big picture." What they mean by this expression is, of course, the importance of having a framework of knowledge about their clients' problems, including every step involved in getting the product from the factory into happy and repeated use by the consumer. Having this framework, they can then relate individual bits and pieces of information to the whole. Short-range problems are seen for what they are. The day-to-day concerns of advertising the product do not become confused with the total problem of marketing it.

What the alert advertising man does more or less impressionistically (or through disciplined intuition) when he looks at "the big picture" provides the key to the kind of research approach that is needed. Essentially, this approach calls for the prior or simultaneous formulation of long-range marketing objectives and the spelling out of the plans, policies, and programs calculated to reach those objectives through the use of the appropriate marketing tools. Describing these goals and plans in detail inevitably exposes the need for certain data which, in turn, leads to a listing of research projects over the same term as the marketing plan. It also suggests a priority order for their completion.

Here, in outline form, are the major steps that some progressive companies are taking in building long-range research programs which develop concurrently with, which parallel, which inform and are informed by the master long-term marketing plan:

1. Decide on long-term marketing objectives.
2. Enumerate in detail the policies, plans, and programs needed to attained the objectives.
3. Identify roadblocks barring progress toward goals and specify the areás where further information is necessary.
4. Define what and how the marketing research function can contribute to information gathering and problem solving.
5. Obtain the agreement of all members of the marketing team to objectives, plans, and programs.
6. Set up a priority order and timetable for the research projects.
7. Allocate the necessary budget, personnel, and facilities for implementing the program.

DEVELOPING THE PROGRAM

Defining a company's long-range goals is a painful, soul-searching process. But, as we have all learned by now, these goals should be as concrete as possible; this helps both in setting up plans and in assessing performance after the programs go into effect. Obvious as this seems, it is surprising how many companies continue to define an objective as "to boost sales" when more down-to-earth statements of sales targets are needed, such as:

Increase unit sales.
Sell the whole line, not items.
Improve share of market.
Concentrate on key accounts.
Introduce new products successfully.
Gain greater immediate profitability.
Open new territories.

Such objectives, alone or in combinaton, are specific enough to help in the choice of tactics to implement the master marketing plan. In the assignment of sensible goals, research can help by turning up data on such questions as:

What share of market is rightfully ours?
What payout period on investment should we strive for?
Are we going after the best markets?
Should we be in this business in the first place?

For example, the marketing plan of a producer in the transportation field was predicated for many years on the oversimplified sales goal of selling as much of its service as possible. This firm believed that all men were potential customers. Hence, the only criterion available to it for the proper use of such tools as advertising copy and media selection was that of reaching adult males. Later, marketing research showed that there was an enormous concentration of potential customers among businessmen who traveled considerably. The sales goal was then defined more specifically so as to concentrate marketing efforts on this crucial market segment. As a result, it was possible to reach the market more effectively and economically.

Effective long-range planning is necessarily a team activity. In addition to the immediate members of the marketing team, headed up by the marketing vice president or his equivalent, many companies have found it wise to have production, finance, and control men participate sufficiently so that (1) they understand and accept the marketing targets established and (2) the marketing goals harmonize with the over-all corporate objectives. In a framework of this kind the researcher can contribute more than he himself is able to see. The value of his data is not limited to what he can infer from it.

The responsibility of marketing to develop such a role for research is exemplified by Westinghouse Electric Corporation's philosophy: "The entire organization (research, engineering, production, and marketing) must work together to determine what the customer wants, how best to produce it, how to motivate its sales, and how to deliver it."[4] To achieve this over-all goal, each division of the Westinghouse organization is bound into the over-all plan and its contributions clearly delineated. Simultaneously, marketing and product research are specified at each phase of the cycle leading from initial customer indications of what they want to their ultimately being sold what they want. Each individual research study is coordinated with the other elements of the program and becomes a part of the whole structure of marketing knowledge.

PROBLEMS AND SOLUTIONS

To understand the planning approach better, let us turn now to some concrete problems. These will help to show the kinds of alternatives that confront managers wishing to make research an integral part of marketing, and the kinds of decisions that contribute to progress.

A good type of problem to begin with is media selection because, for many firms, it is a vital part of the larger problem of developing a unified marketing strategy. Moreover, not only do considerations of product, budget, market position, marketing objectives, and creative strategy affect media choice, but it is also influenced by numerous psychological and personal factors, by the diverse selling activities of media themselves, and by the various individuals in companies and advertising agencies who participate in buying space and time. Exhibit I represents an attempt to portray these relationships schematically.

Here, briefly, is an illustrative case history. In 1958 the Market

---

[4] James Jewell, vice president of marketing, Westinghouse Electric Corporation, in an address before the Marketing Committee of the National Association of Manufacturers, Spring, 1958.

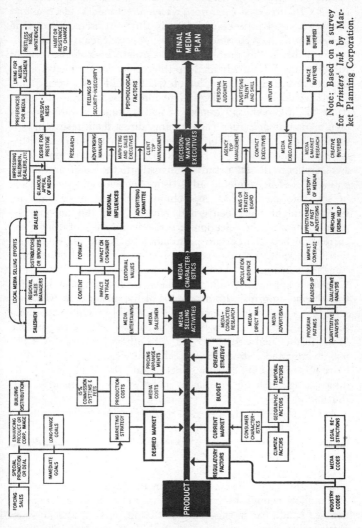

EXHIBIT I. FACTORS AND PEOPLE INFLUENCING MEDIA SELECTION

Note: Based on a survey for *Printers' Ink* by Market Planning Corporation.

Planning Corporation (now Marplan) was commissioned by *Printers' Ink* to assess the forces which affect media selection and to show how advertisers' decisions in this area are reached. One of the alternatives considered by the research team assigned to conceptualizing the problem was to isolate one or two crucial variables and intensively analyze their influence on media selection. Here are three examples of what might have been done. (1) It would have been legitimate for a researcher to design a study to explore the awareness of and attitudes toward media's own marketing activities (advertising, direct mail, research, personal selling, and so on) on the part of advertisers and advertising agency executives. (2) It would have been equally proper for a researcher to design a study to investigate the range and differential roles of personnel at advertising agencies and their clients in selecting media. (3) A technique-oriented motivation researcher might have concerned himself with the unconscious reasons affecting the selection of some media and not others, the correlation between certain personality types and choice of certain media, and the influence of prestige, habit, and other emotion-laden factors.

Another approach would have been to design research which would come to grips with all phases of the problem. It was foreseen that a narrowly designed project would preclude obtaining sufficient information by which to judge the relative importance of the factors analyzed compared with others known to exist but not investigated. However, this alternative presented the difficulty of sorting out numerous factors and, in all likelihood, the disadvantage of being unable to make precise statements about the findings.

At first, therefore, the research team appeared to have a choice between dealing with a small problem with a high degree of scientific rigor or dealing with a large problem with only moderate scientific rigor.

It was then recognized that the advantages of the two research philosophies might be well mated in the form of a plan which would allow enough breadth for rich hypothesis formulation, on the one hand, and means for quantifying some of the findings, on the other hand.

The techniques chosen reflected this hybridization approach, too. For instance, the major instrument of research was that of the "depth" interview, using the "probes" of the psychological researcher to dig deeper after the respondent had exhausted his spontaneous comments, but the interviews were sufficiently structured by question guides to follow a broad outline and thus allow for systematic analysis.

As a result, it was possible to reach conclusions that would not have emerged from a one-dimensional study of one aspect of the problem. If, for example, the study had been more narrowly conceived and been an analysis of reactions to the various tools used by media men to sell space and time, it would have yielded data on how to strengthen media's selling approach—useful but of tactical value only. As it was, the broader approach covered the roles of various executives in decision making, and this produced data of a more basic nature, with more implications for management. Among other things, it was learned that a far greater number of men exercise some influence than had been hitherto suspected, ranging from the lowliest media clerk at the agency up to the chairman of the board of the client firm. This suggested the need for media to reach every decision-influencer, not just the media buyer, the account executive, or the advertising manager.

To make planning effective, it is important to conceive of and set up programs so that a series of research studies can feed into the picture.

In the case just described, for instance, the first research project was followed up by a second designed to probe even more deeply into the factors affecting the selection of major media classes: newspapers, radio, magazines, television, and the business press. Still other studies were projected to evaluate the problems of more specific media groups, such as station representative firms and news magazines. In other words, the over-all, long-range plan was being used to guide the development of individual studies so that they would not only contribute knowledge needed for immediate decisions but would also be helpful in constructing a theory of media marketing that would be useful for the long term.

There is no one rule for systematizing this "feeding-in" process. To a considerable degree it depends on the nature of the problem. For example, in the case of a firm planning a new product, the research process might last at least several years and go from initial consumer research through product testing, analysis of the most suitable channels of distribution, test marketing, and then repeat consumer research to check on product satisfaction and use—with each study being atomistic in design and yet contributing to the over-all picture. By contrast, in the study of media selection just described, "feed in" occurred in two ways: (a) the first study was broad-gauge enough so that its separate parts contributed importantly to the desired whole, while (b) later studies were planned to add more brush strokes to the picture.

Let us turn now to a more detailed problem in new product marketing. The case I shall describe here concerns a leading manufacturer of consumer durables. Since the innovation represented a radical departure from the proven product in its field, the company felt the need for considerable research. As Exhibit II shows, the research followed a logical sequence (dates and some of the details of the plan have been disguised).

Phase I. As soon as the technical feasibility of making the new item was determined, but before the company had committed any significant funds to the idea, consumer and dealer attitudes were sought. Was there enough dissatisfaction with the current product to create a solid foundation for marketing a new one? Would dealers carry and support such a product? What ideas did consumers and dealers have that might improve on the proposition?

Phase II. The response to these questions being encouraging, the company authorized product development and laboratory tests. The latter were conducted both by company personnel and, later on, by an outside testing firm.

With product development proceeding favorably, research went into high gear early in 1958. The marketing research director designed a consumer usage test to measure product performance under normal conditions. As soon as findings became available from this research to serve as guidance, a test was conducted to select the name that would best convey a favorable image of the product. Next several package designs and dealer sales promotion and merchandising materials were prepared and tested.

EXHIBIT II. SIX-YEAR MARKETING RESEARCH PLAN FOR A NEW CON-
SUMER PRODUCT

(Market introduction—Spring 1959)

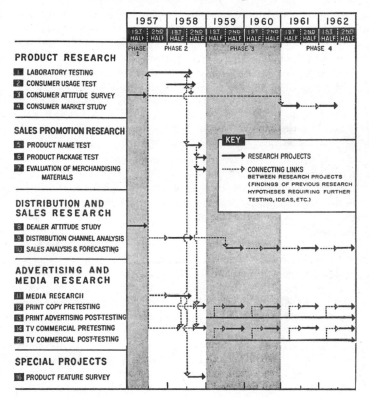

Each research project was feeding into the succeeding one as the
marketing mix for the new product took shape.

In the meantime, the consumer survey had pointed up a possible problem involving one product feature. The problem was
referred back to product development and testing; a modification
in the design was made, and a special consumer test was con-

231

ducted to check the acceptability of the revised feature to consumers. The funds for this research were drawn from a reserve set aside at the initiation of the whole plan for unforeseen problems.

During Phase II the marketing research department also analyzed its dealer organization to help sales management choose the broad classifications of dealers and also the individual dealers particularly well qualified to get the product off to a good start. This step was especially important since there were not enough units produced initially to supply all retailers. As the exhibit indicates, the earlier dealer attitude study was useful in selecting trade channels.

Media research was also undertaken to answer the questions: (1) which media classes to use and (2) which specific media to use. As soon as it was decided that consumer magazines and spot television would be the principal media, the agency began to prepare advertising. The consumer surveys were used extensively in determining creative strategy. Ads and commercials were then pretested to ensure that the most effective appeals possible would be used.

Phase III. During this stage, the company instituted what were to become continuous research projects. These projects included pretesting new printed and broadcast advertising, as well as tests of advertising after it had appeared, using regular rating services for this latter work. The exhibit indicates that the findings from "post-testing" were used to improve the ads subsequently designed and pretested.

Simultaneously, the company began a program of continuing sales analysis, which included breakdowns of sales by categories of retail trade, salesmen, price lines, geographic areas, and so on. This activity was designed to lead to annual sales forecasts that could be used to formulate more accurate production and marketing plans. Territorial sales analysis is also being used to assess salesmen's performance and to set up area potentials, sales quotas, and a sales incentive program.

Phase IV. The company is now in this phase. A large-scale consumer survey is planned for two years after market introduction. Management expects that by this time there should be sufficiently broad distribution and consumer experience with the new product to make such a study informative and practicable from a cost standpoint.

For succeeding years, the firm's marketing research director has recommended repeating from five to ten of the key questions of the large-scale consumer study, either in a mail survey among members of a consumer panel or as part of another national study. The purpose of this continuing research is to trace trends in product penetration and acceptance at low cost.

IN RETROSPECT

Marketing research planning—particularly the long-range variety—is not easy, and the approaches to it contain various pitfalls. But five important advantages of planning show that it is worthwhile to cope with the problems and circumvent the pitfalls.

1. *Those firms which have most successfully used this kind of planning have discovered that it not only helps to pinpoint areas of needed research but contributes to far more sophisticated research.*

For instance, in 1957 a major oil company defined its marketing objectives for the following decade with a view to maximizing its share of the market in each of the states it served. In detailing its plan, it was recognized that more knowledge would be necessary in numerous areas. (There were wide variations in marketing opportunities and in the company's status in each state, which complicated the planning picture considerably.)

Accordingly, demographic and automobile ownership and expenditure trends in each state were studied; trends in public and private transportation and highway growth were considered. Many other questions were examined—for example, the pricing structure of the industry; practices in service station ownership, operation, and personnel; changes in consumer shopping habits; the rising influence of private brands; and pertinent developments in such other fields as highway retailing.

In effect, a study of nearly every factor that conditioned the firm's marketing effort was built into the over-all research program. From a management viewpoint, this resulted in more useful findings than could have been obtained by "bits and pieces" studies of the diverse facets of petroleum marketing.

2. *Another common benefit is a multidimensional quality to the research.* It may have breadth; that is, it may cover different sectors of the marketing front. It may also have depth; that is, more than one type of research may be used in a sector over a period of time.

In the case of a whiskey brand, motivation research was utilized to explore attitudes toward the product. This qualitative study furnished insights of considerable value in planning the creative strategy for the promotion of the brand. Subsequently, it became important to determine exactly how widespread these consumer attitudes were, both geographically and among socioeconomic groups. Accordingly, the attitudinal data were quantified through the use of a structured questionnaire and a large nationwide probability sample.

Market analysis, employing secondary data from trade and government sources, then documented the size, character, and potential of given markets, while a briefer study among liquor retailers identified their reactions to the brand.

Strengthening the multidimensional character of this research was the use of parallel questions to cement the separate studies together. Thus, in the consumer studies respondents were queried about a unique product characteristic. The counterpart of this question was then put to dealers. By relating the findings from both surveys, important conclusions were reached leading to better promotion.

Thus, it was learned that retailers had not been sufficiently motivated (in terms of higher markup, local advertising, special merchandising aids, and so forth) to learn the whiskey's unusual sales appeal, let alone use it to push the brand to their customers. It was thus logical to recommend stronger preselling to consumers coupled with a promotional "deal" for retailers which made it worthwhile for them to stress the brand's unique sales story.

All in all, the sum of this research in terms of value was greater than the mere addition of its parts.

3. *Long-range research planning is economical.* By taking inventory of research needs, it is occasionally possible to combine what would otherwise be two studies into one, with consequent savings.

An industrial goods manufacturer achieved such an economy in this way. His sales department was concerned about negative attitudes on the part of the firm's wholesalers toward a new functional discount policy. The sales manager was interested in having research conducted on this matter. In the meantime, the head of the public relations department was evolving a new campaign and required knowledge of wholesalers' attitudes in the industry. As a result of joint planning, these respective needs were made known, and the research manager was able to map out one trade survey to fill both needs.

Economy also results from the fact that research is permitted a more logical and useful sequence of development.

4. *Planning tends to assure greater application of research to marketing problems.* Fewer reports wind up gathering dust. The reason is plain: by building research into the plan, making it an integral part of marketing activity, and obtaining greater acceptance for it by members of the marketing team, it can be brought to bear on problems far more effectively. Also, of course, a project is likely to be more useful if it has its birth in marketing problems or information deficiencies. Technique is not confounded with problem solving, and research becomes more sensitive to the needs of management.

5. *More marketing problems are anticipated.* This means that research can be provided in sufficient time to eliminate some of the "firefighting" that characterizes the operations of so many companies.

As with any other relatively new procedure, there are "bugs" in long-range research planning which need to be eliminated. The hard lessons from experience of companies in the vanguard of planning can be summarized briefly.

(1) Do not leave the planning to the director of marketing research alone. He is only one of the marketing team; the procedure requires a joint effort to be successful. The research director's contribution during the planning stage is (a) to help isolate problems amenable to research and delineate fuzzy information areas; (b) to outline the scope and method of research which will prove most effective; (c) to indicate the contribution research is ex-

pected to make; and (d) to furnish time, cost, and personnel estimates to help in setting up timetables, budgets, and staff requirements.

(2) Do not attempt to incorporate too much detail into the plan, particularly for any period more than a year away. The usual consequence is to become bogged down in details that lead to frustrations, delays, and, at worst, abandoned plans.

(3) Modify the plan as often as market and other conditions dictate. The very life and value of a program stem from its flexibility and responsiveness to the market place. A static plan soon becomes a worthless plan.

(4) Formalize the plan by committing it to paper and distributing copies to all of the individuals involved in its development and use. Although this may sound a bit naive, it is amazing how many hours are spent in meetings creating a long-range plan without an official record being compiled of the decisions reached. It is also valuable to have responsible officials initial the document. Psychologically, it builds up their stake in the plan's soundness and success.

(5) See that there are sufficient funds, personnel, and facilities for the marketing research department to carry on the bigger job called for by thinking ahead.

CONCLUSION

To serve management better, marketing research must become broader gauge. It must escape its preoccupation with narrow investigations of limited utility. It is true that broad definitions of problems often make for unmanageable research projects, but this is not a major obstacle. The solution suggested is to devise long-range research plans so that they will guide the design of individual studies. Research can then furnish data needed for today's decisions and contribute to the accumulation of information needed for making long-range decisions.

To begin, marketing management must be able to define its long-range goals and detail the action programs necessary to attain those goals. This detailing of plans inevitably highlights problems and information gaps. Marketing research should then be called on to map out long-range plans to solve the problems and fill the information gaps. A timetable should be agreed on, and the plan implemented with the help of the necessary budget aid, personnel, and facilities.

Operating executives in marketing are not the only ones to gain from planning. Research practitioners themselves stand to benefit considerably. We are all familiar with such epithets for researchers as "residents of ivory towers," "the slide rule brigade," and so on. The images thus created, right or wrong, have helped relegate the research function to a position of limited stature. The planning concept, with its emphasis on what research can do for departmental operations, can help to change all this.

It can be reasonably anticipated that the hunger for certainty in marketing operations will result not only in more calls for helpful facts but in increasing demands for measures of marketing effectiveness. The opportunity for research executives is exciting. To the extent that they are able to see a marketing problem in its totality, they will be seeing it as top marketing executives do. By thus being alert to general management needs, they will have won half the battle for greater recognition and acceptance.

13

MARKET TESTING

ERNEST J. ENRIGHT

Several years ago a top executive of one of the country's largest packaged foods manufacturing companies asked, "Where can I find out more about test marketing? Our experiences with the use of such testing have been so varied. One test campaign will return valuable and reliable information for new product planning while the results of the next campaign may be completely misleading."

Another executive, whose company has had notable success with the use of test marketing, commented, "You will find that there are no secret ways of test marketing. Everyone knows how to do it, but I don't want to talk about our experiences because successful test marketing is one of the major reasons for our marketing success."

After study of the subject I can only agree with both of those statements! Actually, there are no secrets to testing the market for a product. The difference between a sound and a poor job lies in the planning and management of this information-gathering process; and testing that is inadequate in this respect is one of the reasons why so many companies fail to market a new product successfully.

Before continuing, let me state at the outset that it seems to me more meaningful, as well as safer, to think of *market testing*

(A. C. Nielsen's phrase) rather than of *test marketing* (the usual term)—not only for the purposes of this paper, but for the purposes of management decision making. The trouble with the traditional concept is that it can lead to treating the testing process as marketing itself; I shall describe some of the consequences of this later. So I would abolish the use of test marketing in favor of market testing, which is more truly descriptive of the actual function that is needed in this preliminary stage of introducing a new product.

AIMS AND VALUES

Market testing of new products involves the trial reproduction on a small scale of the planned full-scale marketing program for a new product. Its purposes are:

To determine the acceptability of the new product and the effectiveness of its accompanying marketing program.

To measure the probable marketing success of the new product.

To find out whether any significant problems have been overlooked in planning the market program.

The marketing and testing elements of such a campaign must be carefully blended, even though they are quite different. Marketing carries with it the idea that the new product is taking its place in the line of products offered by the company and that it is on the market to contribute its share of sales and profit income to the company; its basic objective is profits—action to produce profits. By contrast, testing implies that management is attempting to find out whether it has prepared the new product and its marketing program well enough for full-scale marketing, and what more, if anything, should be done; its basic objective is information—as a prelude to action.

Market testing is undertaken to reduce the risks faced by executives planning national distribution for their new products by providing them with different measures of how well their plans succeed on a small scale, by pointing up those areas in which their plans are inadequate, by providing an opportunity for any unforeseen problems to crop up, and by providing some of the time needed to make adjustments before the far greater risks of large-scale marketing are assumed by management.

The planning of new product marketing strategy usually precedes market testing, and the adequacy of this planning is relatively unpredictable before some marketing to consumers is attempted. This basic planning is subsequently revised or supported by the testing results. In other words, market testing provides executives with some measure of the risks ahead, some insurance against the unseen, and some guides to action.

How extensive is the need for such data? I do not have any conclusive figures, but the fourteen case studies on which this article is based are suggestive. At the beginning of each marketing experience examined, the management team making the market-testing decisions felt that its new product was as ready for marketing as the time and skill available to the company for development and research had been able to make it. These products appeared to have an excellent chance of marketing success. Yet only three of the fourteen studied went through the market-testing process without some moderate change in the product itself, its method of distribution, or its marketing campaign.

> In three instances the production methods had to be changed in order to maintain quality standards.
>
> In three instances the product itself underwent considerable improvement.
>
> In other cases the package, the package fill, or the price was changed.
>
> In most cases some element of the marketing program underwent change as a result of the testing operations.

These changes were made possible because market testing provided executives with various measures of how successful the trial marketing campaign had been. The marketing executive was given sets of marketing facts obtained from studies of the selling campaign. These data were in the form of relative factors, such as share of market. Some information reflected the potential success or failure of the new product from the company's point of view, as given by sales-cost comparisons. Other data reflected the probable trade acceptance of the new product as determined from trade attitude surveys. Still other information measured the acceptability of the product from a 'consumer point of view by means of consumer preference studies.

At times a test was structured to measure the relative effectiveness of alternate methods of selling or advertising. Occasionally the testing company was provided with some measure of the ability of competitors to counteract its new product marketing strategy.

I should add that the results of a market-testing campaign are as much a measure of the resistance to a product's acceptance as they are a measure of its acceptance. If a careful log is kept of the circumstances surrounding the test, the nature of these resistances may be roughly determined.

We should become aware of one other aspect of market testing. Not only is the test campaign a small-scale marketing test, but in practice it also usually represents simultaneously the conclusion of a company's testing preparations and the beginning of its marketing. Executives generally recognize the strong probability that some changes in their product and its marketing program will be needed before the product reaches the national markets. They stand ready to make these changes while the testing with consumers goes on. They do not, however, expect to withdraw the product once the marketing channels are opened unless the expected demand fails to materialize.

Even in those instances where a product fails to command sufficient consumer acceptance for profitable marketing, management may not immediately withdraw the product from the market. Some companies even seem to be willing to supply the few customers created until demand dies out completely.

At the beginning of marketing, therefore, market testing is used as a bridging activity between the research and development phase and extensive marketing. By spending time in the test markets, a company is afforded the chance to alert its manpower to the task of marketing the new product on a wide scale. Like the product and its marketing program, the production system and the sales-training program are open to scrutiny during the test campaign. Several difficult production problems arose during the market-testing period of some of the products included in my study, and the time given to the testing afforded the companies concerned a chance to correct these difficulties before the national campaign began.

In this way market testing serves as a test of a company's readiness in all functional areas to put its marketing plans into operation.

Taking a closer look, we should recognize that an executive may wish to put his new product into test markets because he does not think he can predict its future well enough to risk full-scale distribution. For instance, he may have little or no basis for predicting the probable success of the new product, or for convincing other members of the executive committee how soundly he has prepared certain aspects of the proposed full-scale campaign. While he may have information from previous development and research (or from past experience), he may still feel that he needs additional proof or reassurance.

Market testing, then, can be of particular value to an executive, depending on the extent to which it helps him in decision making. His specific needs may take one or more of these forms:

1. The need for straight merchandising facts—such as knowledge of whether his new product is labeled and packaged properly.

2. The need for some basis for choosing between alternatives—such as a way of determining which is the more effective and economical way of advertising the new product.

3. The need for reassurance and confidence—such as knowledge that the new product is liked and wanted by consumers or that the company is justified in spending large sums for production equipment.

4. The need for realism—such as a recognition that, because of the newness of the product, it will not return a profit to the company for a period of years even though it is marketed wisely.

5. The need for enthusiasm—such as the strong support that successful market testing can build up for a new product among company men and the trade.

6. The need to check for the unknown—such as whether there are any overlooked or unforeseen circumstances that may affect the success of the product.

This list is given because there is sufficient evidence to conclude that executives tend to view the risks of national marketing, and consequently the values they hope to gain from market testing, in terms of their needs. Managers appear to design their test campaigns, select methods of measuring test results, and otherwise manage the outcome of their campaigns in terms of these same needs. Once these needs are satisfied, they are ready to finish testing and to begin marketing.

LEARNING FROM MISTAKES

In a discussion of the frame of mind or the approach with which an executive committee may go about its work of designing and managing a successful market-testing campaign for its new product, one can study the details of highly successful experiences. There are many that can be related. But, as in most recountings of "how to do it," or "how it was done," the process becomes over-simplified, and the problems overcome by successful managements are seldom given their proper emphasis. We may applaud the successful ending without a true realization of the kinds and degrees of difficulties which have been conquered.

For these reasons we will do well to look at some of the failures in market testing—the telling instances where management yielded unwisely to pressure and chose an expedient way out. Such an examination will give us a finer appreciation of management's accomplishment in the many cases where market testing has been successful.

In the discussion that follows I shall assume that management has chosen its objectives well. It should be emphasized, however, that in actual practice this may not be the case. In a sense, market testing is like risk insurance: the company must make a decision as to the coverage desired, and it must pay the money, effort, and time premiums required to obtain this coverage. The desired coverage is outwardly found in the list of "objectives for testing," but frequently management's real reasons for planning and managing its campaign in a particular manner stem from various subjective influences working on executives.

One of the leading errors revealed by my study comes from the temptation to make short cuts. For example, a marketing executive of a leading packaged goods manufacturer made the following comment after a multimillion-dollar mistake: "We found that we had not gone into the test markets long enough to check the effects of the high retail price on repeat purchases before we moved into other markets. We were misled."

His company had paid part of the premium for market testing. It paid some of the usual costs required: expenditure of money, time, and effort to carry out an introductory marketing program; exposure of the new product and its marketing program to scrutiny, analysis, and possible counterattack by competitors; commitment to the board of directors, to the company sales force, and to the trade that the test campaign was adequately designed and managed. But management had been unwilling to pay the full time premium required for sound testing.

In the majority of cases of mismanagement of testing campaigns, executives have been unwilling to pay this particular premium. For instance, in my study of the fourteen test cases I observed companies trying to get results more quickly by:

> Testing before production could manufacture an adequate stock for testing needs.
>
> Testing during the off-season for the product.
>
> Testing before the company had notified its wholesalers of the role that the company wanted them to play.
>
> Testing before the shelf life of the product could be checked.
>
> Concluding the testing phase before the research work designed to provide wanted information could be finished or, in one case, before the research work even began.

In each of those cases more time should have been allotted. In other cases the company did not test on a scale necessary to produce test results of the validity needed by management, because most market testing calls for a sizable out-of-pocket cash drain. For instance, I noticed that one marketing executive had underestimated the costs of his proposed market-testing campaign by at least $100,000. When I questioned him about this, he answered that the executive committee would have turned down his test proposal had it known what the total costs would be.

From the fourteen cases studied it appears that market-testing costs run from $10,000 to $15,000 out-of-pocket for each test area used.

In one sentence, it may be said that management makes its basic mistake by choosing to treat the process of market testing as a marketing rather than a testing procedure. To get a clearer picture of what is involved in the contrast between putting the emphasis on marketing and putting it on testing, we must remember that most manufacturers of consumer goods are looking to new products to provide an important share of their future business. Thus, in 1953 a major packaged goods manufacturer embarked on a five-year plan which had as its goal the doubling of its 1952 sales volume. After examining the company's existing product line and the possibilities of increasing sales of these products, company marketing executives concluded that at least one-quarter of the 1958 sales volume would have to come from new products not then sold by the company.

It is safe to say that a new product is related to the company's over-all marketing strategy—it becomes much more than just a single new product. And there is every evidence in management's actions that it looks on the new product more concretely as an integral part of future marketing strategy as development of the product proceeds. However, we run into a danger here. It cannot be emphasized too strongly that management must look on market testing as the testing of a particular product and its marketing program, and not as if it were the introductory marketing of a new member of the company's product line. Management must not be pressured to fit its market-testing planning into its over-all marketing strategy; testing must be designed according to the needs of the new product under consideration.

I might go on to prove this point by listing many examples, and marketing executives would probably find valuable a comprehensive and exact description of the mistakes made by those who market rather than test. But there have been many articles devoted to this subject. We should find greater value in determining why management acted as it did.

INTERNAL PRESSURES

Members of an executive committee are not allowed the luxury of reaching market-testing decisions in a pressureless and competitorless void. Instead they are under heavy pressure—they have subjective as well as objective needs to be satisfied—and cannot obtain completely reliable answers through testing. They cannot even hope to get enough facts through market testing to prove conclusively that the new product will succeed. It is not difficult to understand, then, why executives fail in certain ways to test their new products adequately.

The pressures working on the executive that influence his market-testing methods may arise from the attitudes of the managers themselves. A good case in point is the mental pressure on management "to get it over with."

Such an attitude is a natural result of the long and costly process involved in the adequate development of a new product idea into an accepted consumer product. Throughout the development period, which may stretch over several years, top management has to devote a great deal of personal time and effort before the product is judged ready for marketing. In some cases any exercise of executive caution, including a decision to market-test the product, can be looked on as an unnecessary delay and is deemed to be another way of running up the vast total of costs already invested in the new product. One marketing executive, for example, explained that he and the other members of his committee had "worked and planned for the new product introduction for so long a time that they found it difficult to hold the product off the market once they had some evidence the product was ready for marketing." He also said he "found it hard to live with the high pitch of enthusiasm and excitement over the new product for such a long time," and he "chafed at the need to spend the extra time required for testing markets." It is easy to see how a product may be rushed prematurely to the markets because of this eagerness to get going.

Another important way in which executive attitudes influence market testing is reflected in the following statement taken from the minutes of an executive committee meeting:

We can never be sure that we are 100% right, but the sales volume of our new product seems apparent. We will be gambling as much by holding back as going ahead.

Against the alternative of holding back for three or four months in order to secure absolutely definite findings and in more markets, we have to weigh the risk of some competitor coming along and attempting to pre-empt this market with a similar product.

Our industry is one of keen competition at all times, not only between established old products but also on the introduction of new ones. *The risks are considerable; the rewards, attractive.*

The executive who said that "we can never be 100% sure" was reflecting a widely held, and a reasonable, management philosophy: that a company cannot afford to get all the facts about a new product before putting it into the national markets. Another executive put the same idea into different words: "We don't want to put ourselves out of business before we have started marketing the product."

Admittedly the foregoing comments provide some justification for an abrupt move in response to competitive pressures. We cannot question the elements of realism in this attitude. But we can question the use to which it is put in market-testing decisions.

The degree to which management becomes emotionally involved in its new product development is often a factor which affects the management of testing campaigns. And it is a most difficult kind of pressure to counteract. In colorful and fairly accurate words, Conrad Jones of Booz, Allen and Hamilton had the following to say:

Most companies that have learned to test effectively still find they have the problem of taking test results seriously enough. The hand has been bet heavily by now, and you start getting the old feeling that 'if you don't play, you can't win.' But the next round of bets is a big one, and the good poker player will still fold his hand—if the pot is too small or his hand too poor.

Nonobjectivity reaches its most dangerous level now. By this time, *top management* is likely to be emotionally attached to the product! Whose cool head will provide the restraining counsel? Furthermore, if a faltering product planning program is bringing nothing else

247

along to take the place of the rejected programs in growth plans, what can the company do *but* take a chance?[1]

My only quarrel with Jones would concern his estimate of the timing of the low point in management objectivity. This point is usually reached before or during the test campaign and vitally affects the soundness of the research done. Proper evaluation requires detachment.

Like impatience to get going, emotional involvement is a major reason why company executives are unwilling to pay the premium required for soundly managed market-testing work. But these attitudes are not senseless, illogical, or unrooted feelings. They are the natural result of the complex, ever-changing, and highly competitive characteristics of the marketing situation in which all companies strive to live and grow.

I do not intend to imply that management should not have such attitudes. However, it is my firm conviction that management must openly recognize that its market-testing design, planning, and execution can be completely changed if there is "no cool head to provide restraining counsel."

EXTERNAL PRESSURES

Let us now look at some of the external pressures that influence management's planning and administration of its market-testing program. I do not intend to determine which pressures are of greatest significance or to determine their validity. But by at least being made aware of these pressures, marketing executives may better realize the several directions from which distractions can come. If they can then identify correctly the pressures working on them in their particular situation, they may avoid some costly market-testing errors.

Many executives have felt a pressure to gain the first position in the markets with their new product. This drive is particularly strong in those cases where the new product embodies a substantially new product idea. In one instance the pressure to be first in the markets led a large food processor to put its new product into a market test without checking into the legality of its

[1] "New Product Selection, Evaluation and Development," speech delivered to American Management Association Research and Development Seminar at Hamilton, New York, July 16, 1956.

pricing structure, since such a move would have provided competition with advance notice of the company's marketing intentions.

A striking example of a company's desire to be first in the markets is that of a large packaged goods manufacturer. This company devoted a great deal of research and development work over a period of six years to ready a new packaged dessert mix for marketing. In the judgment of management this product gave promise of becoming highly successful. When the product reached the stage of marketing, elaborate plans were drawn up for its national distribution. Several months before the date of introduction, the executive committee decided to market-test the product in two areas to recheck its estimate of potential sales of the product. Since time was short, the committee decided to use the size of the wholesalers' initial orders in the test markets as a measure of the probable sales success of the product. The product was introduced widely throughout the country two months after the market test began.

Management should have been forewarned by its own premarketing consumer research, which revealed that the housewife liked the individual characteristics of the product, but much preferred her own homemade product to the new packaged product. However, wholesalers in the test cities responded to the initial product offering by placing orders far larger than those usually placed for such a product. Management made its mistake by not moving to hold up on its expanded marketing plans as wholesalers in the test markets began canceling half of their initial offers.

Many manufacturers of consumer goods have interpreted their experiences to mean that in bringing a new product to consumers ahead of competitive brands they have the greatest opportunity to win consumer association of the product idea and the brand name, and that accordingly they will benefit in sales volume and brand loyalty. Conversely, they feel it is a disadvantage to be second, on the ground that once the trade is stocked with one product of a product class, wholesalers and retailers are reluctant to stock similar or "me too" brands. However, marketing research is now piling up considerable evidence that being first in the markets is a dubious advantage; sometimes it is better to let another company do the costly groundbreaking and make the mistakes of inexperience. The fact remains that such research does not appear to have greatly influenced management thinking—at least as far as market testing is concerned. They still feel impelled to move fast.

The market position of a company's product or product line is being challenged constantly by forces originated by competition, the trade, or the consumer. The degree of consumer acceptance of a brand is known to be a temporary condition subject to drastic change. The manufacturer can gain some degree of protection for his products by the introduction of new products—by being, in a sense, his own competition. The greater the apparent threat to his products' position, the greater is the pressure to move a new product into full-scale marketing.

In one case, a small soap products manufacturer watched the sales volume of its leading product dissolve as newer, soapless products took over its market. In a new deodorant soap, company executives believed they had a product with which they could recover some of their lost sales volume.

A first attempt to market the product widely through drug channels failed. The company then decided to find out through market testing whether it could market the product through a channel wholly new to it, the grocery trade. A sound test campaign was planned and started. However, at the first blush of consumer response to the introductory product offer, store auditing and checking stopped, the testing ended, and the company opened a series of new markets.

A short time later when sales began to fall off in the various markets, company management had no idea why the product had stopped selling; it had cut off the information which market-testing research could have supplied. In a very real sense the test had failed, not the product.

In another case, a major household chemicals manufacturer recently put a new product directly into national marketing to forestall possible moves by competitors. A careful analysis had earlier convinced management that its principal product was in danger of being challenged by a similar product with somewhat different characteristics. As part of its strategy, the chemicals company put the same characteristics into its new product.

It prepared elaborate plans for market testing. Just as the tests were to begin, however, management abandoned them in favor of national distribution. One may well sympathize with the executives' sense of hurry, but it would be difficult to argue that the original reasons for market testing were not as good as ever when the plans were abandoned.

Another strong pressure on the planning and execution of market testing, and one that has led to the development of many new products, is that arising from a company's discovery of unusual marketing opportunities. Many major companies now conduct a continual study of consumer acceptance of all the types of products which they might be able to produce and market. Management interest in this area becomes especially strong when consumer demand for the products it is offering to the market becomes stagnant or begins to fall off.

In one such case, a leading company whose markets had started to level off noted from its field research that consumer acceptance of a product which it was not producing was growing rapidly. Furthermore, no one company dominated this new market, nor, in the opinion of the company executives, was any manufacturer doing an outstanding marketing job. The company's opportunity hinged on its ability to produce a better product in this new field and to put this product into the market before another major company could seize the opportunity. The new product, a highly seasonal household item, was developed. Unfortunately, development was not completed in time for the company to begin its market testing at the beginning of the season for the item. Management was eager to get its new product going, so it began the market test rather late in the selling season. This yielded only limited results.

One of the many companies which leaped into the dried soup field at the beginning of the war and the tin-can shortage saw that canned soup manufacturers would be unable to meet customer demand. With only field research as a basis of information the company bypassed its usual policy of carefully developing a new product, and began a 90-day crash program to ready a product for market testing. This deadline was met. Unfortunately, the end of the 90-day period coincided with the beginning of summer, an off-season for hot soups, and did not allow management time to check the shelf life of its new product. At the conclusion of a six-month test, management found it difficult to give any kind of interpretation to the test results.

Company executives' willingness to meet the requirements of sound market testing is influenced to a large extent by their estimate of consumer loyalty to established brands. If they judge that consumers will respond quickly to a competitor's new product idea, they will be under pressure to react quickly. However, if they feel that consumers will have to be won away slowly from established brands, they will have more time to act and will have to be more certain of the qualities embodied in their new brand before national marketing.

This last consideration was uppermost in the mind of a manufacturer who planned to market a new liquid detergent. Company executives seemed assured that they could take the time needed to make certain that their new product had real advantages over similar powdered products. They were unwilling to stake a great sum of marketing dollars on the possibility that considerable numbers of consumers would abandon their regular brands and adopt the new product quickly. Consequently, they spent substantial amounts of time and effort in developing and market-testing their product.

By contrast, according to all the marketing stories coming out of the cosmetics field, for example, established consumer franchises appear to be lost overnight by new product ideas combined with fast-moving and extensive marketing programs. Thus, a Gillette executive should be under considerably less pressure to short-cut market testing than should a fellow Toni marketing manager, who cannot count on the same kind of consumer loyalty.

Marketing executives also become aware of the pressure from wholesalers and dealers who are not a part of the market-testing program. News about a promising new product and its test campaign spreads quickly, and, as it spreads, various members of the trade will ask the testing company to "send me a supply quick." Marketing management will be sorely pressed to fill these requests and to split its attention between testing and marketing.

In some product fields, too, trade practices governing seasonal selling deadlines may force a company to hurry its market testing or to end such testing prematurely. The testing company must conclude its testing in time to meet such trade deadlines, or lose a large part of its potential sales for that particular selling period.

"WAIT AND SEE"

In contrast to the actions of management in responding to the pressures previously described, it is useful to note the reaction of many large manufacturers when a major competitor has won the race into the markets with a new product. For they often tend to delay their entry of a similar product until their executives can obtain some measure of consumer acceptance of the rival brand, and until further testing shows that their new product is superior to the product being offered. They have the advantage of being able to use the competitive product for purposes of comparison. Also, they can often audit the competitor's market test and thus obtain valuable marketing information for relatively little effort and money.

The "newness" of a new product is a mixed blessing to a manufacturer, for he has first to make the novel quality understood by and familiar to his customers before he can use it to his advantage. Meanwhile, the introducer of a new product provides his competition with a firsthand view of how the consumer responds to the new idea. For instance, the competitors of The B. F. Goodrich Company waited for a period of years watching the sales progress of the original tubeless tire before they marketed a similar product. I suspect that they found this "wait and see" period very useful.

In those cases where the new product can seemingly be imitated with little effort, many companies will do so to take advantage of consumer enthusiasm as it grows. They recognize that the consumer demand of the moment is primary rather than selective in nature. They know that consumers are seeking the advantages offered by the new product idea, and that they have not yet used the new product enough to recognize the qualitative differences between brands. For example, in 1932, when General Mills introduced "Bisquick," the first successful blending of flour and shortening in a packaged product, the product received a tremendous amount of publicity and a corresponding amount of public interest. Within six months of the introductory date some 200 competing brands were placed on the market. With perhaps one or two exceptions, these competing brands were of such inferior quality that consumer interest in such a product virtually disappeared within the next twelve months.

CONCLUSION

Many pressures can make management unwilling to pay the premiums needed for an adequate market-testing job. These pressures can come from such varied outside sources as competitors, consumers, or the trade, and such inside forces as desire to get the testing over with, reluctance to wait for all the facts, and unobjective emotional involvement in the campaign. Whatever the nature of the pressure, it threatens to impel management to begin marketing before testing has been completed.

These pressures will always be present under our competitive marketing system, and they will become stronger as each day of market-testing planning or operations goes by. Management cannot be asked to ignore such pressures; nor should it pretend they are not present. Instead, it should acknowledge them frankly and try to deal with them.

Whenever the executive committee begins to consider the design of a test campaign that can be questioned on grounds that it allows too little time for testing, testing in an off-season, testing on too limited a scale, testing before production can meet the inventory requirements of market testing, inadequate research methods to measure the results of the test campaign, or the closing of the campaign before research can do its work, it is time to stop and think. If executives openly and coolly consider the whole risk proposition with an accurate awareness of the pressures they feel, they are better able to judge whether they can afford to pay the full premium required for market testing.

In my study of market testing I have found no evidence that management wins any great marketing advantage by compromising its market-testing program, when introducing a product. On the contrary, I have seen companies lose a great deal by hasty or expedient market testing, or by launching into full marketing before the testing has a chance to get the facts. In every case I have studied, the company with a new product had to make some change in the characteristics of the product or in the marketing campaign before national distribution was successful. Experience is the best testimonial to the value of market testing or some similar form of sales-testing research. In general, the more important the new product is likely to be in the company's future marketing strategy, the greater will be the need for management to pay the full price of adequate testing.

As a top executive of one of the nations' largest consumer products manufacturing companies commented to me in regard to market testing, "There are no reasons strong enough to justify our skipping it; it is one of the major keys to our success."

14

HOW TO EVALUATE ADVERTISING'S CONTRIBUTION

CYRIL FREEMAN

How much is advertising worth?

Why not spend the money on salesmen?

Does it pay to advertise at all?

For every industrial-product advertising manager, and many consumer-product advertising managers as well, these questions assume increasingly greater importance as today's profit squeezes force all managers to justify their own function's expenditures. Advertising's history of avoiding this type of accountability is obviously an untenable position for today's hard-pressed management—particularly when the amounts of money involved are continuously increasing.

When the sales manager talks to management about the value of adding members to his sales force, he says: "Here is what the additional men will cost in salary, commissions, backup, and so on. And here is my projection of added monthly sales which these men will bring in." This language is easy for management to understand.

Advertising can talk this language, too,—if (1) it establishes a value on its contribution in achieving specific communications objectives, and (2) it relates this value to the selling effort required to accomplish the over-all sales-marketing goals for the particular product involved.

It is the purpose of this paper to show that numbers can be applied to some of the subjective estimates involved in such analyses; and that by putting a specific value on advertising's projected contributions in relation to steps in the total marketing task, advertising dollar yardsticks for management can be formulated.

This method has been developed and applied at Worthington Corporation over the past year, and has provided useful evaluation of a number of promotional programs. Analyses made thus far have produced promotion value estimates which are compatible with the business facts of life. Management has endorsed the approach as a conceptually sound yardstick developed in a language which it prefers. Marketing executives have found little conflict thus far in the course of making the subjective estimates involved, and agree that promotion's contribution to the over-all marketing effort has not only been better pinpointed, but better appreciated by all concerned.

ADVERTISING GOALS

Increasingly, advertisers are coming to accept the fact that advertising is primarily communications. The Association of National Advertisers has published a significant book in which the author, Russell H. Colley, ably develops the concept of a "communications spectrum" within which advertising acts as a major communications force.[1] The author has adopted a management-oriented approach whereby he emphasizes the establishment of specific advertising goals and the measurement of specific advertising results based on the accomplishment of these goals. Examples of such defined objectives are persuading x customers to visit y dealers over a three-month period, establishing new product awareness among $x\%$ of the potential market within y months, and increasing penetration of a particular advertising message from $x\%$ to $y\%$ in z months.

While most companies involved in advertising and sales promotion conduct studies related to "advertising value"—readership studies, buying motivation analyses, and so forth—it is only in auditing the accomplishment of specific advertising goals that

---

[1] *Defining Advertising Goals: For Measured Advertising Results* (New York, 1961).

a perspective on advertising's direct achievements can be gained. This does not mean that other advertising research studies are to be discarded; however, it does mean that measuring the accomplishment of specifically postulated advertising goals requires critical attention. (Advertising is usually the largest part of the promotional package, which also includes all sorts of sales-promotion techniques like display and direct mail, and it often serves conveniently to stand for promotion generally, in contrast to personal selling.)

However even measuring the end results does not go far enough by itself. Management wants such measurements related to value. And, the timing of value estimates most usefully occurs before programs are committed. Companies usually project a reasonable rate of return on investments, resulting from planned, budgeted activities. But the top decision-makers find it hard to evaluate advertising in the same manner. Though not basically concerned with how promotion gets its job done—nor requiring absolute proof of promotion's value—management does want a logical rationale supported by a dollar evaluation.

Accordingly, the problem resolves itself into establishing achievable, defined communications objectives for promotion and then setting a value on them which is related to management's appraisal of the market situation. Since these objectives will only be part of a total marketing plan, it must be accepted that advertising may be successful, and yet sales still fail, if a company's over-all marketing plans are in error.

PROMOTION'S CONTRIBUTION

Here we must go further than the traditional advertising approach of asking "How much *more* will I get through advertising?" That really is not the most significant question for the majority of businesses. With a budget limit established and assuming adequate programing in the past, the questioning should be focused on balancing losses and gains in the total selling process: "What will I stand to lose in quota achievement, regional customer list attrition, or share of market if I discontinue adequate promotion?" versus "What would I gain in using these dollars for strengthening field personnel?"

It should be noted that the promotion dollars in question here are not the total dollars charged as "advertising" in many companies. Only the variable costs of promoting the product (that is, present program costs, plus administration, specifically supporting communications objectives) are relevant to the approach taken in this article. Nonpromotional costs often charged to advertising (such as salesmen's price and data sheets, sales meetings, and so on) or promotion expense that is required regardless of sales objectives (such as advertising in local commemoratives) has to be eliminated. Also, we must disregard residual advertising effects from previous programs, because these constitute the platform from which present plans are projected. (If these residuals did not exist, the proposed plan, objectives, and expense, and the sales quotas, would not exist.)

Exhibit I shows the theoretical framework of the "promotion versus salesman" choice. Consider the sales effort required to reach the market potential as fixed. (Such effort is represented by distance in the exhibit.) There are three different situations. Part A illustrates the sales force effort required to achieve the market quota with minimum sales personnel and no promotion support. Part B illustrates the gains in all selling efforts from advertising and sales promotion's unilateral efficiency; promotion eventually pays off through increased sales personnel capability or time to book orders. Part C illustrates the selective gains to be made by increasing sales personnel in specific areas (geographic or industry) without advertising support.

When considering how to allocate promotion and personnel, the most efficient combination is the one which contributes the most total effort (greatest total distance in the charts) toward attaining the potential. This may be clearer when pictured in three dimensions, as in Exhibit II.

Referring to Exhibit II, we see that a certain portion, the solid color area, of total bookings represents *advertising's efficiency contribution to the total sales effort*, and is the value of a given promotion program. Alternatively, the cross-hatched area represents added bookings derived from investing these same dollars in added salesmen. (For simplicity in this presentation, "salesmen" stands for a company's capability to contact customers per-

EXHIBIT I. THE PROMOTION VERSUS SALESMAN CHOICE

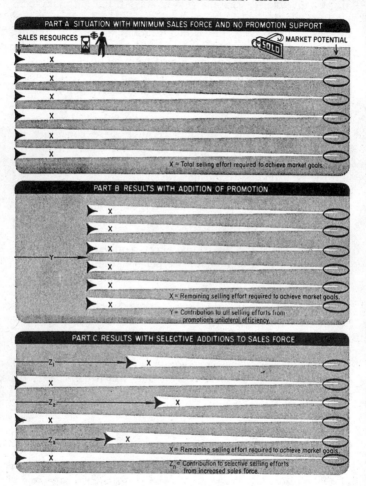

PART A SITUATION WITH MINIMUM SALES FORCE AND NO PROMOTION SUPPORT

SALES RESOURCES   MARKET POTENTIAL

X = Total selling effort required to achieve market goals.

PART B RESULTS WITH ADDITION OF PROMOTION

Y

X = Remaining selling effort required to achieve market goals.

Y = Contribution to all selling efforts from promotion's unilateral efficiency.

PART C. RESULTS WITH SELECTIVE ADDITIONS TO SALES FORCE

Z_1

Z_2

Z_n

X = Remaining selling effort required to achieve market goals.

Z_n = Contribution to selective selling efforts from increased sales force.

sonally, whether directly or by motivating or expanding distribution.) Management has the option of deciding whether either or both of these expenditures should be made. The relationship of these two areas is the crux of the analysis described below.

EXHIBIT II. ADVERTISING'S EFFICIENCY CONTRIBUTION TO THE TOTAL SALES EFFORT

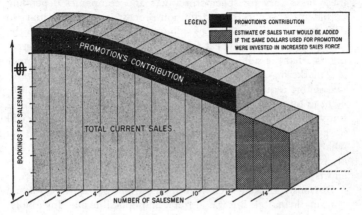

THE EFFICIENCY RELATIONSHIP

But how much does advertising contribute to selling efficiency? *Our basic premise for evaluation is that the total selling effort—salesmen plus promotion—has a value equal to established sales quotas.* (These figures need not be projected on an annual basis. Longer or shorter range projections are equally valid.) The selling process, from original contact through purchase, can be broken down into task accomplishments. By being specific in the setting of advertising objectives, the objectives can be directly related to these tasks.

Marketing management must take on the responsibility for arriving at common agreement within the marketing group on what the selling process and the specific tasks within that process are for any particular product or set of products. This is a requisite preliminary to determining advertising's contribution to the selling effort. The guide as to what represents a selling task is that it exists as a common denominator activity in all sales/distribution efforts. As the task analysis is refined and made more specific, we will automatically limit the opportunity for error in estimating advertising's contribution to any one task, and so to the sum total of these tasks.

The McGraw-Hill Publishing Company has a "standardized" view of the sales process as consisting of six selling tasks. Actually, these tasks vary for specific products and companies depending on the industry and the distribution process involved. Exhibit III depicts a simplified picture of selling task accomplishments in the sales process for one repeat-sales industrial business. After agreeing on what the selling tasks are for the specific business or product, marketing executives must then agree on the percentage of sales effort required within each area of selling task accomplishment to total 100%. In coming to this agreement, use of both intuitive judgment and market-advertising research information will be particularly helpful. Customer studies, such as research on what the salesman does and his importance to the customer, analysis of salesmen's servicing efforts versus their new business efforts, and so forth, are all relevant.

Obviously, making such quantified estimates is hardly a routine or a simple matter. But it is also not an impossible one. Invariably, relatively fair agreement can be reached among marketing executives as to a narrow range within which lies a specific selling task's contribution to the total selling effort. Indeed, experience has shown that with the passing of time, much quicker and closer agreement on such estimates can be attained. Agreement, however, need not be a testimonial to absolute accuracy. Basic agreement on relative task importance is more pertinent—and more useful. In addition, benefits within the marketing executive group are derived from the experience of negotiating these estimates: each subfunction group becomes more conversant with the roles all other groups play in the total sales process. And, as will be seen later, the eventual result is closer agreement on everyone's part as to the values of advertising and sales promotion.

Now let us turn to some specific examples. The case below illustrates the next logical step in the development of an advertising dollar yardstick approach to advertising investment—namely, *the application of estimates of advertising's contribution to each of the selling tasks in the sales process, and the derivation of a dollar value for advertising's contribution.* Then, two specific examples wherein the advertising dollar yardstick approach is utilized are presented in detail, including both the sales process and the advertising contribution analyses. The initial case is a highly simplified representation of a real situation. The latter two examples, while disguised, are based on applications of the technique to actual decision-making situations.

A CASE IN POINT

This is a case based on the company whose sales process is depicted in Exhibit III. The company is a general machinery manufacturer, with present bookings totaling $15,000,000. Its present sales force consists of 30 men who make regular calls on companies in a national, general industrial field.

EXHIBIT III. SIX SELLING TASKS IN A SALES PROCESS

Note: The actual sales process for any particular product or business should be divided into tasks with percentage allocations to each task reflecting its role in the process.

When the company's marketing group analyzed the sales process for its product, they agreed on these task percentage allocations:

Making contact	10%
Arousing interest	15
Creating preference	25
Making specific proposals	15
Closing	10
Keeping sold	25
Total	100%

The advertising manager had developed a $100,000 promotional program with specific communications objectives, budgeting his plan against those objectives. (This task-force budgeting approach is a basic requirement for today's advertising management.)

Market research had shown the company that three bids were generally required in a typical purchasing procedure for the product, and past sales records indicated that the company was seen as a logical supplier by about 30% of its prospects. An obvious goal for the company's promotional program was to increase sharply the number of people influencing purchase decisions who picked the company as one of the three suppliers invited to bid.

How to achieve this? *Advertising research* showed that the present level of market knowledge of the product's three unique features was 38%. The general aim of company advertising was to secure increased buyer knowledge and acceptance of the product. Specifically, advertising was to achieve understanding of the three unique product features among at least 50% of the logical prospects. The advertising manager's analysis was that this was a reasonable result for the recommended program.

In discussing what contribution the achievement of this advertising goal would make to the product's over-all selling effort, the sales manager and the advertising manager agreed that success in their objective would result specifically in:

An increase of 30% in salesman efficiency in his limited contact-making effort.

A one-third increase in salesman's interest-arousing effectiveness.

A nominal increase of 10% in preference-creating effectiveness.

A nominal increase of 10% in preference-creating effectiveness.

No measurable contribution to making proposals and closing orders.

An estimated 10% increase in the job of keeping present customers sold in order to assure reorder business.

(Increased effectiveness, as used in this analysis, connotes a reduction in personal selling effort required to maintain current performance levels.)

Now, by applying these percentages to the defined tasks involved in this product's selling process, we find promotion's contribution to the total marketing effort to be:

Specific selling task	Per cent of sales process	×	Agreed per cent of promotion's contribution to task	=	Total promotion contri- bution
Making contact	10%		30%		3%
Arousing interest	15		33⅓		5
Creating preference	25		10		2½
Making specific proposals	15		0		0
Closing	10		0		0
Keeping sold	25		10		2½
Total	100%				13%

This analysis shows that the total advertising contribution to the projected sales effort is about 13%. This is the key figure with which we can now correlate advertising's revenue contribution to sales. (The potential error here is relatively low because we have estimated promotion's contribution in each task area.) Using the 13% figure for advertising's contribution to this product's selling effort, and the $15-million total sales for the product, the sales revenue contribution from advertising is valued at about $1,950,000.

What of the alternative of salesmen instead of promotion? The marketing manager has estimated that the promotion budget of $100,000 could support four additional salesmen (at about $25,000 total support cost per salesman). He believed these four men could operate at the present average billing level of $500,000 per man. Thus, they would provide $2 million in sales, minus 13% of this amount because of a lack of promotion, leaving a total revenue of $1,740,000, or $210,000 less than the income gained with promotion.

In this case, then, it appears that the promotion support earns more than an equal investment in salesmen. However, before the company's investment decision can be made, a final step in the analytic process must be taken. What will be the company's return on the $100,000 promotional expenditure? This depends not only on the revenue contribution generated by the promotional campaign ($1,950,000), but also on the rate of profit of these sales. If, for example, the profit on sales were 6%, the $100,000 promotional investment would be worth $117,000, or $17,000 more than the cost, or a return of $17,000 ÷ $100,000 = 17\%$. Correspondingly, the salesman return equals 10.4%. The final decision to go ahead with either or both expenditures can then be treated in comparison with other investment opportunities.

Two more detailed and practical examples of this concept at work, presented in Exhibits IV and V, should amplify its application.

EXHIBIT IV. EXAMPLE A

FACTS

Type business: Heavy capital goods, $25,000–$150,000 price class; one of three major suppliers, four competitors.

Present coverage: Regular calls made on engineering departments of all prospect companies, an average of nine contacts maintained per prospect.

Quota: $6,000,000.

Sales force: Equivalent of 15 full-time men.

Proposed promotion variable cost: $50,000.

Cost of fielding men: $20,000 per man.

Market: About 300 companies; national, average 25 influences per prospect company.

Promotion objectives: (1) 80\% of all prospects should list this company as one of two best suppliers for this product, against present level of 60\%; (2) 100 contacts for discussion of product-application of product services; (3) complete dramatization of product benefits in one engineering-salesman presentation for unilateral sales force use.

Projected sales per additional man: $350,000.

From an analysis of Exhibit IV, the choice is clear: salesmen appear to be the better alternative. In making the final decision, management may conclude:

(1) Advertising's proposed program is too expensive for the promised results. The program might be revised to concentrate in those selling task areas where the greatest contribution can be made for the least cost. This would involve reestablishing promotional objectives.

(2) Regardless of promotion's questionable values here as compared to salesman investment, factors such as industry stature, prospect penetration, and so on may dictate that the advertising program be run anyway. Again, the over-all return on the profit generated by the increased sales would decide the wisdom of investing the money at all.

ANALYSIS OF EFFORT

Specific selling task	Per cent of sales process	× Agreed per cent of promotion's contribution to task	= Total promotion contribution
Establishing new company contacts	0	0	0
Developing supplier reputation	5.0%	75%	3.750%
Account service—keeping sold	65.0	5	3.250
Handling specific proposals	[30.0]	—	—
Making influence contacts	5% × 30 = 1.5	15	0.225
Developing interest	10 × 30 = 3.0	30	0.900
Influencing specification	15 × 30 = 4.5	5	0.225
Proposals	10 × 30 = 3.0	0	0
Following engineering detail	20 × 30 = 6.0	0	0
Negotiation	30 × 30 = 9.0	10	0.900
Closing	10 × 30 = 3.0	0	0
Total sales process	100.0%		9.25%

Promotion efficiency contribution

Program value = .0925 × $6,000,000 = $555,000.

Alternate salesman investment = $50,000 ÷ $20,000 = 2½ salesmen × $350,000 sales per man = $875,000, minus 9.25% of $875,000, leaving $794,062 added revenue.

Analysis of Exhibit V shows that advertising and salesmen have about equal value. Again, the company's final spending decision now requires estimating the profit on the sales revenue achieved as a result of the effort, that must provide a satisfactory return on the dollar investment. If, in Exhibit V, the profit on sales were 13%, the company would realize about $76,000 from its $65,000 promotion cost. The return would be $11,000 ÷ $65,000 = 17%. The salesman return would be nearly as attractive.

WHEN TO EVALUATE?

Should this technique be applied to each and every program? Every objective? Probably not. We are not involved here in proving the basic value of the advertising function. Millions of dollars in yearly promotion investment for all classes of business attest to the general soundness and value of advertising and sales promotion activities. Rather, we now have a management tool to be used in making gray-area "go" or "no go" decisions—and for evaluating the over-all soundness of a promotion support effort.

Evaluations of program economics, therefore, should be made when required for the business investment decision. On the other hand, the selling task research basic to these analyses is also the foundation for the proper setting of specific promotion objectives and plans. This should be a continuing fact-gathering activity sponsored by marketing management.

EXHIBIT V. EXAMPLE B

FACTS

Type business: Industrial distributors, $50–$1,000 price class; one of six major suppliers.

Present coverage: National; distributors in all key areas.

Quota: $4,000,000.

Sales force: 20 sales representatives calling on distributors.

Proposed promotion variable cost: $65,000.

Cost of fielding men: $15,000 per man.

Market: National; all plants/industrials.

Promotion objectives: (1) for distribution franchise development, make 30% of nonhandling distributors aware of line benefits and availability; (2) for serving/motivating distributors, increase stocking distributors running promotion programs by 20%; (3) for influencing users, increase from 5% to 50% the number of prospects aware of new distributor stock plan.

Projected sales per additional man: $150,000.

ANALYSIS OF EFFORT

Specific selling task	Per cent of sales process	×	Agreed per cent of promotion's contribution to task	=	Total promotion contribution
Franchise development	[20%]				
Distributor contacts	10% × 20 = 2		33%		0.66%
Developing company business image	35 × 20 = 7		25		1.75
Product-market education	40 × 20 = 8		25		2.00
Negotiate/close	15 × 20 = 3		0		0
Serving/motivating distributors	[40%]				
Help in management procedures	30% × 40 = 12		0		0
Inventory control aids	20 × 40 = 8		20		1.60
Provide customer/market acceptance	10 × 40 = 4		75		3.00
Training—product sales	20 × 40 = 8		10		0.80
Job closing aid	10 × 40 = 4		0		0
Joint customer service	10 × 40 = 4		0		0
Distributor effort	[40%]				
Making user contact	30% × 40 = 12		20		2.40
Developing user interest	20 × 40 = 8		10		0.80
Developing user preference	20 × 40 = 8		10		0.80
Making proposals	10 × 40 = 4		0		0
Closing	10 × 40 = 4		0		0
Account service—keeping sold	10 × 40 = 4		20		0.80
Total sales process	100%				
Promotion efficiency contribution					14.61%

Program value = .1461 × $4,000,000 = $584,400.

Alternate salesman investment = $65,000 ÷ $15,000 = 4% salesmen × $150,000 sales per man = $650,000, minus 14.61% of $650,000, leaving $555,035 added revenue.

CONCLUSION

The dollar-contribution method is an aggressive stand for advertising. We now have an estimate that sales and advertising can agree on as being the level of contribution—in dollars—of a prescribed advertising objective for a budgeted number of variable advertising dollars. An integral part of this approach involves acceptance of the fact that specific measurable advertising goals should be established. Variations in the advertising budget should be achieved by changing objectives and program structures when necessary—not by cutting separate ads or arbitrary management slashing. The advertising dollar yardstick approach is a firm, aggressive position—not a defensive one. It can be applied to all classes of business, and for both product and corporate program evaluations. Finally, it is a way for advertising to talk to top management in the same language as sales.

15

SQUEEZING THE WASTE OUT OF ADVERTISING

RUSSELL H. COLLEY

In its search for new sources of productivity gains, management can find no more fertile field than advertising. A shockingly large share of the $12 billion spent annually for advertising is wasted for one fundamental reason: lack of well-defined objectives.

The blunt truth is that among hundreds of consumer and industrial goods manufacturers it is difficult to find a handful that have gone beyond such vague and obscure objectives as "to increase sales," "to keep our name before the public," or "to establish a corporate image." No wonder there has been such faltering progress in answering management's most persistent question: "What return do we get on our advertising investment?" How could a company conceivably measure results when it has not decided what results it expects to accomplish?

A growing number of advertising and marketing directors are trying to do something about this problem.[1] However, they run head-on into a brick wall if they do not have the full understanding and wholehearted support of general management, sales management, and financial management. It is not enough for the final decision-makers to sit on the sidelines. Top management itself must provide total marketing leadership. Accordingly, this paper will focus on what top management can do to help, en-

[1] See Russell H. Colley, *Defining Advertising Goals for Measured Advertising Results* (New York, Association of National Advertisers, 1961).

courage, and, if necessary, trap its advertising and marketing people into conceiving sound objectives and plans with measured results. More specifically, I shall set forth (a) two simple experiments that the chief executive can conduct which, in all likelihood, will prove to his own satisfaction that his company does not have specific, agreed-on advertising and marketing goals; (b) opposing viewpoints and gross misconceptions of the purposes of advertising that exist among sales, general management, and advertising people; (c) steps to take in formulating a sound program of defined goals and measured results; and (d) a list of provocative questions general management can ask to help get progress started.

In order to analyze these topics in some depth I shall purposely avoid the question of how much of the selling job should be done by advertising. A helpful discussion of this question can be found in Cyril Freeman's paper "How to Evaluate Advertising's Contribution."[2]

CHIPS GROW BLUER

In search of profit and growth, corporate management has focused its attention on the technological aspects of business. In the past, here was where the big productivity gains could be made; and here was where top management felt most competent and comfortable. But improved technology is no longer the whole answer. A drug company president tells me: "Advertising has become the second largest item in our corporate budget. The chips are getting so blue that top management can no longer afford to be uninformed—naive, if you will—about advertising."

A top executive of a billion-dollar industrial corporation phrases it this way: "The executive committee may spend half a day digging into the pros and cons of purchasing a $1-million machine tool. But when a proposal comes up for spending $10 million for advertising, the discussion may last only a few minutes—not because we are not deeply concerned with an expenditure of this size, but because we have no way to get our minds around the subject."

In many industries (for example, automobiles, steel, food,

[2] Chapter 14, above.

chemicals, and petroleum), it becomes increasingly difficult to maintain historic 2% to 3% gains solely through improved technology. Production labor is demanding—and often getting—most or all of these gains. One chief executive in Detroit whom I know observes: "Today we must work very hard to take another three cents out of the cost of building a carburetor. Technological advances are getting harder to come by. Advertising offers big, fat opportunities for getting a greater return per dollar spent."

In marketing, which represents over 50% of United States economic activity, or more than $250 billion annually, the opportunities for productivity gains are so large and numerous that we practically stumble over them. And the *crème de la crème* lies in advertising. To suggest the possibilities for improvement, I am told by Gallup & Robinson, Inc., that the best advertisement in the current issue of a leading magazine like *Life* is not just 10% more effective than the poorest ad, and not just twice as effective, but more nearly in the magnitude of ten or more times as effective. (These comparisons are based on reader recall of specific material in the ads and on favorable attitudes resulting from reading the ads.) Where in the area of materials cost, production methods, or product reliability can ranges like that be found?

Even the most successful advertisers may admit that half of their advertising is wasted (common complaint: "We don't know which half"[3]). Hundreds of lesser lights have little to show for their advertising efforts beyond "a nice warm feeling."

All of this takes on still more significance when we compare advertising expenditures with profits. Whereas profits after taxes have shown little gain in the past decade, advertising expenditures have nearly doubled. Taking all U.S. corporations as a whole, advertising expenditures ($12.0 billion in 1961) were 52% as large as net profits ($23.3 billion in 1961). In analyzing profit data of companies spending over $5 million annually in advertising, I have found that in nearly half of the companies advertising outlays exceed net profits after taxes. Exhibit I shows a few leading firms in different categories of the advertising outlays-earnings ratio.

In the light of these figures it is easy to see how a modest 10%

[3] A statement attributed to John Wanamaker.

EXHIBIT I. AMOUNT SPENT ON ADVERTISING PER DOLLAR OF EARNINGS
IN 16 LEADING COMPANIES

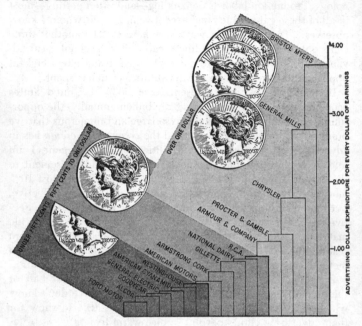

to 25% gain in advertising efficiency could be translated into real
profit improvement. And a 200% or 300% gain in effectiveness
for the same dollar expenditure is not at all fantastic; in many
cases it could be realistically expected if the right approach were
taken. In essence this approach is simply the application to advertising of one of the oldest principles of successful business:
management by objective.

TESTING THE PROGRAM

"But," company executives are likely to say, "we do have objectives for our advertising." If you are one of these men, the first
thing you should do is test the adequacy of present objectives and
plans in your company. This is not hard to do. I shall describe

two simple, eye-opening experiments you can make—both likely, I must warn you in advance, to show that your present program falls far short of the need.

Experiment 1. Ask a dozen people in advertising, marketing, and general management: "What are your advertising objectives?" Chances are you will get a combination of vague platitudes, evasive or facetious answers, and blank looks. Don't be surprised if you find widely divergent views on the purpose of advertising. The sales manager may look on advertising as a device for moving carloads of goods next month. The agency and advertising manager may be striving to build and maintain a strong brand franchise. The president may view present and proposed campaigns with "corporate image" uppermost in his mind.

The result of conflicting objectives is conglomerate, compromise, no-sell advertising. And the reason is obvious: the people who create advertising and those who approve it have not thrashed out in advance the answer to the question: "Specifically what do we want to communicate to whom?" The experiment will pay off if you get one man who says (as some have confessed to me): "I honestly don't know, and if anybody else in our company or agency knows, he is certainly keeping it a secret. This is the heart of our problem—we rush into action without adequate plans. We have no clearly defined objectives. No wonder we can't measure results."

Experiment 2. Ask to see a copy of your company's latest advertising "plan." Don't be surprised if these plan books (a large multidivision corporation may have several dozen reports covering its various product groups) contain little or nothing in the way of definitive objectives. The reports will vary in size from ten pages to ten pounds. Some will contain elaborate statistical tables showing proposed expenditures by product, by month, by media. But such a report is not a plan at all; it is merely a budget. It states how the money will be spent, with little or nothing on why and on what the company hopes to accomplish through the proposed expenditure.

A few reports will contain a short paragraph or so under the heading of "objectives." But the objectives are stated in such broad terms as "to increase sales and profits," "to expand our share of industry," or "to maintain a favorable attitude toward our company among the trade and consuming public." These are not advertising objectives, but total marketing objectives. Further, they are so vague they defy attempts to measure their attainment.

The businessman who takes an open-minded look into this subject will likely be forced to the following realistic (however unpleasant) conclusions: (a) there are no advertising plans worthy of the name in the company (but only budgets and programs), and the same may be true of over-all marketing plans; (b) responsibility for preparing plans is, to say the least, fuzzy; (c) few company people know how to go about the job of writing objectives and plans for carrying them out, and few know what a plan should contain or the steps in the planning process; (d) even those who understand or are willing to learn the process will be stopped cold because of great gaps in the information needed to do an effective planning job.

Who is to blame for this sad state of affairs—the advertising professionals? I think not. A similar inquiry into other areas of the business, especially selling, might reveal equally startling deficiencies in planning. We may as well recognize the fact that, in most instances, people in all phases of the business have been brought up as functional specialists. The transition from doer to planner is not easy, and the man who knows this best is the general management executive.

Rather than condemn advertising practitioners for past negligence, top management should recognize that marketing research, which lies at the very core of all marketing planning, was created, nurtured, and advanced to a very large extent by professional advertising men. The first commercial research department was started 50 years ago under Charles Coolidge Parlin by the Curtis Publishing Company. R. O. Eastman, Daniel Starch, A. C. Nielsen, George Gallup, Arch Crossley, and dozens of other research pioneers were all launched under advertising sponsorship. The fact that U.S. business has failed miserably to utilize the tools of research in its total marketing planning can hardly be a reflection on the advertising business.

It should be further recognized that the cornerstone of modern marketing—the philosophy of consumer orientation, or "the customer is king"—was largely the insight of early advertising men.

It has taken several generations for this philosophy to sink in among the staunch producer-oriented companies. Many have gone little beyond giving lip service to the idea.

After many years of observation and study among leading national advertisers I have come to the conclusion that the main causes of aimless advertising are:

1. Vague notions, misconceptions, often diametrically opposed viewpoints regarding the purpose and function of advertising among the dozens of people in the company and agency who influence advertising decisions.

2. Heavy preoccupation on the part of advertising and other marketing people with day-to-day "doing," gross neglect of goal setting and of plans to achieve goals.

3. Failure to utilize more than a tiny fraction of the present state of the art in customer research.

I do not know of a single national advertiser who has found quick and easy solutions to these problems that lie at the core of wasteful advertising. The best answer appears to lie in long-range personnel development coupled with probing inquiry into the areas of doubt and ignorance. Companies that have taken this approach are already beginning to reap the benefits. Let us examine the basic principles and steps in such an approach.

PURPOSE AND DIRECTION

Advertising today is rarely the product of a single winged pen. Dozens, sometimes hundreds, of people get into the act of creating, constructing, and approving or disapproving an advertising campaign or even a single ad. Chances are we could do little to change this situation, even if it were desirable to do so. Specialization is a fact of mass communication just as it is a fact of mass production.

But we can do something about giving these people a common sense of purpose and direction. If we succeed in doing this, people will not go charging off in six different directions toward what they think the advertising is supposed to accomplish.

An objective (in its most refined and specific state, a "goal") is a device for keeping all eyes on the same ball and heading toward the same green. Let's not concern ourselves at the moment with techniques of sinking the putt, because we have a much bigger problem first: getting all of the players together on the same tee. For what usually happens, fantastic as it may sound, is that the people who get into the advertising act have never got their thinking together on the fundamental issue of what advertising should be expected to do. There is no consensus on such questions as: Do we expect advertising to wrap up an immediate sale? Is advertising's purpose to make our company or brand name well known? Is advertising's main task to introduce new products? Do we expect advertising to create an emotional or rational preference or predisposition toward our brand so that in a specific buying situation the balance scale will tip in our favor? Is the main task of advertising to lighten the communications burden of the salesman, smoke out prospects for sales follow-up, build confidence (and orders) from retailers, or some other job?

Advertising can and does perform all of these tasks and many others with great speed and economy. But it cannot communicate all things to all people all at once. We must be selective and articulate in answering the question, "What do we want to communicate to whom?"

If we cannot answer this question, put the answer in writing, get agreement on it, and stick to it, the many cooks who brew (and taste) the advertising broth will serve up a concoction unfit for human consumption.

The fact that nine out of ten people, when asked the purpose of advertising, will give some variation of the answer, "to make a sale," does not mean that ultimately this is not true in most cases. (The exceptions occur when advertising is used for personnel recruitment, financial goals, political purposes, or public service; here we are concerned only with marketing.)

But when is the sale to be made? Next week? Next month? Several years from now? And is advertising expected to do this job singlehandedly? As Exhibit II shows, there are at least seven other forces that must be blended together to reach the ultimate objective of a sale. Advertising alone does not sell goods. Neither does any one of the other basic marketing functions. Each contributes in some way to the ultimate objective of the sale of a product or service.

Specifically, then, what do we expect advertising to contribute in each particular marketing situation? The deeper we probe, the more we come to grips with the obvious. Advertising does not physically bring buyer and seller together. Its purpose is to communicate something to somebody. And since communications is a process with several stages (see Exhibit III), both the "something" and the "somebody" vary with the situation.

EXHIBIT II. FORCES COMBINING TO MAKE A SALE

For example, suppose an automobile manufacturer is about ready to bring out a new compact car which he has named, let us say, "Venus." At the moment nobody has ever heard of Venus. His first communication job is therefore to make the consuming public aware of Venus. Next, he has certain information and mental impressions he wants to convey; Venus is a lithe, spirited beauty; a roomy, economical compact. He wants *comprehension* of these features. Then he wants to create a favorable disposition (emotional or rational) toward the purchase of his product; he wants to develop public *conviction* about it. Finally he wants to spur the consumer to *action*, which, in this case, might mean persuading the consumer to visit a dealer's showroom and ask for a demonstration. Note that I have carefully avoided including sales as an aim. Here, as in so many cases, the sale awaits other forces,

EXHIBIT III. STAGES IN THE COMMUNICATIONS PROCESS

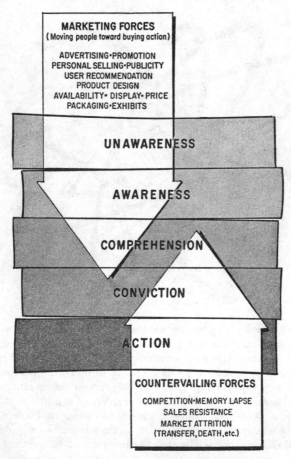

such as an artful demonstration of the car, a design the prospect cannot forget, a price and financing he can afford.

The four steps in the communicating process just described are, under one set of labels or another, as old as advertising and other forms of persuasive communication. It is inconceivable that we can get a consumer to comprehend the advantages of a product until he is aware of it, or to be convinced until he comprehends it. In a few isolated instances (mail-order advertising, for example), a single advertisement is expected to take a reader or viewer through the entire spectrum from unawareness to buying action, but such cases are rare. Most advertisers are building up their reservoirs of prospective buyers at each level, moving them up, one or two levels at a time, closer to the ultimate objective of a sale (or, in the case of such items as cigarettes, food, or toothpaste, repetitive purchases.).

At the same time, there are forces continually at work in the opposite direction. Competitors are constantly trying to switch consumers from our brand to theirs. Memory lapse is a strong countervailing force—people forget, very fast, a brand name or product benefit unless they are incessantly reminded. And so on.

Bear in mind that advertising makes its greatest economic contribution by communicating a selling message better, faster, cheaper than some other means of communication. With one product, let us say an industrial item, advertising's greatest contribution may be to establish brand-name awareness and knowledge of certain product features; with another product, let us say soap or auto tires, it may be to hammer away at brand superiority on some particular product feature. Or its job may be to create a favorable emotional disposition toward a brand (perfume, cigarette, beer). Then again, its main function may be to remind people to buy (soft drinks, razor blades), or to stimulate impulse purchase (food products).

Sometimes, too, the emphasis shifts at various stages of the product's development or at different seasons of the year. The job may be to build brand-name awareness during the introductory period, establish knowledge and preference during the period of growth, and remind consumers once the brand is well established.

This highly condensed discussion serves merely to illustrate a need, and a possible approach, to a long-neglected subject—a company's advertising rationale. Without such a rationale, management efforts to define specific tasks or goals for advertising and to measure results against those goals can be easily sidetracked or frustrated.

GUIDES TO RESULTS

We might define an advertising goal as "a specific communication task to be accomplished among a defined audience to a given degree in a given period of time."[4] Here, from experience and common sense, are six guidelines which management can make good use of in formulating a sound company program:

1. An advertising objective must be distinguished from a total marketing objective.

2. In writing and in conversation, executives should distinguish specific from general aims. I recommend using the word "goal" for the former, and "objective" for the latter. That nomenclature will be used in the remainder of this article.

3. Goals are based on an intimate knowledge of market opportunities and buying motives; they express realistic expectancy, not vain hopes.

4. Goals should be expressed in writing and should be agreed upon before programs or campaigns are undertaken. (Non-advertising people should participate in goal setting, but should leave execution to the experts.)

5. Bench marks are required if progress is to be measured.

6. Methods of measuring accomplishment are a built-in part of the plan.

Why are these guidelines important? How should they be used? Let us examine them in more detail.

It is important to distinguish advertising from other marketing objectives for a very practical reason. Unless we assign specific, measurable tasks to advertising, how are we going to tell whether the increase (or decrease) in sales is attributable to advertising, to product improvement, to more effective selling, to better distribution, to price changes, or to such other variables as weather or economic conditions.

[4] See Colley, *Defining Advertising Goals*, p. 6.

Let us assume that advertising does an outstanding job of increasing the propensity to buy a brand of toothpaste, an automobile, or an industrial chemical. It has made the prospect aware of the brand name, it has informed him of the product features, it has created a favorable disposition or frame of mind toward the product's benefits. It has even persuaded the prospect to take action. But let us say that when the prospect asks for, or reaches for, the brand of toothpaste, the dealer does not have it in stock; that when the prospect visits the auto dealer's showroom, the trade-in price for his old car is not right; that when the prospect inquiries about the industrial chemical, the salesman fails to follow up the lead. Advertising has completely fulfilled its part of the job: communicating. But there is no sale.

In other words, if we wish to define advertising goals, if we want to prepare plans for reaching these goals, and if we expect to measure achievement, then we must separate out of the total marketing complex the particular communicating tasks we will call upon advertising to perform. For example, suppose our product is a make of compact car. Suppose further that we have found out, through painstaking customer research, that the one outstanding feature people want in a compact car is roominess. Our car has 1½″ more headroom, 3″ more legroom, and so forth, than our leading competitor's car has. Our communication objective is to convey the information and the emotional impression or "image" that our car is the roomiest compact of them all. This separates the advertising objective from the over-all marketing objective, which may be to increase sales of the car.

Webster does not distinguish between the terms "objective" and "goal"; they are used interchangeably. A search of the field of management literature reveals little on the subject of an objective other than that it is the first and inescapable step in a plan. But some aims are broad, general, and long-term, and some aims are not; and the difference is significant from a management viewpoint. Let us, therefore, take the bull by the horns and use the following as working definitions:

Objective: a broad aim, a desired end.
Goal: an objective which has been made specific as to time and degree.

Example of a *marketing objective:* to increase sales.

Example of a *marketing goal:* to increase sales 10% in 1966.

Example of an *advertising objective:* to communicate the idea that brand A is a roomy compact.

Example of an *advertising goal:* to increase the number of good prospects for compact cars who get the message that brand A is the roomiest compact of them all, by one million in one year.

Can an advertising goal of the type just described be measured? The answer, in my opinion, is unquestionably yes—not with 100% accuracy, but certainly with quite high accuracy using present-day marketing research tools.

A goal must be realistic and attainable. It must be based on careful research into market opportunity, not on some vague hope that is pulled out of thin air. As an illustration, take the earlier-mentioned goal of registering the car "roominess" message with one million good prospects. First, we must define a "good" prospect. Next, we must have a reasonable estimate of the size of the selected audience. Let's assume it is ten million people. At this point the advertising man is challenged to put his knowledge and faith in advertising on the line. He must go beyond customary audience measurements such as "16% saw our latest magazine ad" or "16 million people viewed our latest television show." He must make a prediction of expected results in terms of changes in knowledge and attitude about the product. Such a prediction requires real depth of research and analysis. It is a tough job. But is it any tougher than predicting the number of people who will buy a new product or a new model (which somebody is forced to do in order for production to tool up to make the new product), or than predicting that the corporation will make 8.5% net on sales in the coming year (which somebody has to do for the sake of financial planning)?

Advertising people have not been accustomed to making such predictions in the past because of lack of information, lack of planning time, and, perhaps most important, the fact that management has not asked for it.

It is a strange state of affairs that many managements that spend millions of dollars for product research are penny pinchers when it comes to original, imaginative customer-attitude research. In fact, many scientifically trained managements are skeptics or agnostics with regard to customer research. They do not realize that a properly designed and executed survey of a few hundred people can be projected to a hundred thousand people or even a hundred million people with a fairly high degree of statistical accuracy.

"Why put it in writing?" some will say. "We know what we want to accomplish." If this is true, then it is no chore to put it in writing.

One or two people—let us say the advertising manager and agency account executive—may have a fair idea of what they personally want to accomplish. But what about all of the other people who get into the advertising act? What about the copywriter and the media man back in the agency—do they know precisely what you aim to accomplish? If not, how can they do an effective job of writing copy and selecting media? How about the people who approve advertising in the client organization—do they all agree?

This is where much of the waste comes in. People have not agreed in advance that this or that is what they want to communicate to whom.

They do not start giving serious thought to this question until they see semicomprehensives of typography, art work, and filmed commercials. Then they say, "But this is not what we want to say at all. Let's get more sell in the commercial about the design of the car or its economy or its price." What a waste of talent! What a waste of expensive materials! And the biggest waste is in compromise advertising—a conglomeration of different people's ideas of what to communicate, with no strong central message that gets through to the only people whose opinions count: the customers.

Lawyers learned several centuries ago that the only satisfactory way to arrive at human understanding is to put it in writing, and get agreement in advance.

We begin to realize why those at the top-management level must be involved in the planning phase. The advertising manager cannot say to his boss, "I want everybody at the final approval level to agree on the goals and then leave the cotton-picking details of art, copy, and media to me to work out with the agency." The boss, himself, must sound this note.

Some ask, "Isn't it enough to decide what we want to communicate? Why do we have to put numbers on it?"

If you want to measure results, the goal must be expressed in concrete, measurable terms. To illustrate with our earlier example of the compact car, we have reached an agreement that the one big idea we want to get across is "roominess." (Other themes, such as design, economy, and so on, are not omitted; they are simply given less prominence.) How many prospective purchasers already know or think this? Is it 10% or 90%, or somewhere in between? Suppose we establish the figure at 20%. Now we can set a goal—not some vain hope such as "we want to tell the world all the wonderful things about our product." We might decide that to raise the awareness figure from 20% to 30% would be a realistic achievement—a gain of one million informed prospects. Now we have some semblance of a logical approach to the big enigma, "How much to spend for advertising?" Research and media experts have something they can get their teeth into (instead of such generalities as "maximum reach" and "depth of coverage"). The cost of the campaign is estimated at $2 million or $2 per informed prospect. Is it worth it? This is for top management to decide. The question is clear and specific, not vague.

The answer to two big questions, "What did we accomplish?" and "Was it profitable?" are found in before-and-after studies of consumer knowledge, attitude, and buying action. One such study showed that the percentage of actual buyers of the product was twice as high among people who received and remembered the advertising message as among people who did not remember the advertising. The cost per delivered message and cost per new customer were so dramatically favorable to advertising, as compared with all other marketing forces, that the president was glad to double his advertising expenditure. Or it could have been the other way.

CASE STUDIES

To show what can be done if the foregoing guidelines are used, I want to cite examples of two cases where companies have come to grips with their marketing and advertising problems. (To avoid disclosure of confidential information, I have disguised data and products in the case examples.) Note that, despite the great contrast in situations, the thinking is similar in the two cases.

The first case involved a corporation selling gasoline in 14 states. The company was faced with the threat of a declining share of the market caused by new competitors entering the areas in which the company had historically held a strong position. It was recognized by marketing management that the first step toward more effective and more profitable advertising was for company and agency personnel to see eye-to-eye on the purpose and function of advertising in the company. Hence, a series of meetings was held in which sales, research, marketing, and general management people of the company met with various people in the agency to discuss and evolve advertising "philosophy" and "strategy."

These meetings were held in an atmosphere in which each participant was encouraged to speak his mind and exchange views and experiences. Discussion with "no holds barred" included such subjects as the following: What advertising can, and cannot, be expected to do in our business; why we advertise and what we seek to accomplish through advertising; and complete analysis of products and services—where we suffer competitive disadvantages, where we are on a par with competition, and points of product and service superiority.

For the first time, as a result of these meetings, the advertising, sales, technical, and financial people began to see eye-to-eye on the true purpose and capabilities of advertising. In previous years, the advertising team had developed an annual "pitch" or budget presentation complete with copy and media recommendations. In the new approach discussions were held many months in advance of the budget and copy approval period. The agenda was restricted to discussion of the question "What do we have to communicate?" Techniques of how to communicate (media, copy, and so on) were off limits at these "think" sessions.

Company executives concluded that six broad marketing objectives should be met:

1. Bring new customers into the company's stations.
2. Make steady customers out of occasional users.

3. Hold present users against competition.
4. Increase ratio of premium grade sales to regular grade sales.
5. Increase the sale of oil, tires, batteries, and accessories to present customers.
6. Enlarge the entire market by encouraging tourism.

They decided advertising was one of several forces that could help accomplish these objectives. Other forces included the stations themselves, the attitude and training of station attendants, the quality of products, product packaging, display, and price. They agreed that advertising could contribute to all of the above marketing objectives. However, if the same ad or campaign tried to do all of these things, they realized, it was not likely to succeed very much in any one of them.

The company and agency decided to define the function and role of advertising as follows. The primary aim of advertising was to get new customers and retain old ones. It could seldom be expected to induce "brand switching" (dramatic product advantages were few and far between). But the company's brand did have superior features; it was not like all other brands, as some people were inclined to think. Advertising's job was to communicate to motorists differences and benefits they were not aware of. These advantages should be put across in simple, homey language. Advertising's job was also to create a certain frame of mind about the company—that it was constantly on the alert to ways of improving the product for the motorist.

Executives realized that these expectations needed to be translated into hard, measurable criteria. The conclusion was reached that advertising effectiveness would be judged on its accomplishment of two tasks: the number of motorists who were aware of the differences and benefits of the company's gasoline, and the number of motorists who considered the brand superior or outstanding.

In order to make these goals specific and measurable it was necessary to conduct research among a representative sample of the motoring public in the marketing area. The first research study was conducted to establish a bench mark. Later studies were conducted to determine the progress in communicating "the intended messages to the intended audiences." Exhibit IV shows the kind of summary data management obtained (the figures are, of course, disguised).

While I shall not describe the research program, I might mention one detail that is indicative of the kind of work done. A representative sample or panel of motorists was selected. Prior to the advertising campaign, and at six-month intervals thereafter, questions similar to the following were asked.

EXHIBIT IV. STUDY OF ADVERTISING RESULTS

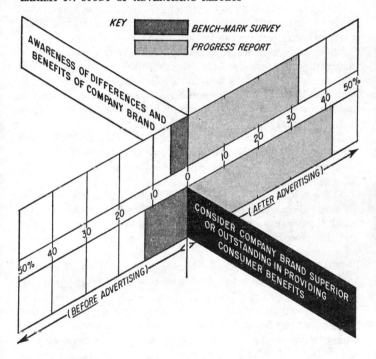

"No doubt you have used or read about several different brands of gasoline. Can you think of any ways in which the gasoline of one manufacturer is different from that of another?" Answers were coded according to whether messages contained in the ads had registered with the consumer. For example, the following verbatim answer was credited as message registration: "They put stuff in the gas that keeps the carburetor and gas lines clean."

"Here are five cards containing the names of brands of gasoline sold in this area. Please tell me what brand you think is doing the best job of providing the motorist with improved gasoline." Consumers were further queried until brands were ranked 1 to 5.

The second case, very different from the first, concerns the manufacturer of a drilling bit used in drilling oil wells. Made of a special alloy steel, the bit lasts longer by 25% than others and leads to important savings in time and costs for drilling firms. The marketing picture can be summarized as follows.

The market consists of oil companies who let the contracts, contractors who drill the wells, and distributors who sell bits and other supplies. The total number of "buying influences" is estimated at 15,000, including engineers, superintendents, and other technical and managerial personnel who have an important voice in the specification and purchase of drilling bits.

Research shows that only 50% of the 15,000 buying influences are acquainted with the new, superior drilling bit. And only 25% are familiar with the claim that this bit reduces net over-all drilling costs.

The company has ten salesmen. The average salesman makes 20 sales calls a week. Each sales call costs an average of $35. It is much too expensive to use salesmen to convey the message that (a) this product exists, and (b) it offers decided cost reduction advantages.

Besides, it would take the salesmen a year and a half to make just one informative sales call on each of the 15,000 buying influences.

In this situation, the salesman's job is to convince prospects that the product can be applied to their particular technical problems, to get buying action, and to aid customers in successful product application. Advertising's job, on the other hand, is to raise the number of "buying influences" who are acquainted with the product from 50% to 75% in one year, and to increase the number who get the message, "reduces over-all drilling cost," from 25% to 50% in one year. This separates advertising's tasks from the total marketing job to be done. Now we can plan to measure how effectively advertising performs in its assigned role.

GETTING ACTION STARTED

An agency executive who has served on the Procter & Gamble account, when he was asked the secret of P & G's success, summed it up in five words: "Meticulous attention to marketing detail." He went on to say, "They drive the ordinary advertising agency man nuts with their probing questions. Who? How? Why? A new man on the account is stumped for the answers. But he doesn't go into the second inning unprepared—that is, not if he wants to stay in the league."

I think this observation is a clue to what top management can do to start real progress in advertising. I refer to the art of asking provocative, penetrating questions. Indeed, it has worked so well where tried that one wonders why every company hasn't used it. For example, the chairman of the board of a leading corporation has said: "Over a period of years, top management has asked some very searching questions to find out whether the proposed programs are based on really sound concepts. Over this same period our advertising has vastly improved. I can say with confidence that our advertising people have developed better techniques and reasons for what they are doing because we make it very clear that we expect a reasoned analysis behind a proposal."

What kinds of questions should the executive ask advertising people? The following checklist has been gleaned from the experience of many successful advertisers.

1. *Whom are we trying to reach with our advertising?* When you ask this question, do not accept vague answers such as "housewives," "farmers," "businessmen," "car owners," "plastic fabricators," and so forth. If your product is cake mixes, you are interested only in those who bake cakes often enough to make themselves worthwhile prospects. If your product is hay balers, you are interested only in those farmers who bale enough hay to warrant mechanized equipment.

2. *What is the size of the audience for the company's advertising?* Insist on specific answers; get to the hard core of the particular audience you want to reach. What you are looking for is data

as factual as these: There are 11,000,000 housewives who serve tea nearly every day; there are 7,500 engineers in aircraft plants who influence the purchase of electronic testing equipment; there are 8,600,000 motorists who say they will give serious consideration to the purchase of a compact car in the coming year. Advertising and market research people can get this kind of information. Many already have it, but the chances are it is buried in some big, thick statistical report.

Insist that it be distilled to the essence and written into the plan. Insist that everyone who has a voice in advertising decisions agrees in advance on the size and character of the audience to be reached.

3. *What are the deciding factors that cause people to buy or not buy our products?* Do not be satisfied with hearsay information that floats back from dealer to salesman to district manager to sales manager to advertising manager to agency. Information that goes through all these layers of insulation is weak and often distorted. Do not be satisfied with warmed-over data gathered by others for some other purpose, or with a "quickie" mail questionnaire. Insist on a professional survey in depth of buying motives, habits, attitudes, and characteristics of the "core group" of customers and potential customers.

4. *What do we want to communicate to our prospects?* This is the key question. With a good solid background on buying motives there is no excuse for vague platitudes such as: "We want them to know we make quality products." Such generalities are an unmistakable sign that the mission of advertising has not been thought through.

If the preceding steps have been done properly, there should be one primary message (plus several subsidiary messages). Examples of a primary message are: "Convey the idea that car A is the roomiest compact of them all," or "Register conviction that brand B hay baler pays for itself in two years."

5. *What combination of media will do the best job, at lowest cost, of registering the intended message with the intended audience?* Too often the media director is brought into the picture in the last stages of the advertising proposal. He is asked to come up with a media schedule for spending so much money. Nobody has told him that management wants to convey this message to

that audience. He is asked to whip together a media package a few days (and nights) before the big pitch.

To avoid this situation the executive making the final decision is well within his prerogative to ask for some good solid reasons as to why the agency recommends, say, a half-hour prime-time weekly network show, full-page newspaper supplements, or a 12-time schedule in three weekly and four women's service magazines, or spot radio in 100 market areas. Why is this particular combination recommended? Has it been compounded according to some theories of "reach," "penetration," and "coverage" and without full consideration of the particular communication job at hand?

6. *How many of the target audience already know or believe the basic message?* We must have a bench mark against which to measure accomplishment in communicating a sales message. This message may be intended to produce:

Awareness of brand or company.
Comprehension of certain product features.
Conviction of certain product benefits.
Action (visit a dealer, asking for information, and so on).

In some cases the goal is to increase the number of people who know, understand, or believe a basic message. In other cases, the goal may be to retain an already high degree of brand awareness through intensive repetition. In any event, we must know where we stand today in the mind of the customer before we can measure progress.

7. *How are we going to measure the results of the proposed advertising campaign?* The measurement program (including techniques, timing, sampling methods, and so on) should be a built-in part of the plan, not an after-thought. It must go deeper than finding out how many people were exposed to the ads, although that may be an important stage of the work. Its purpose is to measure changes in human knowledge, attitude, buying propensity, and buying behavior.

One reason for past failure in measuring results is the attitude that this job should be provided (for free) by the advertising agency. In most cases such an attitude is shortsighted and delusive. For one thing, agencies cannot afford to provide this service with anything approaching the needed depth. Furthermore, it is asking too much to expect the agency to do an unbiased job of measuring its own efforts.

The trend today among astute advertisers is to let copy pre-testing be the agencies' responsibility but to assign the job of measuring results to other firms. While this adds to the indirect costs of advertising, that is, expenses not directly associated with procuring space and copy, it may lead to more effective, more efficient advertising campaigns.

Appendix

In answer to many requests for more detailed figures on advertising-earnings ratios, I have calculated the A/E ratios for the 100 leading advertisers.[5] These figures (see the table below) show that, among nearly half of the 100 leaders, advertising expenditures exceed annual earnings. For example, General Foods spent $1.46 for advertising in relation to each earnings (net profit after taxes) dollar. In four out of five companies, advertising expenditures exceed average quarterly earnings. For example, General Electric spent 26¢ in advertising per earnings dollar.

In addition to the ratios of 100 leaders, the advertising-earnings ratios have been summarized for all United States corporations combined:

	1950	1960	1961	1962*
Advertising (in billions)	$ 5.7	$11.9	$11.8	$12.4
Net profits (in billions)	$22.8	$23.0	$23.3	$25.
Ratio of advertising to net profit	.25	.52	.51	.50

Source: Earnings data from U.S. Department of Commerce; advertising expenditures from *Printers' Ink*.
* Estimated.

This summary shows that corporations now spend 50¢ on advertising for each dollar of profit, compared with an expenditure of only 25¢ per dollar of profit in 1950. Advertising expenditures have doubled in the last decade; profits show little increase.

The A/E ratio is a new concept in the growing field of man-

[5] The author provided this supplementary information in the *Harvard Business Review,* November–December 1962.

agement indexes. Like price-earnings ratios, current assets to current liabilities, and other management tools, it provides quick insight into certain aspects of the business. But, like all ratios, it should be used with knowledge of other factors and with caution against erroneous or fallacious conclusions. In presenting these figures I shall, accordingly, stress some cautions in their use.

Customarily, advertising expenditures have been expressed as a percentage of sales dollars. For example, Chrysler spent 2.2% of its sales dollars in advertising in 1961, a little above General Motors and Ford (both 1.3%), and slightly less than American Motors (2.4%). But differences in the A/E ratio are fantastically large. Chrysler spent $4.26 in advertising for each earnings (net profit after taxes) dollar. Ford's figure, by comparison, was $0.22 on the earnings dollar. So Ford's advertising expenditures were slightly less than its average quarterly earnings while Chrysler's were more than four times earnings for the entire year.

It would be utterly foolhardy to conclude from these figures that Chrysler is spending too much for advertising. Perhaps the opposite is true. If Chrysler had spent more money for advertising (or found ways to make its present advertising dollars work harder), perhaps the net profit figure would have been higher (and the A/E ratio lower).

The A/E ratio is simply a device for bringing dramatically to the attention of top management the fact that advertising is a vitally important profit-creating force. Intelligently and creatively used, advertising reduces the costs of both distributing and producing goods and increases net earnings.

The A/E ratio is a signal to those at the executive committee and board level that they can no longer concentrate their thinking on matters of plant and equipment or finance and neglect advertising because it is a "mystery" to them. An item in the corporate budget that represents something approaching quarterly or annual earnings suggests that steps be taken to dispel the mystery that has surrounded advertising at the final decision-making level.

This is precisely what happened at Ford. Members of top management there told me that the entire executive group was bound and determined to get better answers to the question, "What do we get for what we spend in advertising?"

RATIO OF ADVERTISING EXPENDITURES TO EARNINGS FOR THE 100 LARGEST ADVERTISERS

	Thousands of dollars		A/E Ratio
Company	Earnings	Advertising	
General Motors Corp.	$892,821	$141,500	.16
Procter & Gamble Co.	109,356	132,724	1.22
General Foods Corp.	72,244	105,000	1.46
Ford Motor Co.	409,579	90,000	.22
Lever Bros. Co.	10,500	87,000	8.29
American Home Products Corp.	50,163	65,300	1.30
General Electric Co.	242,100	63,000	.26
Colgate-Palmolive Co.	4,919	57,000	11.59
National Dairy Products Corp.	45,118	53,000	1.18
R. J. Reynolds Tobacco Co.	117,249	50,000	.43
Chrysler Corp.	11,138	47,441	4.26
Sears, Roebuck and Co.	—	46,700	—
Bristol-Myers Co.	12,957	44,000	3.40
General Mills, Inc.	10,154	40,000	3.94
E. I. du Pont de Nemours & Co.	418,000	39,000	.09
American Telephone & Telegraph Co.	1,325,587	37,714	.03
Distillers Corp.—Seagrams Ltd.	30,944	36,802	1.19
Eastman Kodak Co.	130,203	36,500	.28
American Tobacco Co.	68,734	36,000	.52
The Coca-Cola Company	42,487	33,000	.78
Liggett and Myers Tobacco Co.	26,760	33,000	1.23
The Gillette Co.	42,761	32,500	.76
Westinghouse Electric Corp.	45,446	32,500	.71
Campbell Soup Company	43,909	31,625	.72
P. Lorillard Co.	28,419	31,500	1.11
Kellogg Co.	22,287	31,500	1.41
Corn Products Co.	42,571	31,130	.73
Warner-Lambert Pharmaceutical Co.	11,463	31,000	2.71
National Biscuit Co.	28,400	30,000	1.06
Philip Morris, Inc.	21,511	30,000	1.40
Radio Corp. of America	35,511	28,600	.81
Pillsbury Co.	7,671	28,300	3.72
Sterling Drug Inc.	23,464	28,200	1.20
Miles Laboratories, Inc.	5,480	27,500	5.02
Brown & Williamson Tobacco Corp.	—	27,000	—
Goodyear Tire & Rubber Co.	76,189	27,000	.35
Standard Brands, Inc.	18,715	26,600	1.42
Standard Oil Co. (New Jersey)	758,083	26,491	.03
Anheuser-Busch, Inc.	15,115	23,500	1.56
Firestone Tire & Rubber Co.	63,629	23,000	.36
Standard Oil Co. (Indiana)	153,837	23,000	.15
Schenley Industries, Inc.	—	23,000	—
Revlon, Inc.	12,188	22,900	1.88

Source: Dollar figures from *Advertising Age,* August 27, 1962, p. 39.
Note: Dashes represent companies for which information is unavailable.

RATIO OF ADVERTISING EXPENDITURES TO EARNINGS FOR THE 100
LARGEST ADVERTISERS *(Continued)*

| | Thousands of dollars | | A/E |
Company	Earnings	Advertising	Ratio
Borden Co.	30,082	22,500	.75
Johnson & Johnson	16,592	21,000	1.27
American Motors Corp.	23,578	20,700	.88
American Cyanamid Co.	49,353	20,627	.42
Quaker Oats Co.	15,079	20,000	1.33
National Distillers & Chemical Corp.	23,259	19,758	.85
Stanley Warner Corporation	4,301	19,500	4.54
S. C. Johnson and Son, Inc.	—	19,000	—
Jos. Schlitz Brewing Co.	6,972	19,000	2.73
Union Carbide Corp.	142,298	19,000	.13
Swift & Co.	12,049	18,000	1.50
Armour & Co.	13,121	17,820	1.37
Scott Paper Co.	31,141	17,500	.56
Pepsi-Cola Co.	14,368	17,069	1.18
Shell Oil Co.	140,358	16,800	.12
Beech-Nut Life Savers, Inc.	10,312	16,500	1.60
Carter Products, Inc.	8,778	16,000	1.82
Ralston Purina Co.	19,907	16,000	.80
Hiram Walker-Gooderham & Worts Ltd.	26,362	16,000	.61
The B. F. Goodrich Co.	31,035	15,000	.48
United States Steel Corp.	190,200	14,611	.08
Alberto-Culver Co.	881	14,500	16.50
Continental Baking Co.	7,564	14,500	1.92
Gulf Oil Corp.	338,537	14,000	.04
Richardson-Merrell, Inc.	17,025	14,000	.82
U.S. Rubber Co.	27,096	13,550	.50
Olin Mathieson Chemical Corp.	32,125	13,500	.42
Carnation Co.	12,189	13,100	1.07
Chesebrough-Pond's Inc.	5,749	13,000	2.26
Texaco Inc.	430,116	12,900	.03
The Nestlé Company, Inc.	—	12,500	—
Mead Johnson & Co.	9,624	12,300	1.28
J. B. Williams Co.	—	12,100	—
Helene Curtis Industries, Inc.	3,427	12,000	3.50
Columbia Broadcasting System, Inc.	22,037	11,660	.53
Wm. Wrigley Jr., Co.	11,692	11,600	.99
Falstaff Brewing Corp.	5,790	11,300	1.95
H. J. Heinz Co.	14,165	11,300	.80
Pabst Brewing Co.	5,091	11,000	2.16
Aluminum Co. of America	43,048	11,000	.26
Kimberly-Clark Corp.	31,545	10,830	.34
Armstrong Cork Co.	18,506	10,500	.57
Socony Mobil Oil Co.	211,319	10,311	.05
Seven-Up Co.	—	9,768	—
The Mennen Co.	2,000	9,300	4.65
Hunt Foods & Industries, Inc.	12,798	9,000	.70
American Chicle Co.	9,630	8,950	.93

RATIO OF ADVERTISING EXPENDITURES TO EARNINGS FOR THE 100
LARGEST ADVERTISERS (*Concluded*)

| | Thousands of dollars | | A/E |
Company	Earnings	Advertising	Ratio
Dow Chemical Co.	64,439	8,841	.13
Simoniz Co.	—	8,800	—
Trans World Airlines, Inc.	14,745	8,800	.60
Minnesota Mining & Mfg. Co.	74,914	8,570	.11
Block Drug Co.	—	8,300	—
Prudential Insurance Co. of America	—	8,231	—
United Air Lines, Inc.	3,693	8,100	2.20
California Packing Corp.	17,225	7,035	.41
Kaiser Industries Corp.	—	7,000	—
Andrew Jergens Co.	2,295	6,900	3.01

Instead of an annual or quarterly meeting in which advertising
budgets and programs were "presented" to management, top executives moved advertising up to the top of their own agendas.
Weekly reviews were held. Ford launched an advertising and
marketing research program that overshadowed anything ever
seen before in the industry. Top management did not get into the
technical details of copy and media. To quote from one interview,
"The executive who tries to become his own chief engineer or
advertising manager is a fool. Techniques should be left to the
experts." But the chief executive cannot escape responsibility
for evaluating return on advertising investment.

In looking at consumer goods, some of the ratios may seem in-
congruous, especially to executives of producer goods companies.
In cosmetics, Alberto Culver, for example, spent $16.50 in ad-
vertising for every dollar of net profit. "How could this possibly
be justified?" some may ask. The answer may be quite simple. A
relative newcomer to the cosmetic field might decide very wisely
to spend practically all of its profits in the early years in advertising as a means of carving out a brand franchise and share of market. The strategy of pumping all profits back into advertising
during the growth period has paid off handsomely in later years
for some of the most profitable consumer goods companies in the
United States.

In launching a new product it is not unheard of for a company to budget $10 million for advertising with anticipated first year's sales of $10 million. The product is not expected to reach a break-even point for three or more years. Such a strategy is no different from the practice of investing in research and development or tools and dies with the anticipation of long-term payout.

A high A/E ratio such as Lever Brothers' 8.29 or Colgate's 11.59 does not necessarily signify over-spending on advertising. Such ratios might be caused by a heavy schedule of new product launchings. Then again, they could indicate an effort to regain a market position that has deteriorated because of failure to maintain an adequate advertising program in past years.

In the final analysis, there is one key criterion of the success of a publicly held corporation: long-term growth in earnings per share. The trend toward regarding advertising in this light is growing. The practice of setting advertising budgets as a fixed percentage of past or anticipated sales is old-fashioned. In fact, it can be downright dangerous.

Determining how much to spend for advertising, and what the company gets in return for its outlay, is an inescapable function of top management. To reiterate the theme of "Squeezing the Waste Out of Advertising": management is beginning to realize that advertising does not have to remain a dark mystery. Results can be evaluated. Waste can be drastically reduced. But only if top management, advertising management, and agency see eye-to-eye on both marketing and advertising goals.

16

MULTISTAGE APPROACH TO PRICING

ALFRED R. OXENFELDT

Of all the areas of executive decision, pricing is perhaps the most fuzzy. Whenever a price problem is discussed by a committee, divergent figures are likely to be recommended without a semblance of consensus. Although unanimity in marketing decisions is a custom more remarkable in its occurrence than in its absence, agreement in pricing decisions is even more rare.

This paper accordingly presents a long-run, policy-oriented approach to pricing which should reduce the range of prices considered in specific situations and consequently improve the decisions which result. This approach, which to the best of my knowledge is new, calls for the price decision to be made in six successive steps, each one narrowing the alternatives to be considered at the next step.

Is this method just another mechanical pricing formula? Hardly, for it is my conviction that the quest for mechanical pricing methods is unduly optimistic, if not downright naive. Nevertheless, many businessmen consistently employ almost mechanical formulas for pricing. They do this even though they scoff at the claim that there are reliable fixed formulas for handling personnel problems or making advertising or capital outlay decisions. Certainly, experience has not produced recipes that guarantee correct decisions in any sphere of business. The best of them only apply under normal conditions, and it is most rare indeed that conditions resembling normalcy prevail.

On the other hand, many discussions of pricing present a long list of factors to be "taken into account," carefully weighed and balanced, and then subjected to a process called "judgment." While a specific price is thus arrived at, this does not alter the fact that intelligent and experienced business executives using the method will arrive at widely different price decisions—all based on the same information.

Yet, even if mechanical pricing formulas are the hope of the optimistic, it would be excessively pessimistic to resign ourselves to a formless consideration of all the relevant factors and to a random exercise of judgment. Many things are known about the subject that would be extremely helpful to those responsible for making such decisions.

SEQUENTIAL STAGES

In order to organize the various pieces of information and considerations that bear on price decisions, a multistage approach to pricing can be a very helpful tool. This method sorts the major elements in a pricing decision into six successive stages:

1. Selecting market targets.
2. Choosing a brand "image."
3. Composing a marketing mix.
4. Selecting a pricing policy.
5. Determining a pricing strategy.
6. Arriving at a specific price.

The sequence of the stages is an essential part of the method, for each step is calculated to simplify the succeeding stage and to reduce the likelihood of error. One might say that this method divides the price decision into manageable parts, each one logically antecedent to the next. In this way, the decision at each stage facilitates all subsequent decisions. This approach might also be regarded as a process of selective search, where the number of alternatives deserving close consideration is reduced drastically by making the decision in successive stages. Of course, one could arrive at the same result by simultaneously considering all the factors mentioned—but it might require a computer to do so.

While it appears that this approach is applicable over a broad range of industry and trade, the great diversity of business situations precludes the possibility of its being a universally applicable method. No rigid approach, and certainly not the one presented here, offers a guarantee of reaching the best—or even a satisfactory—price decision. It must be adapted to prevailing circumstances; consequently, information, experience, and the application of rigorous logic are required for its optimum utilization.

MARKET TARGETS

A going concern is "committed," confined, and tied down by several important circumstances which can be altered only over a considerable period of time. It must live with many conditions, even while it may attempt to alter them. Also, an operating business possesses specified resources on which it will strive to capitalize in achieving its objectives. For example, a firm will have:

A fixed production location, given physical facilities, and a particular production and sales labor force.

A set of distribution arrangements through which the firm generally sells, including particular distributors with whom it has established relationships.

Contracts with suppliers, customers, laborers, and lenders of funds.

A portfolio of customers who have a definite opinion of the firm's reliability, and the quality of its offerings and service.

These commitments and resources of a firm contain pricing implications. Mainly, they determine the type of product that it can make, the type of service it can render, and its probable costs of operation. What is more, these circumstances form the basis for the most fundamental pricing decision that management should make—namely, the types of customers, or market segments, it will attempt to cultivate.

By virtue of its fixed commitments, then, a firm is limited to the several market segments it can reasonably hope to capture. It has customer connections on which it can capitalize, and it has a variety of strengths and weaknesses that limit its choice among potential submarkets for intensive cultivation.

Two examples drawn from the television industry will help

to clarify this crucial first stage. Certainly, no two firms could possibly exemplify all situations, nor is it possible for an outsider to explain satisfactorily why specific decisions were made in specific cases. However, these illustrations are intended to indicate what factors management must consider if it is to apply the multistage approach. They do not describe how management reasoned or what would have been the best decision under the circumstances.

First, consider the pricing problem of the Zenith Radio Corporation at the time it started to produce television sets in 1948:

This company, which is one of the two largest television set producers now, dropped out of the automobile radio business in order to manufacture television sets. (At that time, it was the largest single producer of automobile radios, but this business was not very profitable.) Zenith possessed these resources and was subject to these commitments and limitations that could have influenced its selection of market targets in the television business.

It had production facilities in Chicago that had been designed for and used in radio production for many years; its labor force and supervisory personnel were familiar with the electronics business. The firm had substantial manufacturing skills in electronics because of its work for the military during and after World War II. Zenith could assess its manufacturing capabilities as very substantial, but not outstanding.

Financially, Zenith was also in a very strong and liquid position and could readily have undertaken heavy expenditures at this time.

But Zenith's outstanding resource was a distributor and dealer organization that was as good as that possessed by any other firm in the nation. Its dealers commanded strong loyalty among their clientele not only in small communities but also in large cities—a most vital fact in view of the technical character of television and the great power that retailers wield over consumer choices of such products. Here Zenith was helped by the fact that it had acquired an excellent reputation for quality products in radios; for many years, it was the Cadillac of the radio industry. Zenith management, like all other radio manufacturers who entered the television business, decided to sell its sets through the distributor organization it had already created; its distributors, in turn, would sell them mainly to dealers already buying Zenith radios.

There were also several other peripheral advantages. Zenith was closely identified, in the minds of many consumers, with hearing aids which were widely advertised as much on grounds of moderate price as in terms of high quality. Further, Zenith started to telecast, experimentally, in the Chicago market even before World War II and had some local identification as a telecaster, as well as a manufacturer. Its products were strongly favored in the Chicago market.

In summary, Zenith Radio could count on its strong distributor and retail organizations as its outstanding resource, while recognizing that it did not possess any particular advantage in costs of manufacture or quality of product and, in fact, that its behavior in the television business was necessarily circumscribed by its radio and hearing aid business. Zenith's management would have required very strong reasons to choose as its market targets customers who were very different from those who bought its radios and hearing aids.

Under these circumstances, Zenith management might have decided to attempt to reach customers at almost all levels of income. Partly, it could do this by including "low-end" and promotional models in its line; partly because television sets were sold on installment credit involving modest monthly charges; and partly because, at least in the early years, television purchases were spread rather evenly over all income groups.

On the other hand, Zenith management, as its first step, might well expect to cultivate particularly those consumers who were conservative and quality-conscious, who felt a strong loyalty to particular appliance retailers, and who were located mainly in small cities and towns. On this basis, the Zenith customer targets would not include "snobs" who, at that time, favored the Dumont brand and, to a lesser degree, the Radio Corporation of America's set. Also they would not include bargain hunters. Rather Zenith's customers would be the kind of people who feel that "you get what you pay for." (Zenith would presumably capitalize on its strong position in the Chicago area by special measures aimed at that market.)

Now contrast Zenith's position with that of Columbia Broadcasting System, Inc., when it started to produce and sell television sets under its own brand name in 1953.

CBS resources and commitments were altogether different from those possessed by Zenith, with the result that the two companies could have been expected to cultivate different market targets. Specifically, in the case of Columbia Broadcasting—

CBS executives were primarily familiar with the management of entertainment talent and the creation and servicing of a network of stations. Although its phonograph record and hi-fi phonograph business did involve a type of production and distribution experience, CBS was completely new to major appliance manufacturing and possessed no suitable distribution facilities whatsoever for appliances.

In addition, CBS acquired production facilities when it entered the television business that were of relatively poor quality. The size, location, equipment, plant layout, and employee facilities of the Air King firm, which CBS acquired, were widely recognized as mediocre or below. Many people familiar with that company and with the television industry strongly doubted that Air King's management was capable of establishing a prestige national brand and producing the high quality product needed to support a quality reputation.

On the other hand, CBS had some genuine pluses in its favor. Its radio and television networks were the largest, and enjoyed great prestige at the time CBS entered the television set business. Also, by virtue of its telecasting facilities, it could advertise its sets during unsponsored programs at virtually no out-of-pocket cost. It could, moreover, get the advertising support—mainly through testimonials from outstanding personalities like Arthur Godfrey, Edward R. Murrow, Jack Benny, and others—for little or no cost.

To what kinds of customers could a firm with these resources and limitations appeal? One way that CBS might have adjusted to its particular combination of resources and weaknesses would have been to select as its chief consumer market target the metropolitan customer who is anxious to be associated with prestigeful figures, vulnerable to advertising over radio and television, prepared to pay a premium price, and relatively unfamiliar with or insensitive to technical performance features. But this market target would hardly have been very large in the first instance; moreover, CBS management must have recognized that many other firms were cultivating this type of customer.

It would appear, then, that CBS was compelled to select its market targets mainly in terms of distributors and retailers, rather than ultimate consumers. Whereas Zenith already possessed a strong distributor and dealer organization, CBS had to construct one. Only after it secured representation on the market could it hope to sell to consumers.

CBS management must have realized that whatever it did in an effort to win distributors and dealers would also influence the kind of customers it could hope to attract. For example, if it had to extend big markups to distributors and retailers to get them to handle its sets (combined with the fact that its production facilities were mediocre), CBS would be compelled to charge a relatively high retail price for its sets. In turn, it would have to rely on intensive advertising to persuade consumers to pay these higher prices and find methods of making its sets appear luxurious and worth the high price.

In addition to having to accept the fact of a relatively high-price product, CBS would feel pressure to concentrate on customers in the large metropolitan centers, because of the need to build large sales volume rapidly in order to get its production costs in line with those of its competitors. Even as early as 1953, the large metropolitan markets were pervaded by severe price competition among set manufacturers and relatively little emphasis on quality and brand loyalty on the part of retailers. Independent distributors were leaving the business because of great manufacturer pressure to gain heavy sales volume. Hence CBS could not have much hope of obtaining strong independent distributors for its line in most metropolitan markets, but would have to look ahead to a considerable period during which it "supported" both distributors and key retailers to obtain an organization that would distribute its sets.

Zenith and CBS have been cited as companies that would have been justified in placing relatively little weight on price in their selection of target submarkets. These companies mainly had to avoid alienating customers by charging prices that were far out of line with other companies' prices. Not all television set manufacturers could have taken this approach, however. Thus, companies like Admiral, Emerson, and producers of private brands were under pressure to cultivate customers who place heavy emphasis on price. Why? Because in some cases they lacked the personnel and financial resources to sustain a claim of quality and style superiority; or, because their experience in the major appliance business before adding a line of television receivers could have indicated that they had won acceptance mainly among customers who want moderate quality at prices below the average; or, finally, because their chief asset was a very efficient manufacturing organization that could imitate the products of their more progressive rivals at low cost.

Other industries offer clear examples of firms that selected as market targets persons who were not particularly interested in high intrinsic quality or style. A fairly obvious example is the Scripto pencil, which offers satisfactory performance at minimum cost. Apparently the customers Scripto selected for intensive cultivation were those who would want a pencil to write with and not for display, a pencil they could afford to lose or misplace. Similarly, some producers of private brands of aspirin have selected as market targets those persons who know of the fundamental similarity of aspirin quality and who actively desire to minimize their outlays for this product.

These examples illustrate a point that may not have been particularly clear in the discussion of the Zenith and CBS examples: one important criterion in the selection of market targets is customer awareness of and sensitivity to price.

BRAND "IMAGE"

Once management has defined the submarkets it wishes to cultivate most actively, it must select the methods it will use to achieve its goal.

Success in the market place for more and more products seems to depend on creating a favorable general image (often vague and formless) of the product or company among prospective customers. The selection and development of this image become of prime importance and have a direct bearing on price, as will be explained subsequently. A favorable image is especially important when one sells consumers' goods, but only rarely is it completely unimportant even in the sales of producers' goods. Buyers' very perceptions are affected by their prior attitudes, the actions and opinions of others, first impressions and early associations. It is a rare firm that can ignore the total impression its potential customers have of it and of what it is selling.

The firm's selection of its company and brand image should be dictated by the types of customers it is trying to attract. Submarkets may be likened to targets at which the seller is firing, and "images" are powerful weapons that can be used to hit the targets.

Almost every going concern has invested—often very heavily —in the creation of a favorable image. Most businesses know what image they wish to achieve and are concerned lest they or their products fail to have a favorable "meaning" to potential customers. At the very minimum, almost every management knows there are certain images that customers might have of it and its product that would prove disastrous.

The type of image a firm can create of itself and its wares depends to a considerable degree, again, on its fixed commitments and resources. With its physical and personnel resources, there is a limit to what it can do to alter the prevailing opinions—for they reflect all that the company was and did in the past. In that sense, the basic commitments limit the type of image a firm can establish, how much time it will require to establish it, and the cost. Even as brand image is frequently an effective weapon in cultivating particular submarkets, price helps to create the brand image. It is for this reason that the selection of a brand image which is consistent with the firm's market targets implies particular forms of price behavior.

Let us carry our original examples a little further. Given the market targets that they might have selected, as explained earlier, what brand image could Zenith and CBS try to create? As in the selecting of market targets, every firm has only a few reasonable alternatives from which to choose its desired image.

For example, Zenith already possessed a brand image that contributed strongly to its success in the radio and hearing aid business. Even if another image might have been advantageous for its television business, Zenith's management could hardly afford to injure the bird already in hand. Consequently, Zenith would be obliged to perpetuate for its television line the brand image it had already established in its other activities. As it happened, that image was altogether suitable for its television set business.

To implement this line of thinking, Zenith would be obliged to establish the image of a "premium" product and of a company that was oldtime, conservative, and mainly concerned with quality and craftsmanship. Above all, it would seek to avoid high-pressure selling, emphasis on price, and shoddiness of product. In styling, it could pursue a safe policy of including a wide variety of styles, while being especially careful not to alienate its conservative small-town customers with models too far in the vanguard of modern design.

CBS faced a very different choice with regard to brand image. It, too, could not afford to jeopardize its eminent position in the radio and television network field, for those activities were very profitable and would always remain its major sources of income. Except for this limitation, CBS had a relatively free choice of brand images.

CBS could well undertake to be the style leader in the industry. This image would be consistent with relatively inefficient manufacturing facilities, concentration on selling in the metropolitan market, and the necessity of charging a high retail price. It would appear that few brand images other than for advanced styling and for gimmicks would have been consistent with the resources and limitations on CBS at this time.

In contrast to Zenith and CBS, other television set producers sought a brand image that did have an important price ingredient. Again, most producers of private brands, Admiral, Emerson, and others, often featured price in their advertising and apparently sought to sensitize prospective customers to price. They could purposely become identified as firms that were not afraid to discuss price and that seemed confident they offered better values than their competitors.

Many firms outside the television set industry attempt to establish a brand image that has a heavy price ingredient. Among producers, one finds Caron boasting that its Joy perfume is the most expensive, and Chock Full o' Nuts implying much the same thing about its coffee. Without being explicit, some retailers seem to claim that no stores charge more than they—and, strangely, this image is a source of strength. The retail world is full of stores that claim that they are never knowingly undersold; on the other hand, it is difficult to name manufacturers who claim that their product is the cheapest on the market—probably because of the implication that theirs is also the brand of lowest quality. (Automobile manufacturers occasionally claim to be the "cheapest of the low-price three," but none has occupied that position long.)

MARKETING MIX

The third stage in multistage pricing calls for the selection of a combination of sales promotion devices that will create and reinforce the desired company and product brand image and achieve maximum sales for the planned level of dollar outlays. In this stage, a role must be assigned to price. The role in which price is cast should be selected only after assessment is made as to the relative effectiveness and appropriateness of each sales promotion device that might be employed. The short-term gains of certain sales promotion devices may entail injury to the image objectives of the firm. Conflicts of such a nature must be resolved at this stage.

Then, too, a firm might achieve precisely the desired image and still find customers very hard to get. It is not enough to establish the desired image; it must be an effective image. Furthermore, even though a firm may establish highly favorable impressions of itself and its wares, the company and its products must live up to the image they foster. Not only must its product be "within reach" in price, but it must be accessible by being offered through convenient channels of distribution, and must be sold in outlets where customers like to buy.

The third stage builds directly upon the second. The need to conform to the prior decision about company and brand image greatly limits the number of price alternatives that a price setter can reasonably consider.

The marketing mix decision at this stage need not be translated into specific dollars and cents amounts to be devoted to each sales promotion device; however, it does at least call for crude answers to the following questions:

How heavily to advertise?
How much for salesmen?
How much for product improvement?
How much of an assortment to carry?
How large an inventory to hold?
How best to provide speedy delivery?
How much emphasis on price appeal?

The composition of a marketing mix (arrived at by answering the type of questions just listed) is admittedly very difficult and highly subjective. But the job is facilitated greatly when answers are subjected to the test of conforming to the desired company and brand image and to the firm's fixed commitments.

Few firms can afford to switch "images," usually because they have invested heavily in them in prior years and should, therefore, not abandon them lightly. Moreover, past images persist and blur any future attempts at image building. Although it cannot easily scrap its brand image, a firm can vary its marketing mix within moderate limits and remain consistent with the image it seeks to create. Thus, the selection of an image sets limits and gives direction to the decision about the elements to be included in the marketing mix. In that way, it facilitates the decision and also increases the likelihood that it will be correct. However, it does not isolate a single marketing mix as the only correct one.

How might have Zenith, CBS, and other television set manufacturers composed a marketing mix, if they had reasoned about market targets and brand image along the lines of the foregoing discussion?

In Zenith's case, price clearly would have had to be subordinated as a sales appeal. The company could have placed major emphasis on quality of product, subdued advertising, and reliable service, while placing its product with retailers who would enhance the reputation of the brand. By these measures, Zenith could have reinforced the image of a high quality and reliable producer.

In the case of CBS, the role of price in the marketing mix would not have been subject to much control. As explained, it might have been forced to charge a high price; if so, most of its other actions would have been dictated by that fact. It could have relied very heavily on radio and television advertising to generate consumer preference, and justified its high price by adding externals to the set—particularly attractive styling, an expensive furniture appearance, or special features of some sort. It could not have reasonably hoped to get very much support from retailers who commanded strong loyalty among their patrons.

Other television set producers adopted quite different market mixes from those that Zenith and CBS would have selected if they had reasoned along these lines. Some, however, apparently had no conscious marketing mix philosophy and, therefore, seemed to improvise and stumble from one crisis to another. Nevertheless, in their bids for patronage, some television set producers apparently placed relatively heavy reliance on advertising (including mainly RCA, General Electric, Westinghouse, and Sylvania). Others made strong quality claims (like Dumont and Andrea). Still others placed chief emphasis on styling (Magnavox).

DETERMINING POLICY

The fourth stage in multistage pricing calls for the selection of a pricing policy. But before a pricing policy can be determined, answers to the following questions must be obtained:

How should our price compare with "average" prices in the industry? Specifically, should we be 2% above or 4% below the average? And, when we speak of the average, which firms' prices are we going to include in the computation?

How fast will we meet price reductions or increases by rivals?

How frequently will it be advisable to vary price? To what extent is stability of price advantageous?

Should the firm make use of "fair trade" price maintenance?

How frequently should the firm run price promotions?

These are simply illustrative of the aspects of a pricing policy which management can and should spell out—in proper sequence. By virtue of having made the evaluations and decisions called for in the first three stages, management will find itself limited in the number of choices on these points.

In addition, each company must take account of the valuations placed on its product-service "package" as well as the valuations of rival products by the market segments it is most anxious to cultivate. On the basis of such considerations, plus its target market segments and marketing mix, it will decide whether it can afford to charge much more or less than its rivals.

Before proceeding further, let us summarize. Surely, a price setter would be some distance from a specific price decision even after completing the fourth step. We must ask ourselves whether he would not also have covered considerable distance toward a price decision. By taking account of the firm's basic commitments and resources, the images it desires to establish, its decision about marketing mix, and the selection of a detailed pricing policy, has not the price setter reached the point where he is very strongly circumscribed in the price decision he will ultimately make? To illustrate step four, let us carry our two main examples—Zenith and CBS—about as far as they can be taken and see what pricing policy these companies might have adopted.

If the Zenith management had selected the market targets set forth here and made the same decisions regarding brand image and marketing mix, it would have had little trouble in selecting a pricing policy. It would have felt obliged to charge a price somewhat above the average in the market and to minimize emphasis on price in its advertising. Moreover, it could have varied price relatively infrequently to the consumer—except possibly in some of the large metropolitan markets where neither consumers nor retailers are loyal to anything or anyone, except their own pecuniary interests.

In Zenith's pricing policy, the preservation of distributor and retailer loyalty would have figured very prominently in its thinking. It would be compelled to sacrifice long-term price advantages in order to protect its distributors and retailers from financial loss due to price change.

CBS, on the other hand, need not have concerned itself much with dealer and retailer loyalty. It had none and must have realized that it would not have been able to create a loyal distribution structure unless it were willing to make very large financial outlays. If it had reconciled itself to a not-too-loyal distributor and dealer organization, CBS could have conducted sales promotions and varied price frequently and by large amounts. It could have emphasized price in these promotions, but presumably only when combined with strong emphasis on alleged high quality and superior styling. CBS need not have felt obliged to match the prices charged by its competitors, but it could not have afforded to have its retailers' margins be out of line on the low side.

Since it commanded no loyalty from its retailers, CBS was, in fact, compelled to buy their sales support. This it could do, primarily by offering a higher than average margin. (CBS could also have attempted to solve its distribution problem by granting exclusive privileges to a small number of retail outlets. In the case of the television industry, such a policy has been used successfully by Magnavox. However, this company had already sewed up the strong quality retailers who were capable of producing large volume. As a result, CBS was shut out of this pattern of distribution.)

Although Zenith and CBS apparently would have been obliged to charge more than the average by the foregoing line of thinking, other television producers were wise to take a very different tack, mainly because of their different resources and commitments. For example, Admiral and Emerson have tended to charge somewhat less than average, while General Electric has not adopted a very consistent price position.

PRICING STRATEGY

It is difficult to draw a sharp line between policy and strategy, but it is possible and useful to make some sort of distinction between them. Policy is formulated to deal with anticipated and foreseeable situations of a recurrent type. However, markets frequently are beset and dominated by special situations that basic policy was not designed to meet. For example:

A Congressional committee might threaten to investigate the company's or the industry's pricing arrangements.

A sizable firm may have fallen into a desperate financial situation so that it was forced to raise cash through a liquidation of its inventories.

A large new firm may have entered the market.

Business may have fallen off precipitately for the entire industry or economy.

The company may have introduced a model that is either a "dud" or a "sure winner."

Special situations like these ordinarily require an adjustment in price—and the formulation of a strategy to guide management in setting price during the time that the special situation endures.

There generally are several strategies which would be compatible with the firm's basic commitments and resources, its market targets, its image objectives, its convictions about the relative emphasis to attach to various elements in the marketing mix, and its specific pricing policies. Others would be incompatible with earlier decisions and therefore might endanger precious values. A threat to one's very survival might justify a scrapping of these, but impetuousness, shortsightedness, or avarice would not. Explicit recognition of these earlier stages of the pricing decision should prevent hasty short-run actions that are painful, but quite common.

No effort will be made to discuss the Zenith and CBS examples in connection with the formulation of a pricing strategy. They have already been stretched far enough to illustrate the application of the multistage approach to pricing—especially in the most difficult stages. The reader might, however, speculate about how, within the framework of the approach outlined here, both Zenith and CBS management could have responded to a great pricing crisis in the television set industry. This occurred in the fall of 1953 when Westinghouse suddenly reduced its television sets by approximately 20% during the very heart of the selling season. We may speculate that adherence to decisions regarding market targets, brand image, marketing mix, and price policy would have prevented both Zenith and CBS from reducing their prices to the levels set by Westinghouse Electric Corporation.

Specific Price

Here is the final step—the selection of a specific price. At this point, the price setter will usually find himself sharply circumscribed in the specific sums he can charge. Nevertheless, he usually will have some range of price possibilities that are consistent with the decisions made in the preceding five stages of the price decision. How may he best select among the alternatives?

To the extent that he is able, he should be guided by the arithmetic of pricing—that is, by a comparison of the costs and revenues of the alternative prices within the zone delimited by the prior stages of his pricing decision. Once he has taken into account his market targets, brand image, marketing mix, pricing policy, and strategy, he can afford to ignore everything but the calculations of costs and revenues. *The first five stages of decision are designed to take account of the business considerations which may be ignored if one selects price solely on the basis of prevailing cost and revenue conditions.*

It often is impossible to obtain reliable information about sales at different prices; this difficulty is present whatever method of pricing one employs. But the multistage policy approach facilitates research and experimentation into demand conditions by limiting the number of alternatives to be considered.

The price that would be established under this multistage policy approach would rarely be the same as that set by balancing marginal cost and marginal revenue. The former probably would exclude, as incompatible with the firm's basic commitments and resources, desired brand image, and so on, the prices that would be most profitable in the very short term.

The Advantages

First, this approach breaks up the pricing decision into six relatively manageable pieces. In that way, it introduces order into the weighing of the many considerations bearing on price. This approach, therefore, should increase the likelihood that all major factors will be taken into account and that their large number will not overwhelm the price setter.

Second, this method of pricing reduces the risk that the price setter will destroy the firm's valuable investments in corporate and brand images. Also, it requires the price setter to determine and take into account the limitation on the firm's freedom of decision. In that way, it would discourage the pricing executive from undertaking what he is powerless to accomplish. Similarly, the multistage policy approach should militate against a short-run policy of opportunism that would sacrifice long-term values.

Third, the multistage policy approach to pricing should be valuable to those executives who are compelled to delegate pricing responsibilities. In the first place, high-level executives are virtually required by the method to make the decisions for several stages, which thus limits their dependence on their subordinates. In the second place, as explained, it simplifies the making of a price decision so that greater success can be expected. Then, too, its use should make it easier for subordinates to raise questions and obtain advice from their superiors, should they be unable to reach a decision.

Fourth, this approach to pricing puts considerable emphasis on the intangibles that are involved in pricing—particularly on the total impression that customers have of the vendor and of the things he sells. Price is far more than a rationing device that determines which potential customers will be able to afford to make a purchase. Generally it is one of the most important actions in creating an impression of the firm among potential customers. Especially as tangible differences among rival products shrink, these intangibles will grow in significance for marketing success.

THE LIMITATIONS

This approach does not indicate all the considerations that should be taken into account at each stage in the pricing decision. In other words, the price setter is compelled to isolate the significant factors operating at each stage and weigh them for himself.

Second, this approach does not indicate what price to charge in any specific situation. The most that can be claimed for it is that it narrows down the zone of possible prices to the point where it may not matter a great deal which particular price is selected. As stated at the outset, one must beware of any pricing method that does lead to a single price, for such a method could not possibly take into account all of the special circumstances which are relevant to a price decision and which vary so greatly from market to market and from time to time.

Third, this method does not guide price setters in recognizing the factors that dominate the market at any time and in knowing when to switch basic strategies. Also, there may well be more than one dominant condition which must be considered in selecting a basic strategy.

On balance, then, the multistage approach to pricing at best only takes an executive fairly close to his ultimate destination. Although the multistage policy approach does not do the whole job of pricing, the part of the job that is left is relatively easy to finish in many cases. Where this is not so, one can only assume that the task would be almost hopeless without the assistance of a method that reduces the pricing decision to a series of relatively manageable steps in a prescribed sequence.

CONCLUSION

The multistage policy approach outlined here differs from usual approaches to pricing in two major respects. First, it demands a long-range view of price by emphasizing the enduring effects of most price actions on company and brand image. One might say this approach constructs a policy framework for the price decision. And, second, it allows the price decision to be made in stages, rather than requiring a simultaneous solution of the entire price problem.

17

PRICING POLICIES FOR NEW PRODUCTS

JOEL DEAN[*]

How to price a new product is a top-management puzzle that is too often solved by cost-theology and hunch. This paper suggests a pricing policy geared to the dynamic nature of a new product's competitive status. Today's high rate of innovation makes the economic evolution of a new product a strategic guide to practical pricing.

MARKET BEHAVIOR

New products have a protected distinctiveness which is doomed to progressive degeneration from competitive inroads. The invention of a new marketable specialty is usually followed by a period of patent protection when markets are still hesitant and unexplored and when product design is fluid. Then comes a period of rapid expansion of sales as market acceptance is gained. Next the product becomes a target for competitive encroachment. New competitors enter the field, and innovations narrow the gap of distinctiveness between the product and its substitutes. The seller's zone of pricing discretion narrows as his distinctive "specialty" fades into a pedestrian "commodity" which is so little

[*] For major assistance in preparing this article, I am indebted to Stephen Taylor of Joel Dean Associates. Professors James Bonbright and Carl Shoup and Mr. Samuel Richman of the Graduate School of Business, Columbia University, were kind enough to read the manuscript and make helpful suggestions.

differentiated from other products that the seller has limited independence in pricing, even if rivals are few.

Throughout the cycle, continual changes occur in promotional and price elasticity and in costs of production and distribution. These changes call for adjustments in price policy.

Appropriate pricing over the cycle depends on the development of three different aspects of maturity, which usually move in approximately parallel time paths: (1) technical maturity, indicated by declining rate of product development, increasing standardization among brands, and increasing stability of manufacturing processes and knowledge about them; (2) market maturity, indicated by consumer acceptance of the basic service idea, by widespread belief that the products of most manufacturers will perform satisfactorily, and by enough familiarity and sophistication to permit consumers to compare brands competently; and (3) competitive maturity, indicated by increasing stability of market shares and price structures.

Of course, interaction among these components tends to make them move together. That is, intrusion by new competitors helps to develop the market, but entrance is most tempting when the new product appears to be establishing market acceptance.

The rate at which the cycle of degeneration progresses varies widely among products. What are the factors that set its pace? An overriding determinant is technical—the extent to which the economic environment must be reorganized to use the innovation effectively. The scale of plant investment and technical research called forth by the telephone, electric power, the automobile, or air transport makes for a long gestation period, as compared with even such major innovations as cellophane or frozen foods. Development comes fastest when the new gadget fills a new vacuum made to order for it. Electric stoves, as one example, have risen to 50% market saturation in the fast-growing Pacific Northwest, where electric power has become the lowest cost energy. Products still in early developmental stages also provide rich opportunities for product differentiation, which with heavy research costs hold off competitive degeneration.

But aside from technical factors, the rate of degeneration is controlled by economic forces that can be subsumed under

(1) rate of market acceptance and (2) ease of competitive entry

By market acceptance is meant the extent to which buyers consider the product a serious alternative to other ways of performing the same service. Market acceptance is a frictional factor. The effect of cultural lags may endure for some time after quality and costs make products technically useful. The slow catch-on of the "electric pig" (garbage-disposal unit) is an example. On the other hand, the attitude of acceptance may exist long before any workable model can be developed; then the final appearance of the product will produce an explosive growth curve in sales. The antihistamine cold tablet, a spectacular example, reflects the national faith in chemistry's ability to vanquish the common cold. And, of course, low unit price may speed market acceptance of an innovation; ball-point pens and all-steel houses started at about the same time, but look at the difference in their sales curves.

Ease of competitive entry is a major determinant of the speed of degeneration of a specialty. An illustration is found in the washing machine business before the war, where with little basic patent protection the Maytag position was quickly eroded by small manufacturers who performed essentially an assembly operation. The ball-point pen cascaded from a $12 novelty to a 49-cent "price football," partly because entry barriers of patents and techniques were ineffective. Frozen orange juice, which started as a protected specialty of Minute Maid, is speeding through its competitive cycle, with competing brands now crowding into the market.

At the outset the innovator can control the rate of competitive deterioration to an important degree by nonprice as well as by price strategies. Through successful research in product improvement he can protect his specialty position both by extending the life of his basic patent and by keeping ahead of competitors in product development. The record of the International Business Machines punch-card equipment illustrates this potentiality. Ease of entry is also affected by a policy of stay-out pricing (so low as to make the prospects look uninviting), which under some circumstances may slow down the process of competitive encroachment.

STEPS IN PIONEER PRICING

Pricing problems start when a company finds a product that is a radical departure from existing ways of performing a service and that is temporarily protected from competition by patents, secrets of production, control at the point of a scarce resource, or by other barriers. The seller here has a wide range of pricing discretion resulting from extreme product differentiation.

A good example of pricing latitude conferred by protected superiority of product is provided by the McGraw Electric Company's "Toastmaster," which, both initially and over a period of years, was able to command a very substantial price premium over competitive toasters. Apparently this advantage resulted from (1) a good product that was distinctive and superior, and (2) substantial and skillful sales promotion. Similarly, Sunbeam priced its electric iron $2 above comparable models of major firms with considerable success. And Sunbeam courageously priced its new metal coffee-maker at $32, much above competitive makes of glass coffee-makers, but it was highly successful.

To get a picture of how a manufacturer should go about setting his price in the pioneer stage, let me describe the main steps of the process (of course the classification is arbitrary and the steps are interrelated): (1) estimate of demand, (2) decision on market targets, (3) design of promotional strategy, and (4) choice of channels of distribution.

The problem at the pioneer stage differs from that in a relatively stable monopoly because the product is beyond the experience of buyers and because the perishability of its distinctiveness must be reckoned with. How can demand for new products be explored? How can we find out how much people will pay for a product that has never before been seen or used? There are several levels of refinement to this analysis.

The initial problem of estimating demand for a new product can be broken into a series of subproblems: (a) whether the product will go at all (assuming price is in a competitive range); (b) what range of price will make the product economically attractive to buyers; (c) what sales volumes can be expected at various points in this price range; and (d) what reaction will price produce in manufacturers and sellers of displaced substitutes.

The first step is an exploration of the *preferences and educability of consumers,* always of course in the light of the technical feasibility of the new product. How many potential buyers are there? Is the product a practical device for meeting their needs? How can it be improved to meet their needs better? What proportion of the potential buyers would prefer, or could be induced to prefer, this product to already existing products (prices being equal)?

Sometimes it is feasible to start with the assumption that all vulnerable substitutes will be fully displaced. For example, to get some idea of the maximum limits of demand for a new type of reflecting-sign material, a company started with estimates of the aggregate number and area of auto license plates, highway markers, railroad operational signs, and name signs for streets and homes. Next, the proportion of each category needing nightlight reflection was guessed. For example, it was assumed that only rural and suburban homes could benefit by this kind of name sign, and the estimate of need in this category was made accordingly.

It is not uncommon and possibly not unrealistic for a manufacturer to make the blithe assumption at this stage that the product price will be "within a competitive range" without having much idea of what that range is. For example, in developing a new type of camera equipment, one of the electrical companies judged its acceptability to professional photographers by technical performance without making any inquiry into its economic value. When the equipment was later placed in an economic setting, the indications were that sales would be negligible.

The second step is marking out this *competitive range of price.* Vicarious pricing experience can be secured by interviewing selected distributors who have enough comparative knowledge of customers' alternatives and preferences to judge what price range would make the new product "a good value." Direct discussions with representative experienced industrial users have produced reliable estimates of the "practical" range of prices. Manufacturers of electrical equipment often explore the economic as well as the technical feasibility of a new product by sending engineers with blueprints and models to see customers, such as technical and operating executives.

In guessing the price range of a radically new consumers' product of small unit value, the concept of barter equivalent can be a useful research guide. For example, a manufacturer of paper specialties tested a dramatic new product in the following fashion: A wide variety of consumer products totally unlike the new product were purchased and spread out on a big table. Consumers selected the products they would swap for the new product. By finding out whether the product would trade even for a dish pan, a towel, or a hairpin, the executives got a rough idea of what range of prices might strike the typical consumer as reasonable in the light of the values she could get for her money in totally different kinds of expenditures.

But asking prospective consumers how much they think they would be willing to pay for a new product, even by such indirect or disguised methods, may often fail to give a reliable indication of the demand schedule. Most times people just do not know what they would pay. It depends partly on their income and on future alternatives. Early in the postwar period a manufacturer of television sets tried this method and got highly erratic and obviously unreliable results because the distortion of war shortages kept prospects from fully visualizing the multiple alternative ways of spending their money. Another deficiency, which may, however, be less serious than it appears, is that responses are biased by the consumer's confused notion that he is bargaining for a good price. Not until techniques of depth interviewing are more refined than they are now can this crude and direct method of exploring a new product's demand schedule hold much promise of being accurate.

One appliance manufacturer tried out new products on a sample of employees by selling to them at deep discounts, with the stipulation that they could if they wished return the products at the end of the experiment period and get a refund of their low purchase price. Demand for frozen orange juice was tested by placing it in several markets at three different prices, ranging around the price of fresh fruit; the result showed rather low price elasticity.

While inquiries of this sort are often much too short-run to give any real indication of consumer tastes, the relevant point here is that even such rough probing often yields broad impressions of price elasticity, particularly in relation to product variations such as styling, placing of controls, and use of automatic features. It may show, for example, that $5 of cost put into streamlining or chromium stripping can add $50 to the price.

The third step, a more definite inquiry into the *probable sales from several possible prices,* starts with an investigation of the prices of substitutes. Usually the buyer has a choice of existing ways of having the same service performed; an analysis of the costs of these alternatives serves as a guide in setting the price for a new way.

Comparisons are easy and significant for industrial customers who have a costing system to tell them the exact value, say, of a fork-lift truck in terms of warehouse labor saved. Indeed, chemical companies setting up a research project to displace an existing material often know from the start the top price that can be charged for the new substitute in terms of cost of the present material.

But in most cases the comparison is obfuscated by the presence of quality differences that may be important bases for price premiums. This is most true of household appliances, where the alternative is an unknown amount of labor of a mysterious value. In pricing a cargo parachute the alternatives are: (1) free fall in a padded box from a plane flown close to the ground, (2) landing the plane, (3) back shipment by land from the next air terminal, or (4) land shipment all the way. These alternatives differ widely in their service value and are not very useful pricing guides.

Thus, it is particularly hard to know how much good will be done by making the new product cheaper than the old by various amounts, or how much the market will be restricted by making the new product more expensive. The answers usually come from experiment or research.

The fourth step in estimating demand is to consider the *possibility of retaliation by manufacturers of displaced substitutes* in the form of price cutting. This development may not occur at all if the new product displaces only a small market segment. If old industries do fight it out, however, their incremental costs provide a floor to the resulting price competition and should be brought into price plans. For example, a manufacturer of black-and-white sensitized paper studied the possibility that lowering his price would displace blueprint paper substantially. Not only did he investigate the prices of blueprint paper, but he also felt it necessary to estimate the out-of-pocket cost of making blueprint paper because of the probability that manufacturers already in the market would fight back by reducing prices toward the level of their incremental costs.

When the company has developed some idea of the range of demand and the range of prices that are feasible for the new product, it is in a position to make some basic strategic decisions on market targets and promotional plans. To decide on market objectives requires answers to several questions: What ultimate market share is wanted for the new product? How does it fit into the present product line? What about production methods? What are the possible distribution channels? These are questions of joint costs in production and distribution, of plant expansion outlays, and of potential competition. If entry is easy, the company may not be eager to disrupt its present production and selling operations to capture and hold a large slice of the new market. But if the prospective profits shape up to a substantial new income source, it will be worth while to make the capital expenditures on plant needed to reap the full harvest.

A basic factor in answering all these questions is the expected behavior of production and distribution costs. The relevant data here are all the production outlays that will be made after the decision day—the capital expenditures as well as the variable costs. A go-ahead decision will hardly be made without some assurance that these costs can be recovered before the product becomes a football in the market. Many different projections of costs will be made, depending on the alternative scales of output, rate of market expansion, threats of potential competition, and measures to meet that competition that are under consideration. But these factors and the decision that is made on promotional strategy are interdependent. The fact is that this is a circular problem that in theory can only be solved by simultaneous equations.

Fortunately, it is possible to make some approximations that can break the circle: Scale economies become significantly different only with broad changes in the size of plant and the type of production methods. This narrows the range of cost projections to workable proportions. The effects of using different distribution channels can be guessed fairly well without meshing the alternatives in with all the production and selling possibilities. The most vulnerable point of the circle is probably the decision on promotional strategy. The alternatives here are broad and produce a variety of results. The next step in the pricing process is therefore a plan for promotion.

Initial promotion outlays are an investment in the product that cannot be recovered until some kind of market has been established. The innovator shoulders the burden of creating a market— educating consumers to the existence and uses of the product. Later imitators will never have to do this job; so, if the innovator does not want to be simply a benefactor to his future competitors, he must make pricing plans to recover his initial outlays before his pricing discretion evaporates.

His basic strategic problem is to find the right mixture of price and promotion to maximize his long-run profits. He can choose a relatively high price in pioneering stages, together with extravagant advertising and dealer discounts, and plan to get his promotion costs back early; or he can use low prices and lean margins from the very outset, in order to discourage potential competition when the barriers of patents, distribution channels, or production techniques become inadequate. This question is discussed further below.

Estimation of the costs of moving the new product through the channels of distribution to the final consumer must enter into the pricing procedure, since these costs govern the factory price that will result in a specified consumer price, and since it is the consumer price that matters for volume. Distributive margins are partly pure promotional costs and partly physical distribution costs. Margins must at least cover the distributors' costs of warehousing, handling, and order taking. These costs are similar to factory production costs in being related to physical capacity and its utilization, that is, fluctuations in production or sales volume. Hence these set a floor to trade-channel discounts. But distributors usually also contribute promotional effort—in point-of-sale pushing, local advertising, and display—when it is made worth their while.

These pure promotional costs are more optional. Unlike physical handling costs the have no necessary functional relation to sales volume. An added layer of margin in trade discounts to produce this localized sales effort (with retail price fixed) is an optional way for the manufacturer to spend his prospecting money in putting over a new product.

In establishing promotional costs, the manufacturer must decide on the extent to which the selling effort will be delegated to members of the distribution chain. Indeed, some distribution channels, such as house-to-house selling and retail store selling supplemented by home demonstrators, represent a substantial delegation of the manufacturer's promotional job, and these usually involve much higher distribution-channel costs than do conventional methods. Rich distributor margins are an appropriate use of promotion funds only when the producer thinks a high price plus promotion is a better expansion policy on the specialty than low price by itself. Thus there is an intimate interaction between the pricing of a new product and the costs and the problems of floating it down the distribution channels to the final consumer.

POLICIES FOR PIONEER PRICING

The strategic decision in pricing a new product is the choice between (1) a policy of high initial prices that skim the cream of demand and (2) a policy of low prices from the outset serving as an active agent for market penetration. Although the actual range of choice is much wider than this, a sharp dichotomy clarifies the issues for consideration.

First, let us take up the policy of skimming price. For products that represent a drastic departure from accepted ways of performing a service, a policy of relatively high prices coupled with heavy promotional expenditures in the early stages of market development (and lower prices at later stages) his proved successful for many products. There are several reasons for the success of this policy:

(1) Demand is likely to be more inelastic with respect to price in the early stages than it is when the product is full grown. This is particularly true for consumers' goods. A novel product, such as the electric blanket or the electric pig, is not yet accepted as a part of the expenditure pattern. Consumers are still ignorant about its value as compared with the value of conventional alternatives. Moreover, at least in the early stages, the product has so few close rivals that cross-elasticity of demand is low. Promotional elasticity is, on the other hand, quite high, particularly for products with high unit prices such as television sets. Since it is difficult for the customer to value the service of the product in a way to price it intelligently, he is by default principally interested in how well it will work.

(2) Launching a new product with a high price is an efficient device for breaking the market up into segments that differ in price elasticity of demand. The initial high price serves to skim the cream of the market that is relatively insensitive to price. Subsequent price reductions tap successively more elastic sectors of the market. This pricing strategy is exemplified by the systematic succession of editions of a book, sometimes starting with a $50 limited personal edition and ending up with a 25-cent pocket book.

(3) This policy is safer, or at least appears so. Facing an unknown elasticity of demand, a high initial price serves as a "refusal" price during the stage of exploration. How much costs can be reduced as the market expands and as the design of the product is improved by increasing production efficiency with new techniques is difficult to predict. One of the electrical companies recently introduced a new lamp bulb at a comparatively high initial price, but with the announcement that the price would be reduced as the company found ways of cutting its costs.

(4) Many companies are not in a position to finance the product flotation out of distant future revenues. High cash outlays in the early stages result from heavy costs of production and distributor organizing, in addition to the promotional investment in the pioneer product. High prices are a reasonable financing technique for shouldering these burdens in the light of the many uncertainties about the future.

329

The alternative policy is one of penetration price, using low prices as the principal instrument for penetrating mass markets early. This policy is the reverse of the skimming policy, in which the price is lowered only as short-run competition forces it. The passive skimming policy has the virtue of safeguarding some profits at every stage of market penetration. But it prevents quick sales to the many buyers who are at the lower end of the income scale or the lower end of the preference scale and who therefore are unwilling to pay any substantial premium for product or reputation superiority. The active approach in probing possibilities for market expansion by early penetration pricing requires research, forecasting, and courage.

A decision to price for market expansion can be reached at various stages in a product's life cycle: before birth, at birth, in childhood, in adulthood, or in senescence. The chances for large-volume sales should at least be explored in the early stages of product development research, even before the pilot stage, perhaps with a more definitive exploration when the product goes into production and the price and distribution plans are decided upon. And the question of pricing to expand the market, if not answered earlier, will probably arise once more after the product has established an elite market.

Quite a few products have been rescued from premature senescence by pricing them low enough to tap new markets. The reissues of important books in the 25-cent pocket-book category illustrate this point particularly well. These have produced not only commercial but intellectual renascence as well to many authors. The pattern of sales growth of a product that had reached stability in a high-price market has been known to undergo sharp changes when it was suddenly priced low enough to tap new markets. A contrasting illustration of passive policy is the recent pricing experience of the airlines. Although safety considerations and differences in equipment and service cloud the picture, it is pretty clear that the bargain-rate coach fares of scheduled airlines were adopted in reaction to the cut rates of nonscheduled airlines. This competitive response has apparently established a new pattern of traffic growth for the scheduled airlines.

An example of penetration pricing at the initial stage of the product's market life, again from the book field, is Simon &

Schuster's recently adopted policy of bringing out new titles in a $1, paper-bound edition simultaneously with the conventional higher priced, cloth-bound edition.

What conditions warrant aggressive pricing for market penetration? This question cannot be answered categorically, but it may be helpful to generalize that the following conditions indicate the desirability of an early low-price policy: (1) a high price-elasticity of demand in the short run, that is, a high degree of responsiveness of sales to reductions in price; (2) substantial savings in production costs as the result of greater volume—not a necessary condition, however, since if elasticity of demand is high enough, pricing for market expansion may be profitable without realizing production economies; (3) product characteristics such that it will not seem bizarre when it is first fitted into the consumers' expenditure pattern; (4) a strong threat of potential competition.

This threat of potential competition is a highly persuasive reason for penetration pricing. One of the major objectives of most low-pricing policies in the pioneering stages of market development is to raise entry barriers to prospective competitors. This is appropriate when entrants must make large-scale investments to reach minimum costs and they cannot slip into an established market by selling at substantial discounts.

In many industries, however, the important potential competitor is a large, multiple-product firm operating as well in other fields than that represented by the product in question. For such a firm, the most important consideration for entry is not existing margins but the prospect of large and growing volume of sales. Present margins over costs are not the dominant consideration because such firms are normally confident that they can get their costs down as low as competitors' costs if the volume of production is large. Therefore, when total industry sales are not expected to amount to much, a high-margin policy can be followed because entry is improbable in view of the expectation of low volume and because it does not matter too much to potential competitors if the new product is introduced.

The fact remains that for products whose market potential appears big, a policy of stayout pricing from the outset makes much more sense. When a leading soap manufacturer developed an additive that whitened clothes and enhanced the brilliance of colors, the company chose to take its gains in a larger share of the market rather than in a temporary price premium. Such a decision was sound, since the company's competitors could be expected to match or better the product improvement fairly promptly. Under these circumstances, the price premium would have been shortlived, whereas the gains in market share were more likely to be retained.

Of course, any decision to start out with lower prices must take into account the fact that if the new product calls for capital recovery over a long period, the risk may be great that later entrants will be able to exploit new production techniques which can undercut the pioneer's original cost structure. In such cases, the low-price pattern should be adopted with a view to long-run rather than to short-run profits, with the recognition that it usually takes time to attain the volume potentialities of the market.

It is sound to calculate profits in dollar terms rather than in percentage margins and to think in terms of percentage return on the investment required to produce and sell the expanded volume rather than in terms of percentage markup. Profit calculation should also recognize the contributions that market-development pricing can make to the sale of other products and to the long-run future of the company. Often a decision to use development pricing will turn on these considerations of long-term impacts upon the firm's total operation strategy rather than on the profits directly attributable to the individual product.

An example of market-expansion pricing is found in the experience of a producer of asbestos shingles, which have a limited sale in the high-price house market. The company wanted to broaden the market in order to compete effectively with other roofing products for the inexpensive home. It tried to find the price of asphalt shingles that would make the annual cost per unit of roof over a period of years as low as the cheaper roofing that currently commanded the mass market. Indications were that the price would have to be at least this low before volume sales would come. Next, the company explored the relationship between production costs and volume, far beyond the range of its own volume experience. Variable costs and overhead costs were estimated separately, and the possibilities of a different organization of production were explored. Calculating in terms of anticipated dollars of profit rather than in terms of percentage margin, the company reduced the price of asbestos shingles and brought the annual cost down close to the cost of the cheapest asphalt roof. This reduction produced a greatly expanded volume and secured a substantial share of the mass market.

PRICING IN MATURITY

To determine what pricing policies are appropriate for later stages in the cycle of market and competitive maturity, the manufacturer must be able to tell when a product is approaching maturity. Some of the symptoms of degeneration of competitive status toward the commodity level are:

Weakening in brand preference—this may be evidenced by a higher cross-elasticity of demand among leading products, the leading brand not being able to continue demanding as much price premium as initially without losing position.

Narrowing physical variation among products as the best designs are developed and standardized—this has been dramatically demonstrated in automobiles and is still in process in television receivers.

The entry in force of private-label competitors—this is exemplified by the mail-order houses' sale of own-label refrigerators and paint sprayers.

Market saturation—the ratio of replacement sales to new equipment sales serves as an indicator of the competitive degeneration of durable goods, but in general it must be kept in mind that both market size and degree of saturation are hard to define (for example, saturation of the radio market, which was initially thought to be one radio per home and later had to be expanded to one radio per room).

The stabilization of production methods—a dramatic innovation that slashes costs (such as prefabricated houses) may disrupt what appears to be a well-stabilized oligopoly market.

The first step for the manufacturer whose specialty is about to slip into the commodity category is to reduce real prices promptly as soon as symptoms of deterioration appear. This step is essential if he is to forestall the entry of private-label competitors. Examples of failure to make such a reduction are abundant. By and large, private-label competition has speeded up the inevitable evolution of high specialties into commodities and has tended to force margins down by making price reductions more open and more universal than they would otherwise be. From one standpoint, the rapid growth of the private-label share in the market is a symptom of unwise pricing on the part of the national-brand sector of the industry.

This does not mean that the manufacturer should declare open price war in the industry. When he moves into mature competitive stages, he enters oligopoly relationships where price slashing is peculiarly dangerous and unpopular. But, with active competition in prices precluded, competitive efforts may move in other directions, particularly toward product improvement and market segmentation. Product improvement at this stage, where most of the important developments have been put into all brands, practically amounts to market segmentation. For it means adding refinements and quality extras that put the brand in the elite category, with an appeal only to the top-income brackets. This is a common tactic in food marketing, and in the tire industry it was the response of the General Tire Company to the competitive conditions of the 1930's.

As the product matures and as its distinctiveness narrows, a choice must sometimes be made by the company concerning the rung of the competitive price ladder it should occupy—roughly, the choice between a low and a not-so-low relative price.

A price at the low end of the array of the industry's real prices is usually associated with a product mixture showing a lean element of services and reputation (the product being physically similar to competitive brands, however) and a company having a lower gross margin than the other industry members (although not necessarily a lower net margin). The choice of such a low-price policy may be dictated by technical or market inferiorities of the product, or it may be adopted because the company has faith in the long-run price elasticity of demand and the ability of low prices to penetrate an important segment of the market not tapped by higher prices. The classic example is Henry Ford's pricing decision in the 1920's.

SUMMARY

In pricing products of perishable distinctiveness, a company must study the cycle of competitive degeneration in order to determine its major causes, its probable speed, and the chances of slowing it down. Pricing in the pioneering stage of the cycle involves difficult problems of projecting potential demand and of guessing the relation of price to sales. The first step in this process is to explore consumer preferences and to establish the feasibility of the product, in order to get a rough idea of whether demand will warrant further exploration. The second step is to mark out a range of prices that will make the product economically attractive to buyers. The third step is to estimate the probable sales that will result from alternative prices.

If these initial explorations are encouraging, the next move is to make decisions on promotional strategy and distribution channels. The policy of relatively high prices in the pioneering stage has much to commend it, particularly when sales seem to be comparatively unresponsive to price but quite responsive to educational promotion. On the other hand, the policy of relatively low prices in the pioneering stage, in anticipation of the cost savings resulting from an expanding market, has been strikingly successful under the right conditions. Low prices look to long-run rather than short-run profits and discourage potential competitors.

Pricing in the mature stages of a product's life cycle requires a technique for recognizing when a product is approaching maturity. Pricing problems in this stage border closely on those of oligopoly.

18

HOW TO SET REALISTIC PROFIT GOALS

BRUCE PAYNE

Why is it just as serious an error for companies to set short-term sales and profit goals that are too low as it is to set goals that are too high?

Why does pressure from top management so often lead division managers to purposely understate their profit targets?

What can be done to encourage managers to set more realistic and challenging goals?

What steps and policies will help to make short-term planning more consistent with top management's long-range strategy?

Sporadic postwar recessions have done more than anything else to spotlight the strengths and weaknesses of American management. They have served, for example, to emphasize the tremendous gains that medium-size and large companies can make through realistic, aggressive short-term planning tied to long-range needs and objectives. Many companies have taken advantage of planning to improve their profit positions even during the past year. In these firms executives knew where to try to reduce costs, what kinds of orders to concentrate on, what revisions in inventory levels to make, what changes to make in staff assignments, and so on.

In many industries, however, such companies have been the

exception. It seems to me that more firms have been erring in setting and working toward short-term goals than in any other aspect of management. So often it has been my experience—and many others could confirm it—that executives of organizations hard hit by the recession could not even describe very well what the trouble was.

In a dynamic economy change is continuously taking place. Look into the pace-setting companies, whether large or small, and you will see executives who are always learning, adapting, adjusting, reorganizing. But by its nature practically every organization also has a certain amount of rigidity and resistance to change in the system. As one group of authorities has concluded: "The natural dynamic processes of change do not occur fast enough to keep pace with the very rapidly changing conditions of our world today."[1] It is in reducing this lag—in keeping the company up to date with its opportunities and potentials for profit improvement—that an aggressive, intelligent short-term planning effort is indispensable.

UNDERSTATING GOALS

Every executive knows about the difficulties caused when divisions fall short of their sales and profit targets for the year. The repercussions range from the factory, where workers often must be laid off, right up to the division head's office, where a shake-up in the staff may have to be plotted to appease top management. What we commonly overlook, however, is that it is almost as bad for divisions or departments to set goals that they exceed by a wide margin—goals that are unrealistically low. The effects are of a different kind, to be sure, and an executive may feel more comfortable discussing them; but they can create just as much havoc in the corporation.

For example, if a division reports its sales goal for the next year or two on the unrealistically low side, top management may well decide that some of the funds which to date have been used to support the organization's sales will no longer be required and can be used elsewhere. Then, when sales go over the target figure and capital is required to support additional inventories,

[1] Ronald Lippitt, Jeanne Watson, and Bruce Westley, *Planned Change* (New York, Harcourt, Brace and Company, 1958), pp. 10–11.

accounts receivable, or such, the funds will not be available; the company will either have to enter the market at a disadvantageous time for short-term borrowing or not make the sales at all.

As a practical matter, of course, it is most unlikely that management will refuse sales if there is any way of financing them. However, it is equally unlikely that a company will go out and get the added sales that it could get unless it has the extra manpower and facilities actually available—unless, in other words, it has committed itself in all departments to the higher sales goal.

The firm may run into still other financial problems. Suppose that management takes the divisions' sales and profit estimates for the next few years and decides that by 1967 growth will have proceeded to a point where new financing will be necessary. It plans to go to the banks then and talk about a large loan, knowing that in the meantime it must take steps to make sure that there will be reasonable debt-asset ratios on the balance sheet for the bank officers to see. Now suppose that, the estimates having been made too low, the divisions overshoot their sales targets by a large margin so that it becomes necessary to go to the banks earlier—in 1965, say, or in 1966. If the balance sheet is not overextended in the way of debt at that time, fine. But what often happens in the case of growth companies is that the balance sheet *is* overextended, with the result that management is not in a good position to ask for an increase in its debt. Unable to borrow when it needs to, the company may then be helpless to finance the additional expansion needed to take advantage of a growing market for its products.

It is mistakes of this nature that often frustrate long-range plans and short-range programs as well. The division head is apt to say: "My operation is just a part of the corporation, and surely it won't make so much difference if only my sales go 10% over plan." What he forgets is that if six or seven division managers all do the same thing, each going 10% or 15% over his estimate, the financial men at headquarters will be tearing their hair out.

Moreover, if management does not expect the profits that it actually gets, how can it use them properly? Will it take the calculated risks that it should take? Will it have the extra mill ready to start production, or the new advertising campaign all planned, or the additional inventories waiting in branch warehouses? After the profits come in, management will be willing to make these moves; but the delay in timing may be a costly one in a highly competitive economy.

The effects of pegging goals too low are particularly noticeable in companies committed to maintaining designated turnover and return-on-investment ratios. The number of such firms is steadily increasing; for, with the increase in the amounts of investment required, it has become increasingly important to measure the effectiveness of the capital employed as well as the margin of profit—all the more so if the firm is expanding or must plan closely during the short term to maximize the use of its assets.

To illustrate how opportunities for increasing return on investment are missed, let us take a hypothetical example. As everyone knows, the percentage return on investment can be simply arrived at by dividing the total investment of the corporation into the net profit; however, such a short cut loses sight of the significant relations between sales, investment, and profit. Accordingly, more and more top executives are looking at the turnover factor and using the formula

$$\frac{\text{net profit}}{\text{sales}} \times \frac{\text{sales}}{\text{investment}} = \text{return on investment.}$$

Using this formula, a firm with a tangible net worth of $1,000,000 sets its sales goal for next year at $3,000,000. Such a goal, while overly conservative, enables the firm to get a 30% return on net worth, as shown in the left-hand column of Exhibit I.

EXHIBIT I. EFFECT OF BORROWING ON RATE OF RETURN

	Without borrowing	With borrowing
Tangible net worth	$1,000,000	$1,000,000
Liabilities	0	250,000
Investment	1,000,000	1,250,000
Turnover of investment	3	3
Sales	3,000,000	3,750,000
Profit percentage	10%	10%
Profit amount	300,000	375,000
Return on tangible net worth	30%	37.5%

Let us suppose, however, that a more realistic goal would be $3,300,000 with the present capacity, and $3,750,000 with a 25% increase in the investment. If management realizes this and "trades on the equity" to add facilities and man power, it can achieve a 37.5% return on investment, as shown in the right-hand column of Exhibit I. Note that the turnover and profit ratios are exactly the same as in the left-hand column.

While this example is hypothetical, it shows what a liberal borrowing policy can do for numerous companies. But management is unlikely to visualize these potentials, and to go on to exploit the leverage available in its borrowing position, if the sales and profit targets set up by the divisions are understated.

Many companies should be planning to meet increasing demand in 1965 and 1966—and they can get credit on favorable terms to do so. But if division and departmental goals are understated because of recession thinking, the opportunities to increase the rate of return will not be realized.

Of course, the financial implications of understating goals are but part of the story. The effect upon organizational efficiency is equally serious. As one of my associates commented once in a discussion of this problem: "The trouble is what your organization *didn't* do—because it was not committed to do it." In other words, the company has the people but does not make full use of them.

Conversely, the company may be caught with a shortage of personnel. If sales are a good deal higher than budgeted, will there be sufficient foremen and maintenance men in the plant to handle the increase? Time after time, the answer is no.

The problem is aggravated for growth companies that are acquiring smaller firms in the course of expanding. Frequently the newly purchased firm has a good product or plant that is needed, but it has had poor management. The parent corporation may struggle along trying to stretch its own staff to handle the inadequacies of the subsidiary's management, postponing the decision to go out and buy good managers for the new operation simply because it does not anticipate the profits necessary to get good men. (Or, just as bad, it may decide against buying the smaller firm because it does not see that it can afford to buy a better management team for the subsidiary.)

Again, failure to anticipate sales and profits correctly may result in poor pricing. Generally speaking, what management should do is determine what price will bring a sales volume that will maximize the ratio of marginal contribution to investment. This can be done as follows:

1. Project prices at various levels through a reasonable range, and make forecasts of the sales volumes which can reasonably be expected at each price level.

2. Calculate the direct costs for the various volumes.

3. Figure the required investment at the various volumes, and compute the ratios of marginal contribution (price less direct costs) to investment.

4. Establish the price where the ratio of marginal contribution to investment is greatest.

But if the company foresees a tight cash situation as the result of unrealistically low profit goals, it may decide instead to set prices that will maximize the profit margin instead of the rate of return; there will not be so much volume and turnover, in other words, but the profit percentage for what there is will be greater than for any larger volume. This will mean, assuming the market is sensitive to price, that the company will lose some volume and profits to its competitors—needlessly, of course, because of its overly conservative price-cost forecasts.

PLAYING SAFE

Not long ago I was in conference with a division manager of a medium-size corporation that was struggling with the problems of long-range planning. We were discussing the targets which the division was going to report to the New York office, and in a frank moment the manager happened to remark, "Of course, I set my goals as low as I can get them."

I cannot say that every division head tries to do this, but it certainly seems to be a very prevalent tendency. And it is a very natural one, too. For so often what top management wants to be able to say, at year's end, is: "We made more money than we thought"; or to cite its staff help to the divisions and say: "We helped them to do better than they expected." It takes no genius in the divisions to figure out how to keep headquarters happy in that situation—especially when aggressive presidents are forever trying to keep the divisions on the defensive!

Local managers close to the production and selling situation can peg their goals comfortably under the marks they expect to attain in innumerable ways. As a very simple illustration, by rating the sales performance of his seven different territories according to the metropolitan buying index for the various cities covered, the division manager may know that sales in two territories are excellent; sales in three territories, fair; and sales in two territories, poor. Simply by bringing the poor ratings up to fair, he can increase total sales 25%; by bringing up the sales of any one of the three fair territories to excellent, he can increase the total by 15%. However, since top management sees only the over-all result and has only the past to judge it on, the division head can safely set a 5% increase as a goal for existing products, and use any new products to make the over-all increase look impressive.

Such practices are quite common in industry, and I believe that top executives are just kidding themselves if they do not recognize what is going on. Ordinarily, facts about the exact amount of understatement will be extremely hard for the senior officers to get (although an outsider may be able to get the story more easily). But if management will work hard and long and patiently to build up a frank and open relationship with the divisions, it will commonly find plenty of past evidence to support my contention.

An event like a recession is likely to make the tendency toward understatement more pronounced than ever. Even if the company's sag in sales was light and temporary, the memory of it will linger for some time in managers' minds—the more so if top management kept the telephone ringing and made things uncomfortable for them. Perhaps one of the worst consequences of a recession, in fact, is the unrealistic conservatism it introduces into many company planning efforts.

Another unfortunate effect is what happens to management appraisals and, in some cases, compensation. If division and department heads get patted on the back only for exceeding their sales and profit objectives, the individualists who depart from the general practice and set challenging goals for themselves will not look as well by comparison as they should. Of course, everyone suffers in the end—top management, stockholders, the whole company—but in the everyday struggle that is not so obvious.

Sometimes top management is quite aware of what is going on. Assuming that the goal first reported by the division is understated, it answers by suggesting a goal a good deal higher—as unrealistically high, perhaps, as the division's opening bid was, unrealistically low. This kind of bargaining will probably do little to improve the situation. It only increases the division's determination to justify low goals, without regard for the effect of its policies on other parts of the company and on the over-all planning effort. And this in turn, of course, makes top management's position more extreme.

Many instances where divisions and departments have failed to reach their goals because they were set too high can be attributed to the situation just described. Accordingly, much of the discussion that follows is applicable to the problem of revising targets downward, when that is needed, as well as revising them upward.

WITHIN REACH

"A man's reach should exceed his grasp." This line from Robert Browning seems very pertinent to me in discussing short-term profit improvement. We want division managers to set goals that they have to reach for—goals which can reasonably be attained with an aggressive, intelligent effort, but goals which exceed what the divisions can grasp with certainty if they proceed as usual. In other words, we do not want goals that anybody can accomplish; we want targets that will put the managers under a little pressure, targets that will test managers' skills as planners and doers.

Goals of this kind demand a positive, constructive approach by top management. If it is dissatisfied with the targets first proposed by a division manager, top management should not insist on raising them until it can first outline the changes needed to accomplish the increase. Unless it can do that—working, of course, through the division's own personnel—the division cannot be blamed for poor planning.

But how is the top executive to tell whether a goal is a "reaching" one? How is he to tell whether it can reasonably be improved on?

One of the most helpful things he can do is ask the division to outline a plan of action and then, in discussing that plan, determine just what improvements in performance are anticipated. Is the division simply maintaining the same levels of performance in the factory and in sales as last year, or is it planning to better these levels? Are incentives the same, or are they being improved on? Will management work with the same control data, or will it have better figures? Questions such as these quickly direct attention to the assumptions on which objectives are defined.

This step alone, however, is not enough. In fact, the real need is for a more fundamental approach. For, as experience has so often demonstrated, getting managers to sit down and work objectives out thoughtfully is a hard thing to do, especially when they are not in the habit of doing it. Somehow or other top management has to create an atmosphere in which these men will be willing to talk frankly. It may take a series of meetings—four or five—in which the seniors do the listening and questioning and leave it up to the division men to talk and give suggestions. It may take some kind of training program. It may take a "traveling circus" from headquarters that spends its time consulting with the divisions, tactfully and gradually getting them to open up. These and other methods can be very effective.

The value of open and friendly discussion to short- and long-range profit planners in headquarters is, of course, obvious. It is also good for the division and department managers themselves —a point often overlooked. If, for example, a particular research and development program is in trouble, management needs to know how many sales dollars are likely to be returned from the products and processes research and development is about to turn out, what the relation of research emphasis is to the needs of the sales department, what the cost will be, and so forth. But I know of many instances where a discussion of such questions was of at least as much value to R & D itself as to top management, for until the meetings R & D did not really know what it was supposed to be doing.

Another great value of the profit-planning activity is that it identifies areas where improvement may be needed and launches special studies to find out what, if anything, needs to be done. I cannot overemphasize the potential importance of these investigations. We all hear and read about examples of what this or that company did to cut its costs by so much or increase its sales by so much. But the question that we are often left wondering about is: How did they learn what the real problem was in the first place? There is no end of possible problems; the difficult thing is to identify the most important one without wasting too much time. Working back from objectives and identifying the role that one operation plays in the complex of company activities—all in the kind of atmosphere I have just described—is, in my opinion, the most effective approach.

How specific should division or departmental plans to improve short-term profits be? What kinds of opportunities should executives look for when setting "reaching" goals? Obviously, it is difficult to generalize, but a few examples may suggest the type of approach I have in mind.

Marketing emphasis—A division making parts for electronic equipment lists the existing and new products it will be selling during the next two or three years, estimates the sales for each product, and comes out with an average increase in total sales of about 5% per year. This assumes that the profit on the sales dollar will be about the same, so the profit total will also increase about 5%. So far, so good; many managements would be content to stop here.

Suppose, however, that while the division has always maintained a fairly good profit margin, it has not been at the top in this respect. Motivated by a philosophy of "reaching" goals, then, top management might ask the division to (a) compute the direct costs on each existing product and estimate the direct costs on each new product, (b) subtract these costs from the sales price to obtain what is called the marginal contribution, and (c) compute the percentage of that contribution on the estimated present or additional investment needed to produce and market the product.

If the results of the analysis are at all typical of industrial experience in the past, it will be found that certain products are contributing much more to the return on investment than others are. Thus a way is found to increase the profitability of the division simply by shifting the emphasis in marketing and R & D —and without calling for greater total sales volume.

Production cost control—During a series of planning conferences the production managers of a Midwestern firm manufacturing home appliances point out that "we are doing the best job possible and nothing further can be done in manufacturing." Questioning reveals, however, that little has been done or is expected to be done in the way of better industrial engineering. This is the kind of "lead" that often justifies a special study.

Here a study reveals that incentives have been based on historical experience, with new rates having been set by analogy to established rates. This has resulted in wide disparities between rates on specific operations. Foremen have controlled earnings by allocating "good" work in situations where the group incentive has not provided the necessary "averaging" mechanism. Everyone has unblushingly accepted as sound the practice of workmen holding back finished production against a "rainy day." (This situation is not, of course, unique. It is typical of others I have observed.)

In this plant, production managers are fairly well insulated from the details of cost control. By putting them in charge, and by having them develop tools for effective control, the door can be opened to dramatic improvements in production and profit goals.

Analyzing equipment needs—A division with an expanding marketing operation proposes a substantial addition to present capacity. The corporation is hard-pressed for funds, however, and the division's real need for so much new capacity is questioned. Some men with experience in other plants and industries think the added investment is justified; others do not. The products and manufacturing processes are not common ones, making close comparison difficult.

One alternative is to argue it out in the office and let the most articulate man win; another is to try to work out a reasoned answer. If the latter alternative is decided on, here are a few of the steps that can be followed to reach a solution (assuming that a line-flow concept of operations can be used):

1. Convert the proposed product plan from dollars to units, by years and by product group.
2. Let the plant manager select for each item the route sheet that represents, in his opinion, the average manufacturing time for the current products. (As for future products, he can make estimates on the basis of time for current products with the most similar manufacturing processes.)
3. Multiply the manufacturing hours for each product by the unit-volume forecasts for each year.
4. Increase these figures by 50% (or whatever is a more reasonable figure) to cover setup time, sampling error, inefficiencies, and sales fluctuations. This gives the total operation hours for each product.
5. Subtract the total operation hours represented by inventory on hand.
6. Convert the difference into the number of pieces of equipment needed or the bench requirements.

Whether or not such an analysis supports the division's proposal, it is likely to contribute to short-term profit improvement. If it does not support the proposal, the corporation will save the expense of unneeded investment. If it does back up the proposal, the profit planners can then proceed with conviction to find other proposed outlays—either in that division or in other divisions—which can more profitably be diverted to the expansion in question.

So far I have mentioned looking only at the strengths and weaknesses of the planning organization itself. Actually, management will also want to look at the weaknesses of competitors —information best secured from working with customers. Many companies have made great gains by directing their short-term strategy to take advantage of a competitor's quality problem, a temporary failure in merchandising or service, or inept product planning.

There are two parts to the problem of setting realistic goals. One part, that just described, is to make the goals "reaching" in character. The other is to make sure that the division gets credit for what it does accomplish. This is important because, by definition, a "reaching" goal implies that it might not be attained. It is only a reasonable expectation.

If the division is constantly battling to set its sales and profit targets on the low, safe side, there is perhaps some justification for top management to badger the manager with telephone calls —"You didn't make much money last month," or "You made 25% but you should have made 30%." And headquarters may also be justified, when the division surpasses its goal by a wide margin, in trying to raise next year's target by a large amount. A very different psychology is called for, however, if goals are set in the manner I have recommended. Then, if the objective is surpassed, management can give full credit to the division for an excellent job. And if the division barely attains the goal, or just falls short of it, the managers still deserve a good deal of credit. Experience in a great many industries leaves no question in my mind as to the tremendous value of such an approach.

The value of a plan of action in protecting a division against unjustified criticism is enormous. Suppose, for example, that the plan calls for concentration on increasing sales effectiveness in four weak territories to increase profits. If the division succeeds in bettering sales in only two territories, it will not attain its goals; but since the target was predicated on improvement, it will be apparent that what was accomplished still took some good work. No one can reasonably infer (as might be done without planning) that, because the goal was not attained, the division is slipping. At the same time, the division's "post-mortem" on why the goal was not accomplished is of inestimable value in mapping and executing future plans.

Up to this point I have limited my discussion to the division's accomplishment in making profits. As more and more thoughtful businessmen are coming to realize, however, there are other objectives than short-term profits. (Here it is well to distinguish between the objectives of a business, which I like to think of as referring to its broad, long-term aims, and management goals which refer more to detailed, measurable tasks with a time factor added.) A corporation lives not only for next year but for the years a decade or more in the future. Its long-run investments in research, organization, public relations, institutional advertising, and so forth, may divert profits in the immediate future; but, as we all know, they are necessary to continued health and profitability.

Accordingly, it is essential to give a division credit for what it did not do in increasing the short-term profits as well as for what it did do. For example, did it make a good profit-and-loss showing without cutting back its investment in manpower, supervision, and training? As Rensis Likert has pointed out, a division can "milk the franchise" in the organizational sense as well as in the accounting sense, and the danger is an ever-present one when the pressure is on to cut costs.[2]

Often the division's ambitions conflict with the needs of the corporation as a whole. In such cases, it is only natural to expect the division head to work hardest in the way he knows best. But he should be given enough confidence in the broader corporate objectives, and enough motivation, so that he will continually keep them in the framework of his short-term planning. Here is a case of the kind of thing I have in mind.

One division of an eastern furniture manufacturer is managed by a competent and experienced executive who is ambitious to expand sales volume. Because of a family situation, he is tied to the city where his division is located; his chances of making a name for himself as a builder are all bound up in what he can do with his plants. To justify more production facilities, he must push his volume up. He is constantly making decisions toward this end.

Recently the question arose as to whether or not to add a plant to his division which could supply other parts of the company with certain materials needed in production. By inclination, the manager would (and, at first, did) oppose the plant; it would not increase his sales as much as added production facilities for his main product line would. From the corporation's viewpoint, however, the plant would be very desirable because two profits

[2] "Measuring Organizational Performance," *Harvard Business Review*, March–April 1958, p. 41.

could be made from it—the internal profit on sales to other divisions and also the profit on outside sales of products made from the materials manufactured at the plant.

In meetings of the top-management planning committee, of which he is a member, the manager admitted that the corporation would be better off if he took the plant. More profits could be made through vertical integration than through expansion of his production with the same investment. Moreover, as a result of planning there was so much incentive—and pressure—to contribute to the corporation's profit position that he decided to favor the acquisition.

In another case, a western division of a large, nationally known corporation had five product lines. Two were new items with good future potentials; one was a well-established product in the "mature" stage of its life cycle; the remaining two were in the last stages of being profitable.

The division was under the management of a young man who wanted to "make his mark" with a good profit showing in order to be promoted to a larger division or to an office in headquarters. Because the costs of missionary sales work, advertising, and promotion were heavy for the two new products, he could have increased his short-term profits considerably by cutting back these expenses. At the same time, he knew that would delay the marketing success of the new products and thwart the corporation's longer-range marketing objectives—and that, in turn, might have "meant his neck." So he chose to push the new products and go along with the carefully defined program for a steady, general increase in sales volume. (In this company's case, more emphasis was being placed on long-run volume than on specific profit and rate-of-return objectives.)

We might generalize in various ways about the "moral" of the foregoing cases. I like to think of them as pointing up the importance of mutual respect among managers for one another's goals. This is more than understanding, more than communication; it means that to each manager the objectives of other managers in his division and in other divisions are important enough so that he keeps his courses of action generally consistent with their courses of action.

Short-term profit goals should not, therefore, be set by division and department managers acting alone. They should be set by these men acting as part of a corporate team, so that each manager is committed to them. Equally important, they should be set in such a way that changes do not reflect personally on the managers concerned. Creating the proper atmosphere and incentives for this kind of work is the responsibility of top management.

CONCLUSION

The idea of long-range planning has cropped up from time to time during the preceding discussion, and there is a very good reason for it: short-term profit improvement takes part of its meaning from long-range planning, and long-range planning in turn takes part of its meaning from short-term programs.

I think that businessmen today tend a little too much to think of long-range planning only on a five- or ten-year basis. That is the proper perspective for them to think in, but it should never be carried so far that it leads to the conclusion, for instance, that "if we want to be flexible, we have to throw out long-range planning."

In broad terms, the job of short-term profit improvement is to make the long-range plan a vital, living document. This means putting much emphasis on realistic "reaching" goals for the next year and the year after that, and capitalizing on short-term opportunities that arise, even if they are inconsistent with certain steps in the long-range plan as originally drawn—but only if they are consistent with the basic philosophy and ultimate objectives of the plan.

In other words, identification of long-range goals comes first. Then, as the strategic program is renewed and extended from year to year, these goals may be revised and reformulated. But they always provide the framework within which short-term decisions should be made. The more successful top management is in keeping this framework flexible and up-to-date, the more effective its leadership is likely to be in short-term profit improvement. Many instances could be cited of where a "standpat" attitude toward the plan has resulted in operating managers taking over, by default, the job of revising production and marketing goals. This is because in a dynamic competitive economy plans and policies have to undergo change from year to year. The question is really not whether they will be revised but by whom.

One more point needs to be stressed: as far as I know, no one has yet found a universally good formula or prescription for management to follow in setting realistic short- and long-term goals. Everything seems to depend on the personality of the top-executive group. One group is ambitious; it wants to make the company a monument to its pioneering efforts. Another group is more easygoing, more interested in assured income. One company will have a few top executives of tremendous ability who completely overshadow the men under them, while its competitor may have very able division managers but quarreling owners.

The implications for planning are clear. The need may be for top management to maintain a strong, gentle, continuous pressure through meetings and conferences to instill more drive and ambition at the operating level; it may be to appoint division or department managers to the top planning committee; it may be to pick some able staff people from market research, industrial engineering, control, and other functions and tell them: "You're in charge of planning. Go to it!" Or the need may be for another, different approach. There is only one way to tell in a particular case, and that is to look at the personnel, organization, competitive position, know-how, and other factors which determine what that particular company can do best. You cannot take anything out of a book or from a short course in management.

Challenging short-term goals, profit improvement, sound long-range planning—all three are bound up together. Each in a sense is the key to the others and to the success of management in developing the company personality and corporate image.

INDEX

Abelson, Robert, 112

Admiral television, 307, 309, 314

Advertising: as communications force, 256–258, 263, 292; complexities, 6, 18, 86–87, 115, 125–127; dollar yardstick technique, 256–257, 262–270; inclusion in computer simulations, 111, 112; of product features, 156–159; purpose and function, 272, 275, 277, 278–279, 287, 288; relation to selling and marketing, 53–54, 55, 63, 68, 74, 224, 256, 258, 261–269, 278–282, 286–291. *See also* Brand advertising; Mass communication; Media selection

Advertising Age, 128

Advertising agency, 124–127, 174, 228, 291, 293–294

Advertising budget, 203, 270, 272, 286, 295, 299

Advertising decisions, 5, 20, 277, 300, 306, 311, 312, 327

Advertising director, 256, 264, 265, 271, 275, 285

Advertising-earnings ratio, 294–299

Advertising effectiveness, 5, 88–89, 98, 153, 208, 225, 232, 273–274; measurement, 241, 242, 257, 291–294, 299

Advertising expenditures, 69–70, 271, 294–299, 350; comparison with profits, 273–274

Advertising goals, 257–258, 261, 264, 266, 268, 270

Advertising objectives, 282–284; demonstrable inadequacy, 271–272, 274–276; measurement of results against, 271, 282, 284, 286, 288; need for advance agreement by all parties, 275, 277–278, 282, 285, 287, 299

Advertising plans, 275–276

Advertising profession, 71, 124–125

Advertising research, 257–258, 264

Advertising strategy, 142, 154, 162–166, 178, 291–292. *See also* Marketing strategy; Promotional strategy; Sales strategy

Advertising waste: causes, 271, 273, 277, 285; proposed remedy, 277–282, 299

Alberto-Culver Company, 298

American Management Association, 74

American Motors Corporation, 295

American Petroleum Institute Quarterly, 44

Andrea television, 312

Association of National Advertisers, 257

Automation, 1, 14

Automobile industry, 29, 320, 333; advertising, 5, 158, 160, 163–166, 279–281, 283, 286, 310; competition, 167, 169–170, 176; consumer preference, 9, 36–38, 56, 85, 93, 223; market simulation, 106

Barter equivalents, 324

Barzun, Jacques, 26, 46

Benny, Jack, 305

Benton & Bowles, 113

Big Change, The, 85

Book-depository technique, 12–13

Booz, Allen and Hamilton, 247

Borrowing, 338, 339–340

Brand advertising, 116–117, 119, 155, 200

Brand awareness, 278, 281, 283, 293

Brand competition, 198, 199, 205, 207–208, 212, 214, 215, 241, 247, 249, 253, 320

Brand differentiation, 319–320, 322; based on company image, 171, 278; based on product features, 116, 155–156, 170–171, 177–178, 333; market-limiting, 174–177. *See also* Consumer discrimination

Brand evaluation, 115-116, 118, 120–121, 127

Brand franchise, *see* Consumer franchise

Brand identification, 53–54, 56, 119

Brand image, 94, 115, 119–120, 122–124, 125, 155, 174, 177; relation to price, 301, 307–310, 311, 312, 315–318

Brand loyalty, 54, 92, 96, 107, 249, 252, 302–307, 312, 313; consumption rates of brand-loyal families, 130, 132, 150–151; distribution within product class, 129–130, 142; effect of deals, 130, 132, 146–148, 154; existence proved, 129, 154; proneness, 129, 132, 142–146, 152; relation to store loyalty, 130, 132, 148–150; share-of-market concept, 131, 132; single and dual, 132, 136–141, 146–147, 153; socioeconomic characteristics of brand-loyal families, 130, 132, 151–152, 153–154

Brand-loyalty analysis: basic assumptions and decisions, 131–138; data from consumer purchase panel, 133–138, 150, 151–152; findings on single- and dual-brand loyalty, 136–141, 146–147; possibility of chance in findings, 141–142, 143, 152; present status and further steps needed, 128, 153–154

Brand preference, *see* Brand differentiation

Brand switching, 107, 281, 288

Breakeven point, 184–185, 299

Bright, James R., 1

Brookings Institution, 113

Brown, George H., 128

Browning, Robert, 343

Buick, 85, 163

Business characteristics, as components of product policy, 182–191

Business cycle, 187–188

Business resources, 302–307, 308, 313, 315

Business schools, 71, 98, 100

Businesses, difference between big and small, 182–185, 188, 190–191

Buyer vs. seller conflicts, 73, 75–76

Cadillac, 85, 86, 163

Capital budgeting, 82

Capital investment, *see* Plant investment

Captive production, *see* Manufacturing, vertical integration

Caron's "Joy," 309

Chamberlin, E. H., 67

Changing American Market, The, 85

Chemical industry, 28–29

Chevrolet, 165

Chi-square test, 152

Chicago market, 303–304

Chicago Sun-Times, 118

Chicago Tribune, 101, 102, 118; consumer purchase panel, 133–138, 150–152

Chock Full o' Nuts, 309

Chrysler, 163, 295

Coefficient of rank correlation, Spearman's, 138, 143, 146, 150, 151

Colgate-Palmolive Company, 299

Colley, Russell H., 257

Columbia Broadcasting System, Inc., 305–315

Communication process, 96–97, 127; four steps, 279–281, 293. *See also* Mass communication

Company image, 170, 171, 275, 278, 352. *See also* Brand image

Company resources, components, 181–191, 197

Competition, 81, 347; for new products, 187, 319, 320, 321, 322, 326, 331, 333–334, 335; handicap, 49, 50–53, 54, 55, 56, 57, 59, 67–68; innovistic, 49–50, 52–53, 55–57, 58, 59, 60–61, 62, 63, 67–68; monopolistic (imperfect), 49, 53–55, 56, 67; perfect, 49, 53, 67. *See also* Brand competition; Price competition

Competitive behavior, 166–170

Computer simulation: advances over earlier techniques, 105–107; operation and checking, 108–112; potential advantages to marketing, 114; of several complex systems, 112–113

Consumer: as human being, 84, 86, 92–94, 98–101; Negro, 90–91; woman, 91–92, 93–94, 95–96, 98

Consumer acceptance, 4, 250, 251, 253; of new product, 241, 242, 319, 320, 321

Consumer attitudes, 3, 6, 94–95, 107, 115, 117, 124, 127, 199–200, 201, 208, 234

Consumer behavior: based on needs, 41, 44, 45, 50, 55, 60, 68; patterns, 107–

108, 135, 153; social and economic factors, 85, 88. *See also* Brand loyalty

Consumer cooperatives, 75

Consumer discrimination, 198–199, 204–205, 208–210, 211, 214, 217–218. *See also* Brand differentiation

Consumer franchise, 76–77, 80, 275, 298

Consumer goods, 245, 249, 298, 308, 329

Consumer market, *see* Industrial market

Consumer orientation, 24, 25, 36, 45, 47–48, 56, 198, 199, 205, 215, 220, 221, 276

Consumer preference, 198, 200–204, 312; for new product, 241, 323, 324–325, 335; patterns and trends, 8, 9, 205–208, 210, 211–213, 214, 216–218

Consumer purchase panels, 132, 153, 200, 233, 289–290; limitations, 133–135. See also *Chicago Tribune*

Consumer research, 210, 230, 283, 286, 288–289; areas needing study, 84–98, 107–108, 200; depth interviews, 120–122, 229, 324; failures of conventional techniques, 36, 98–103, 115–116, 202; unexploited value, 4, 277, 285. *See also* Market research; Motivation research

Convenience foods, 96, 98, 249

Copeland, Melvin T., 186, 190–191

Corning Glass Works, 25–26

Correlation analysis, 221

Cost analysis, 82, 184–185

Cost estimating, 180, 326, 327

Cost reductions, 336, 345

Costs, 38, 316; direct, 341, 345

Credit, 340

Crossley, Arch, 276

Curtis Publishing Company, 276

Customer service, 1, 74

Cyert, R. M., 113

Dean, Joel, 188

Demand: elasticity with respect to price, 316, 324–325, 329, 331, 333, 334; for new products, 322–326, 335; seasonal, 187, 251–252, 253

De Soto, 165

Detergents and soaps, household, 53–54, 96, 108, 116–117, 210–213, 252, 331–332

Discount houses, 50, 51–53, 57, 58–59, 75, 85

Discounts, 324, 327–328, 331

Discrimination parameter, 209, 217–218

Distribution, 72–73, 198; small- vs. full-scale, 241–242, 248–251, 254–255

Distribution channels, 77, 186–187, 302–307, 310, 313–314; for new products, 230, 232, 322, 326, 327, 328, 335

Distribution cost analysis, 21, 71

Distribution costs, for new products, 320, 326, 327, 329

Distribution problems, 50, 60, 62

Distribution trends, 6, 11–12, 15, 19

Dumont television, 304, 312

Du Pont de Nemours, E. I., & Company, 25–26, 31, 58, 67, 68, 183

Eastman, R. O., 276

Economy, competitive, 88, 337, 352

Edison, Thomas A., 32

Edsel, 171

Ekco Products Company, 63

Electric utilities, 27

Electrical industry, 17

Electronics industry, 28–29, 42–44

Emerson television, 307, 309, 314

Employee relations, 84, 100

Ethics, in business, 79, 81

Executive decision-making, 6–7, 88, 190–191, 229, 241–243, 336–337, 342, 344. *See also* Management decisions

Executive leadership, 45–48, 351

Executive responsibility, 71, 195, 196, 220; for pricing decisions, 317–318; in advertising and marketing, 127, 271–272, 285–286, 291–294, 298, 299

Executive selection and training, 2, 22, 101

Expected value, 141–142, 217–218

Fair trade, 49, 50–51, 52–53, 62, 63, 67, 68, 77, 312

Fashion merchandising, 190–191

Federal Reserve Board studies, 10

Felton, Arthur P., 57, 68, 72

Ford, Henry, 37–38, 334

Ford Motor Company, 67, 85; overhaul of advertising program, 295–298

Fortune, 6

Freeman, Cyril, 272

Furniture industry, 89, 349–350

Galbraith, John Kenneth, 35

Gallup, George, 276

Gallup & Robinson, Inc., 273
General Electric Company, 50, 51, 294, 312, 314
General Foods Corporation, 63, 294
General Mills, Inc., 253
General Motors Corporation, 31, 163, 295. *See also names of individual cars*
General Tire Company, 334
Gillette Company, 252
Goals, specific, vs. long-range objectives, 283–284, 348–349. *See also* Advertising goals; Profit and sales goals
Godfrey, Arthur, 305
Goodrich, B. F., Company, 253
Grant, W. F., Company, 63
Greenewalt, Crawford H., 183–184
Growth industries, 24–28, 338–341

Hamberger, Michael J., 113
Human behavior, 84–86, 97–100

Incentives, 346
Income-tax rates, 79
Indian Head Mills, 8
Industrial engineering, 4, 346, 352
Industrial management courses, 100–101
Industrial market, vs. consumer market, 19, 73, 186, 188
Industrial research, *see* Research and development
Intermediate products, 196
International Business Machines Corporation, 113, 321
Inventory level, 3, 80, 311, 336, 337, 339

Jobbers, specialty, 13, 190
Jones, Conrad, 247–248

Kaiser Aluminum & Chemical Corporation, 26
Katz, Robert L., 16, 71
Kuehn, Alfred A., 113

Lever Brothers Company, 299
Life, 273
Likert, Rensis, 349
Loewy, Raymond, 63
"Luxury of not bothering," 79

McGraw Electric Company, 322
McGraw-Hill Book Company, Inc., 262

McPhee, William, 113
Magnavox television, 312, 314
Maguire fair-trade bill, 67
Mail-order houses, 56, 281, 333
Majority fallacy, 202–203, 207, 215
Management, strengths and weaknesses, 1, 24, 26, 40, 247–248, 336–337
Management decisions, 179–181, 193–197, 201; on brand image, 122–124, 127; on investment, 79–80, 300, 349–350; on market testing, 239, 243, 246–255; on marketing, 69–70, 219–220, 261–262, 268, 291–294; on pricing, 300–318; on product features, 177–178. *See also* Executive decision-making
Managerial skills, three kinds, 71–72
Manufacturing: relation to retailing, 59–67; value added by, 189–190; vertical integration, 193, 195–196, 350
Manufacturing costs, *see* Production costs
March, J. G., 113
Marginal contribution to investment, 341, 345
Margins, 51–53, 59, 77, 190; new-product, 314, 327–328, 331–333, 334
Market dilution, *see* Market segmentation
Market penetration, 328, 330–333
Market Planning Corporation (Marplan), 226–228
Market research, 21, 71, 74, 82, 84, 153, 177–178, 180, 195, 234, 262, 264, 352; current limitations, 98–103, 201, 219–223; feed-in studies, 219, 223–224, 225–226, 227–230, 233–234; history, 99–103, 220, 276; importance of master program, 219, 220, 223–237; methodology and techniques, 114, 172, 221–223, 228, 235. *See also* Consumer research; Motivation research
Market saturation, 333
Market segmentation, 156, 172–178, 201, 202–203, 205, 207–208, 212–213, 214, 302, 308, 313, 325, 329, 334
Market share, 240, 287, 298; for new product, 320, 326, 332, 333
Market targets, 301, 302–307, 313, 315, 316, 322, 326
Market testing: cost, 244–245; functions and value, 194–195, 230, 239–243, 245, 254–255; need for care in planning, 180, 238, 239; reasons for

failure, 114, 243–253, 254; wait-and-see attitude, 253–254

Marketing: as a form of combat, 73, 81; conceptual approach, 2–3, 16–23, 50, 68, 72–74, 76, 219–220; dynamic quality, 2, 6–16; horsetrader approach, 74, 80–82; investor approach, 74, 77–80, 81, 82; planning and control, 2, 6–7, 69–83; purchasing-agent approach, 74, 75–77, 81, 82; relation to other elements, 2, 3–5, 31, 35–36, 43, 45, 46, 278–282, 288, 290–291. See also Advertising; Brand advertising; Distribution; Promotion; Selling

Marketing costs, 69, 80

Marketing data, 3–4, 9, 10–11

Marketing director, 73–74, 76–77, 78, 104, 111, 112, 198, 220, 223, 225, 226, 233, 235, 271

Marketing leadership, 2–3, 271

Marketing mix, role of price in, 301, 310–312, 315, 316, 327, 334

Marketing objectives, 6–8, 224–225, 276, 282, 287–288, 290–291, 326; difference from goals, 282–284

Marketing problems and complexities, 1–2, 5, 8–9, 23, 69–72, 106–107, 220, 237, 345–346

Marketing strategy, 2, 245; formulation, 128, 153; importance of product features, 155–156, 170–171, 177–178, 210; influence of market segmentation, 172; pretesting on computers, 104–114. See also Advertising strategy; Promotional strategy; Sales strategy

Markup, 50, 51, 68, 332

Marplan, see Market Planning Corporation

Martineau, Pierre, 170

Mass communication, 86, 117, 126, 277

Mass production, 29, 35–42, 68, 190, 277

Massachusetts Institute of Technology, 113

Massachusetts Supreme Judicial Court, 50

Mathematical programing, 82

Maytag washing machines, 321

Media selection, 127, 225, 226–230, 232, 292–293

Merger, 22–23

Merton, Robert K., 221

Miller-Tydings fair-trade bill, 67

Minute Maid orange juice, 321

Monopolies, 27, 54

Montgomery Ward Company, 63

Moore, C. G., 113

Motion-picture industry, 24–25, 26

Motivation research, 2, 18, 21, 82, 87, 97–98, 99, 100, 115, 200, 210, 222–223, 234. See also Consumer research; Market research

Murrow, Edward R., 305

National Sales Executives, Inc., 101

National Wholesale Grocers Convention, 28

Negroes, as consumers, 90–91

New Jersey Retail Grocers Association, 28

New products, 179, 180, 186–187, 193–195, 199, 210; degenerative cycle, 319–321, 333, 335; demand, 322–326, 335; effect on present products, 187, 191–193; first in the market, 248–250, 253–254; pricing, see Pioneer pricing; promotional strategy, 230–233, 238, 240, 320, 322, 326–328, 335; relation to over-all marketing objective, 241, 245, 278, 298–299, 350; usual need for modification, 240, 241, 254–255. See also Competition; Distribution channels; Market testing; Production methods; Sales volume

New York Daily News, 118

New York Times, 118

Newspaper personalities, 118–119

Nielsen, A. C., 239, 276

Objectives, long-range, vs. specific goals, 283–284, 348–349. See also Advertising objectives; Marketing objectives

Office of the Secretary of Defense, Resources Division, 159

Oldsmobile, 85, 163–164

Operations research, 82

Packaging, 6, 18, 20, 54, 56–57, 68, 74, 198, 240, 242

Paired-comparison tests, 201–218

Parlin, Charles Coolidge, 276

Patent protection, 170, 178, 181, 188–189, 191, 319, 322, 327

Penney, J. C., Company, 63

Per-share earnings, 299

Personnel decisions, 300, 340. See also Employee relations

INDEX

Petroleum industry, 29–34, 39–42, 44–45, 233

Pilot production, 180, 194, 330

Pioneer pricing: market penetration policy, 328, 330–333, 335; skimming policy, 328–329, 331, 335; steps, 322–328

Plant investment, 21–23, 57, 68, 182–183, 185, 187, 300, 320, 326, 327, 346–347

Pocket books, 329, 330–331

Polk, Sol, 58–59

Pool, Ithiel de Sola, 112

Population expansion, 29, 30–34

Preference distribution analysis, 201; detailed procedure, 216–218; example of use, 210–213; steps and advantages, 204–210, 213–215

Preference testing, 200–204. See also Consumer discrimination

Price: effect on brand loyalty, 130, 132, 146–148, 154; of new product, 240, 248–249; relation to consumer choice, 117, 214, 307; retail, 49, 50–52, 55, 68; specific, 301, 316, 317–318

Price adjustments 312, 313–314, 315, 320, 325–326, 333–334

Price competition, 306, 307, 309, 312–313, 314, 322, 326

Price-earnings ratio, 295

Price elasticity, see Demand

Price premium, 322, 325, 330, 332, 333

Price range, 300, 310, 316, 317, 341; for new products, 319–320, 322, 323, 326, 335

Pricing: of mature products, 333–334, 335, 350; multistage approach, 300–318; policy and strategy, 74, 187, 300–301, 312–315, 316, 318, 341

Printers' Ink, 228

Probability, 80, 107–111, 207, 209

Probability samples, 223, 234

Procter & Gamble Company, 291

Producers goods, 308

Product design and development, 4, 18, 63, 74, 215, 230, 246, 319, 330

Product differentiation, see Brand differentiation

Product features, 234, 281, 283, 331; adoption rate, 156, 159–162; as basis for brand differentiation, 116, 155–156, 170–171, 177–178, 333; duplication by competition, 156, 166–170, 178; market-limiting, 172–177; matching to consumer preferences, 198, 200, 204, 212–213, 216–218,

231–232; number advertised per company, 156–159, 162–166; scale of feasible values, 204–205, 209, 211, 213, 214

Product improvement, 31, 38–39, 42, 155, 161, 199, 210, 311, 320, 321, 329, 332, 334

Product line, 179, 239, 326, 332

Product maturity, 320

Product obsolescence, 26–29, 32–35, 56, 179, 185, 187, 193, 196

Product orientation, 24, 25, 29, 36, 40, 42–43, 44, 45–46, 56, 277

Product policy: analysis of company resources, 181–191; application, 193–196; formulation, 191–193; importance and functions, 179–181, 196–197

Product quality, 303–307, 309, 311, 314, 322, 325; means of determining, 198–218

Product strategy, 179, 191–192, 197, 205, 210, 347. See also Marketing strategy

Product styling, 85, 155, 171, 176, 177

Product testing, 199, 200, 203–204, 230

Production cost control, 346

Production costs, 60–63, 64, 65–66, 68, 215, 306, 307; of new product, 320, 326, 327, 329, 331, 332–333

Production facilities, 302–307, 309, 349–350

Production methods, for new product, 240, 241–242, 326, 327, 329, 332, 333

Profit, 65, 68, 179, 196, 239, 242, 268, 272, 295, 326, 330, 335; comparison with advertising expenditure, 273–274. See also Advertising-earnings ratio; Return on investment

Profit and loss estimates, 180, 193, 349

Profit and sales goals, 8; importance of realistic setting, 343–352; understatement, 336, 337–341; tendency to play safe, 341–343

Profit estimates, 332–333, 338

Profit margin, 339, 341, 345

Profit maximization, 78–79, 327

Profit planning, see Profit and sales goals

Profit utilization, 338–339

Promotion, 5, 8, 198, 214, 215, 234, 310, 314; role of advertising, 258, 262

Promotion value estimates, 257, 258. See also Advertising, dollar yardstick technique

Promotion vs. salesman choice, 259–260, 265–269

Promotional costs, 259, 328, 329, 350

Promotional strategy, for new product, 230–233, 238, 240, 320, 322, 326–328, 335. *See also* Advertising strategy; Marketing strategy; Sales strategy

Psychological testing, 101

Psychometric techniques, 153

Purchasing cycle, 131

Quality control, 199

Radio Corporation of America, 304, 312

Railroads, 24, 26, 46–47

Raw materials, 181, 182, 189, 195

Recessions, 336, 337, 342

Research and development, 57, 84, 156, 159, 170, 177, 179, 188–189, 193–195, 320, 344–345; at expense of marketing, 42–46. *See also* New products; Product design and development

Retailing, 50–53, 87; conceptual approach, 57–59, 68; costs, 60, 61–63; relation to manufacturing, 59–67

Retailing Daily, 50

Return on investment, 50, 51–53, 58–59, 61, 65–66, 68, 258. 332, 339–340, 346

Return-on-investment ratio, 339, 341

Reynolds Metals Company, 26

Riesman, David, 221

Rockefeller, John D., 31

Sales analysis, 71, 82, 232

Sales-cost comparisons, 240

Sales effort, 327–328

Sales forecasting, 180, 232, 335, 338, 341

Sales manager, 3, 71, 100, 101, 186, 235, 256, 264, 275

Sales-marketing goals, and promotion, 256–257, 261–263

Sales organization, 2, 6, 7, 14–16, 17–18, 20, 78, 311; training, 186–187, 241

Sales strategy, 129, 142, 153, 276. *See also* Advertising strategy; Marketing strategy; Promotional strategy

Sales targets, *see* Profit and sales goals

Sales volume, 1, 7, 182, 185–186, 191, 250, 332–333, 341, 345, 349; of new product, 249, 306, 310, 321, 322, 327–328, 330, 331; quotas, 8, 261, 346, 348, 350

Sampling variation, 218, 347

Scalora, Frank, 113

Scripto pencil, 307

Sears, Roebuck and Company, 57, 63, 64–67, 89

Seller vs. buyer conflicts, 73, 76

Selling: effectiveness, 12, 115, 241; institutional, 163; relation to advertising and marketing, 35–36, 46, 74, 272, 278–281; task accomplishments, 261–269

Semantic differential technique, 223

Shopping centers, 55, 57, 85

Simon & Schuster, 330–331

Simulation, 104–105. *See also* Computer simulation

Smith, Adam, 49, 53, 67

Smith, Wendell R., 172

Social mobility, 97, 117–118

Solar energy, 27, 40

Specialization, 7, 181, 188, 222, 276, 277. *See also* Market segmentation

Starch, Daniel, 276

Statistical research, 101, 102, 115, 127

Store loyalty, 130, 132, 148–150

Store personality, 87

Submarket, *see* Market segmentation

Substitutes, 26–29, 31, 32, 34, 319, 323, 325

Suburban living, influence on buying, 89–90, 97

Sunbeam appliances, 322

Supermarkets, 20, 28, 52, 55, 56, 57, 61; automobile, 13–14

Sylvania television, 312

Technology, 1, 272

Television industry, 11, 24–25, 329, 333; new features, 158, 160, 161, 167–169, 173; pricing decisions, 302–315, 324. *See also names of individual brands*

Test marketing, *see* Market testing

Textile industry, 4, 5, 8, 10, 25, 27

Theory of games, 80, 82

Thomas, William I., 222

Trade acceptance, of new product, 240–241, 242

Trade association reports, 10

Transportation industry, 24, 26, 225

Turnover, 51, 58–59, 68, 339–340, 341

Twentieth Century Fund studies, 85

University of Michigan Survey Research Center, 94

University of Wisconsin, 113

Warehousing, 12–13
Westinghouse Electric Corporation, 51,
171, 187, 226, 312, 315

Women, as consumers, 91–92, 93–94,
95–96, 98
Worthington Corporation, 257

Zenith Radio Corporation, 303–315

Other MENTOR Books of Related Interest